NO ORDINARY PRESS BARON

A Life of Walter Layton

David Hubback

Weidenfeld and Nicolson
LONDON

First published in Great Britain by
George Weidenfeld & Nicolson Limited
91 Clapham High Street, London SW4 7TA

British Library Cataloguing in Publication Data

Hubback, David
No ordinary press baron.
1. Layton, Walter 2. Journalists—Great
Britain—Biography 3. Economists—Great
Britain—Biography
I. Title
070.4'092'4 PN5123.L33/

ISBN 0-297-78472-2

Acknowledgement is made to
The Hallam Press
151 Great Portland Street, London W1

Typeset and printed in Great Britain
at The Pitman Press, Bath

To Walter Layton's children and grandchildren.

Contents

	LIST OF ILLUSTRATIONS	ix
	FOREWORD	xi
	PREFACE	xiii
1	Growing Up	1
2	Walter and Dorothy, 1909–14	24
3	An Economist at War, 1914–19	34
4	Walter Layton, the Man, 1919–39	50
5	New Policies for the Liberal Party, 1920–9	67
6	The *Economist*	82
7	Economic Adviser in Europe and India, 1925–9	98
8	The Crisis Years, 1929–32	112
9	The *News Chronicle*, 1927–35	127
10	The Coming War, 1936–9	149
11	Arms and the Plan for Total War, 1940–3	167
12	The *News Chronicle*: the War Years and After	196
13	The Search for a United Europe	205
14	The Search for the Field Brothers	219
15	The *News Chronicle*: the Last Decade	230
16	Keeping Going, 1960–6	246
	NOTES	254
	INDEX	265

Illustrations

Between pages 114 and 115

Walter and his brother Wilfred
Walter's parents at Stanley House about 1905
The Layton family about 1905
Dorothy, 1910
Walter, 1912
Reception by the Tsar, February 1917
With Lloyd George at Churt, 1927
The family home, Brett House (*Country Life*)
Plan of Brett House
Ministry of Production, 1942: a cartoon by Low
Walter at Twittens, 1942
Walter and Dorothy at Twittens, 1942
Walter with Churchill and Lady Violet Bonham-Carter, 1948 (*Keystone Press Agency*)
Walter and Dorothy with their seven children, 1955

Foreword

A biographer recounts the thread of a person's life in the web of history. Walter Layton, who was born a hundred years ago, was brought up in Victorian times and he was already in his prime in the early 1930s.

The rate of change in many aspects of public life accelerated markedly from the beginning of the twentieth century. Three changes must be mentioned. The first was the way in which affairs of State became irretrievably enmeshed in economics and statistics. The second was the great change in international affairs. The world became smaller and the problems of conflict between national interests have had more and more to be handled by new regional and world wide institutions. The third was the explosion of news and information. In all three Walter Layton became deeply engaged. He was sustained in his work by a wide range of people at home and abroad who were searching for new ways to resolve problems, and were not prepared to accept either socialism or the wait-and-see attitude of the Conservative establishment.

Walter was not a politician but was throughout his life deeply involved in the economic and political questions of the day, and so remained closely in touch with leaders of the Liberal Party and the formulation of their policies. The slow disintegration of that party after the First World War imposed severe limits on what he could achieve.

My father was no popular star but this biography had to be written *pour encourager les autres*. Empty vessels make the most sound but there are other tales to tell and this is one of them.

As David Hubback has said, other men of his time managed to work their way by scholarship from school to university to become dons, and later did well in government service, business or politics, but it is difficult to find a parallel to Walter Layton's many-sided career and to do justice to it. It is a story with many chapters, both personal as well as historical. He wrote his own Memoirs during the latter part of his life, and these provide the bare bones of much of the tale. He treated his many activities, however, so dispassionately that the man behind was hardly discernible. What mattered to him were the activities.

It has only been by diligent research and with the help of surviving friends and relatives that David Hubback, a warm friend of the family, has been able to discover the man. This book could never have been written without their help, which has given colour to the story of his life, particularly his latter years.

DAVID LAYTON
March 1984

Preface

This book could not have been written without the whole-hearted cooperation of Walter Layton's family. In particular, I have been greatly helped by the present Lord Layton, who made his father's papers* available to me and by his brother David, who provided me with an office and much encouragement. I owe special thanks to his secretary Daphne Bonner who typed my manuscript with great skill and good humour. Walter Layton's younger children, Jean Eisler, Olive Gellhorn, Ruth Pegna and Christopher Layton all responded generously to my questioning, as did his son-in-law Alfred Geiringer, his cousin Dr Winifred Layton Gaubert, his nieces Joan King and Monica Urquhart and his nephew Trevor Layton.

I have drawn extensively from Walter Layton's unpublished Memoirs on a draft of which he was working at the time of his death. Where I quote from these Memoirs I mention my source. I have also made great use of Layton's private papers, especially his letters to his wife and his considerable correspondence with the Cadbury family. These papers have not yet been archived. So when I quote from them it has not been possible to cite any reference other than the date.

I am grateful for the helpful comments on various draft chapters made by: David Bensusan-Butt, Mrs Joyce Cadbury, Michael Curtis, Elma Dangerfield, Kate and Hermann Field, Willie Forrest, Sam Mervyn Herbert, David Hopkinson, Graham Hutton, Douglas Jay, Gwyneth McCleary, Richard Mayne, Professor Sir Austin Robinson, Cosmo Russell, Robert Skidelsky, Sir Hugh Weeks and Paul Winterton.

I have also greatly benefited from talks and correspondence with:

* Now in the library of Trinity College, Cambridge.

Ron Arnold, Tom Baistow, Paul Bareau, the late Vernon Bartlett, Roland Bird, Mark Bonham-Carter, Arthur Brittenden, Ivor Bulmer Thomas, the late Lord Byers, the late Laurence Cadbury, Sir Alec Cairncross, James Cameron, Sir Christopher Chancellor, Sally Chilver, Brian Connell, Sir Geoffrey Cox, Margaret Cruikshank, the late Dunstan Curtis, Miss Dellow, Lord Drogheda, François Duchene, Ruth Edwards, Joyce Egginton, Lord Franks, Martin Gilbert, George Goyder, D.M. Hodson, H.V. Hodson, David Holloway, Sir Tom Hopkinson, Lt General Sir Ian Jacob, Professor Stephen Koss, Elizabeth Layton, Mrs Margaret Linell, Dr W.J. Macpherson of Caius College, Mde Paul Mantoux, the late Lord Noel Baker, William Pattinson, Sir Dennis Rickett, Lord Roll, Jasper Rootham, L. P. Wilkinson and Lady Steuart Wilson.

I would like to thank the following publishers for permission to reproduce quotations: Oxford University Press: *Anglo-American Collaboration in Peace and War* by Sir Richard Clarke; Curtis Brown Ltd: *Montagu Norman* by Andrew Boyle; David Higham Associates Ltd: *Lloyd George – A Diary* by Frances Stephenson; Collins Publishers: *Dorothy* by Walter Layton; *Country Life* for permission to reproduce a photograph of Brett House.

I owe much to my own family and in particular to my wife Judith, whose twin skills as a Jungian analyst and editor of a learned journal helped me over several difficult patches.

DAVID HUBBACK
June 1984

CHAPTER ONE

Growing Up

Choirboy

Walter Layton might well have become an eminent musician rather than an eminent economist. At the time he was born in Chelsea on 15 March 1884, both his parents were professional musicians. His mother, Mary Johnson, a keen fighter for women's rights, became the first woman Fellow of the Royal College of Organists in 1872 at the age of twenty-three, against considerable opposition. His father, Alfred Layton, went into the drapery business but his firm failed and he was then persuaded by his wife, a very forceful character, to become a professional singer. To make ends meet, they ran a hostel for students from the Royal College of Music in their house in Milner Street in Chelsea, where Walter described his father's role as staff officer. Alfred had a lovely voice and sang in the St Paul's special choir. With his patient friendliness and tolerance he was a good foil to his wife's highly strung artistic nature.

In his old age Walter wrote of his mother: 'Her strong personality dominated the household. ... If I inherited from my father his equable temperament, I inherited from my mother her keen intelligence, her sense of history and her quick appreciation of the public affairs of the period.'[1] She had begun her teaching career in her teens as a governess, but having been brought up by her parents to be interested in both art and music, she went on to the newly founded South Kensington School of Art to study painting. Here she showed her independence by cutting her hair short, and quickly fell in love with Hubert Herkomer, a fellow student. It seems her love was reciprocated at first, but nothing came of the affair, although she kept in touch with him for many years. Perhaps because of her disappointment she decided to leave the School of Art and study music instead, and in particular the organ. While still in her teens she became the organist at the Markham Square Congregational Chapel in Chelsea. Once more she singled herself out by becoming the first woman to apply to become a Fellow of the Royal College of Organists. This aroused great opposition from those who maintained that women could not possibly be eligible for fellowships – their skirts would be bound to get in the way of the pedals. But the charter of the college did not expressly rule out women, and at her second attempt Mary Johnson was awarded her fellowship. Even so, as a woman, she was not allowed to teach at the Royal College of Music and so set up her own school in Milner Street.

Both Walter's grandfathers were of radical nonconformist stock and both were schoolmasters much taken up with their local Congregational chapels, which had difficulty in getting premises in which to start their schools. In Chelsea, Walter Johnson taught in attic rooms built by lifting the roof of the chapel. At Pirbright, Thomas Layton taught in a barn lent to him by a farming relative until a schoolroom was built alongside the chapel. Walter's father and mother were second cousins, each from families of seven children. So Walter, together with his two brothers Wilfred and Gilbert and his sister Margaret, was brought up in an atmosphere of music and teaching. All three boys were to go to choir school and Margaret was to become a concert singer. Walter was a delicate child and at a very early age developed rickets, then quite a common disease. His earliest memory was of being wheeled about in a large chair-like pram, and of being inordinately proud of the splints he wore to straighten his legs.

By the age of five the rickets were cured and two years later, when he was seven and a half, Walter followed his elder brother Wilfred to boarding school at Windsor to join the St George's Chapel Choir. He was much the youngest candidate and there were not many vacancies but he had long been able to read music easily and was a good and accurate singer. He was used, too, to singing grace before meals at home. He always believed he was accepted because, when sitting on the Dean's knee and asked to read the *Te Deum* from a prayer book, he did so without a mistake, largely because he already knew it by heart.

It is remarkable that the Choir School, which usually recruited from Church of England families near Windsor, accepted the two Congregationalist Layton boys. Their singing must have been outstanding. At that time, November 1891, the school had just moved down from a small Tudor house high on the castle walls, where the twelve choirboys were taught in one room, to more extensive buildings below the walls. Even so, the education provided, other than music, was limited to the three Rs. A choirboy's life was then more like that of an apprentice than that of a middle-class schoolboy. The sons of respectable but badly off parents were being taught a trade early.

The day's routine, which started at 7.30 am with a Bible reading and went on to include two sung services in St George's Chapel and at least one choir practice, left little time for games. With only twelve boys in the school, divided between two classes, Walter should have had a lot of personal attention, but the choir master, Mr Bransome, left soon after he arrived and the matron, Mrs Wright, took over. It seems she was quite incapable of keeping order. The school attendance book, filled in by the boys themselves, records that 'the Dean and Mr Dalton came down to settle various rows of long duration between Mrs Wright and the boys'. The book also records that Wilfred Layton was kept in for a week for lying.

Walter did well as a choirboy from the start and was chosen to sing for Queen Victoria and her guests in the private chapel on Sunday mornings. He and his brother Wilfred were also chosen (being the smallest of the boys) to lead the procession of choir and clergy at the funeral of the Duke of Clarence in 1892 from the Great West Door to where the coffin rested in the Chancel. Walter wrote later that:

> Sir Walter Parratt was stationed at the organ screen, all poised to give the signal to the choir drawn up on either side of the nave below, his deputy being seated at the organ. The Dean was at the Great West Door and in his nervous excitement could not imagine the two little boys could be safely left to fall into place behind the bearers of the regalia who were to precede the procession of the choir. So, in the few moments when the coffin was being drawn on its gun carriage through the entrance gateway of the castle, he bustled forward and taking my brother and myself by the arm, led us back from our stations on either side of the centre aisle to the Great Door, whence he could make sure that we moved off at the right time. But, alas,

> Parratt caught sight of the coffin coming up the steps, and, thinking he must have missed his cue, hastily gave the signal to the organist and to the choir in the nave below. Result – confusion! The leaderless choristers moved off and some began to sing. For a moment the centre aisle was full of a shapeless choir and the Dean, who still had the Layton brothers imprisoned by the open door, had somehow to get the choir to stop singing and return to their places. Fortunately, in a matter of seconds, all realised that it had been a false start and the aisle was quickly cleared, but the smallest of the two small boys was inwardly seething with contempt for fussy people who interfered with boys who knew exactly what they had to do.

While Walter did well as a choirboy, he just was not strong enough to stand the strain of one choir practice and two services every day in addition to ordinary schooling. He was most probably homesick, especially as holidays were short since the choir was expected to sing in chapel throughout the year, and missed his elder sister Margaret, to whom he was very close right through his life. He was ill for a month at Easter 1892. On his eighth birthday she sent him an elaborately illustrated birthday card with a tune, 'Thoughts of Windsor', she had composed. On it she wrote some verses by her mother, ending:

> When you play it, Walter dear,
> In your castle by the river,
> Just think of those who love you here
> And especially the giver.

Whatever the reason, Walter started to have nightmares and to sleepwalk, to the alarm of the other boys in the dormitory, who tried to deal with the trouble by tying him into bed. In the end he was taken away from St George's and given six months at Hastings staying with an old family friend to recover. This worked, and he spent some of the time in learning how to knit and crochet.

The two years away from home, leading the intense communal life of a choir school, made a great impact on Walter. The reserve and self-sufficiency that characterized him throughout life may have been due to the shell he had to grow to protect himself against fellow choirboys who were nearly all bigger and older than he. Perhaps that shell had already begun to form even younger as a defence against his mother's strong personality. A very active and loving person, she could also be demanding. His younger brother Gilbert was also introverted but kept his end up by playing the fool and teasing his elder brothers.

The choral singing Walter learnt at St George's, and later as a member of other choirs until his voice broke, proved a first-rate training in concentration, accuracy and self-discipline. The ability he later showed in mathematics and statistics was developed by his having to learn when very young to be methodical and meticulous. His parents set him an example of working hard which he followed. Both parents were busy seven days a week giving singing and organ lessons and running their hostel for music students. With so many people in the house each of the four children had to find its own way. It may be that Alfred Layton provided most of the sympathy they needed, but Mary, too, had a strong streak of Victorian sentimentality. She kept a green cloth-covered book in which she wrote verses about her children for over twenty years from 1886. These were printed as *Leaves from the old Green Book* in 1920. Of Walter at St George's she had written in 1892:

> The younger, Walter, fair and sweet
> With quaint old thoughts beyond his years
> A mind too full of questionings deep,
> And dreams too solemn even for tears.

Having already started earning his living by singing, Walter continued to do so on Sundays in the choir of the Temple Church while from the age of ten attending King's College School in the Strand. Walford Davies was choir master. By way of encouragement, he instituted prizes, some of which Walter won for oratorios and sight-reading. Before his voice broke, he sang from the steps of St Paul's Cathedral at the Diamond Jubilee of Queen Victoria and the next year at the funeral of Mr Gladstone in Westminster Abbey.

Walter thus got used to appearing in public early. He also acquired confidence as a choirboy through being able to read music easily and hold perfect pitch. When older, he recalled a time when the choir was practising Walford Davies' *Te Deum*:

> I was singing on the decani side. Three times, the cantoris failed to come in. Losing patience, Walford Davies called out from the organ loft, 'Walter, change places with Bob Minion.' I did so, but this time, though

the cantoris came in on time, it was the decani who missed their cue. 'You will have to sing both at once' remarked the bass behind me.

From the age of fifteen, after his voice had broken, his education – by then at the Westminster City School – was financed by scholarships and various earnings, such as playing the organ at Sunday services at the Cancer Hospital and at Chelsea Infirmary, and collecting cheques for a Stock Exchange firm on the fortnightly settlement days. Indeed, Walter was proud of the fact that his parents never had to pay anything for his education, either at school or university. So Walter became self-reliant and emerged early from the usual dependency of teenagers. He also acquired a liking for early morning swims, at that time in the Serpentine, and ran there from Chelsea.

Walter does not record whether his mother pressed him to take up music professionally like his brother Wilfred, who became an organist, and his sister Margaret, who became a concert singer. It is possible that at some time he considered music as a career. Perhaps fortunately for him, in view of his later wide-ranging interests, the academic standard at Westminster City School was high (five boys of his year went on to Cambridge), and a particularly inspiring master called Satchel persuaded him to go to University College, London, to read history. Walter was the only one of his family to go to university. In later life he never had any real doubts that he had followed the right calling.

Undergraduate and Don

Walter Layton was fortunate in having a broad education both at school and University College, London, where he took a degree before going on to Cambridge. At school he had to study a wide range of subjects in addition to all his choral singing and music, instead of specializing from the age of fifteen or sixteen, as often happens now with really bright boys and girls.

He did not specialize either when he went to University College in September 1901. Instead, he enrolled for lectures in Latin, Greek, mathematics and economics as well as his main subject of history, which included Ancient Greek history as well as Modern history, both European and English. The formidable task he had set himself was made more interesting by the calibre of some of the lecturers, the poet A.E. Housman (lecturing on Cicero and the *Rudens* of Plautus), Professor Arthur Platt (on Euripides) and a number of outstanding Cambridge economists who lectured at University College as well as at Cambridge. These included Professor Foxwell, the young Pigou, then aged twenty-four years, who was to beat Foxwell for the Cambridge professorship in 1908, and C.P. Sanger of Trinity College, a first-class statistician. Layton was not so lucky with his professor of history, Montague, who read his thirty lectures on English constitutional history monotonously from an exercise book.

While he was kept busy at University College he was still living at home and there seems to have been little social life in the college, even though numbers were small by modern standards. In all there were 1,100 students of whom 400 were women. University College had always welcomed women (as well as dissenters), and in 1901 already had more women students than Cambridge. There is, however, no mention in Walter's Memoirs of any friends. Indeed, he wrote:

> My fellow students made little definite impact on my mind; nor did I often meet them outside the lecture rooms. I was very fortunate that from my earliest years the function of personal tuition was performed for me so adequately by my mother's wide interests and flair for teaching. For the first twenty years of my life I grew up in a home atmosphere which was always lively and exciting, but the life of a student at a non-residential university can become very lonely. It is an arid environment in which to spend one's formative years.

The man who made the biggest impact on Walter was C.P. Sanger, who took a small class in statistics in his flat overlooking Trafalgar Square. Leonard Woolf described this remarkable man (who had written a very interesting pamphlet on Emily Brontë while working on the use of mathematics in economic theory): 'A gnome-like man with the brightest eyes I have ever seen and the character of a saint, but he was a very amusing, ribald, completely sceptical saint with a first class mind and an extremely witty tongue, a mixture which I never came across in any other human being.'[2] He was also an

Apostle, a member of the highly select and secret Cambridge Conversazione Society.

Apart from Layton there were only two other members of Sanger's class, both women. One was Clara Collet, then aged about forty and a Fellow of University College, who had been a factory inspector and had worked with Charles Booth on his monumental study of life and labour in London. The other was Sophie, C.P. Sanger's younger sister, who had gone up to Newnham in 1900 and later devoted most of her life to the International Labour Organization. Layton probably had these people in mind when he wrote in his Memoirs: 'My years at University College certainly contributed to my background knowledge of international affairs and brought me into touch with a few more people whose idealism I shared and understood.'

It was thanks to Sanger too, that Layton became interested in statistics and put his knowledge to good advantage in the summer vacation of 1903. At that time the Board of Trade was in difficulties, having been asked by Balfour, then prime minister, to make a quick report on the state of British trade and industry, but not having the staff for the job. Sanger only agreed to help if he could bring Layton with him as an assistant, and he was very willing to earn £5 a week for five weeks, collating the scanty available statistics of wages in various overseas countries during the previous half century. As soon as that job was finished Hugh Meredith, an economic historian from King's College, Cambridge, got Layton to help him during the next five weeks in producing statistical ammunition for the campaign then being fought by the Free Trade Union, a society opposed to any introduction of tariffs.

Mainly because of being deflected onto all this statistical work, history was pushed on one side and Walter only got a third class degree. But his academic ability had already led earlier to his winning prizes in both economics and history. Moreover, after taking his history finals in October 1903, he went on to take a second class in economics in 1904 and attended M'Taggart's lectures on philosophy. Though his student career was not brilliant, he was to return to University College to give the Newmarch Lectures on statistics for three years from 1909, and in 1912 he became a Fellow of the College.

While Layton had only managed to scrape through his history

finals, Sanger clearly had a very high opinion of his abilities and urged him to sit for a scholarship at Trinity, Cambridge, although the examination was only six weeks off. He wanted him to take the new Economics Tripos which had just been instituted at Cambridge. Layton records in his Memoirs: 'I said no. I was nearly twenty years of age, I had seen a little of the world and I had long been financially independent and was not anxious to go back and make a fresh start as a student. But he was very insistent and finally I agreed to sit for the examination on the understanding that even if successful it would remain an open question whether I should go up to Cambridge or launch out on my career.' In the event, he failed to get a major scholarship, but he got other awards worth about £75 a year. This, of course, would not have been enough to support him at Cambridge. At that time it was reckoned that the minimum an undergraduate needed to pay his Cambridge bills was £120 a year, and this amount only looked after six months of the year and did not include clothing. To be comfortable and keep up with the majority £180–£200 was needed.

So Layton remained undecided about Cambridge for some time, but very soon other chances of earning money cropped up through his flair for statistics. He wrote a chapter on working-class household budgets for the Board of Trade and in February of 1904 was appointed assistant secretary to the Royal Commission on the Supply of Food and Raw Materials in Time of War. By the summer he had accumulated £150 of savings from his various earnings and another award had come his way, thanks to Parry, a Trinity don, who nominated him for a Fishmonger's Company scholarship.

Now that the money obstacle had been overcome he was persuaded of the soundness of Sanger's advice, that he should take the Economics Tripos at Cambridge. So, rather unwillingly, Layton went up to Trinity College, Cambridge, in October 1904 to read for the new Tripos. Probably he had doubts about taking another degree after a not very brilliant performance at University College. Perhaps, too, he feared he would feel out of place at Trinity among the public school boys, who would be mostly younger than he. Moreover, he had been lonely and unsociable at University College and still depended a good deal on his mother and sister. Nevertheless, in spite of these self-doubts, he took the plunge.

Trinity College and indeed, the whole university of eighty years ago, were very different from today, yet they are surprisingly recognizable. The sheer beauty of the college buildings along the Backs has not changed, even though there are some intrusions since Walter Layton's time. Trinity College itself has not changed, above all Great Court and Neville's Court with Wren's Library are as perfect as ever. Fortunately, the buildings which Trinity had planned in the nineteenth century to put up on the Backs were never constructed. Admittedly, Layton, after a year in lodgings in Portugal Place just behind the Norman Round Church, had rooms in Whewell's Court, a poor late nineteenth-century Gothic Revival building. To offset the noise at night from the street outside his window, he acquired the ability to go to sleep at will, which was to prove invaluable to him in later life when he worked very long hours.

Trinity was, then as now, a large college with 600 undergraduates as against its present 800. But the university was much smaller, a little over 3,000 men undergraduates and 300 women.[3] The mixture of social classes at Cambridge was also very different in 1904 and indeed remained so up to the Second World War. The freshmen of 1904 came very largely from public schools, although bright grammar school boys were appearing in increasing numbers.[4] Layton was one of this minority, but perhaps because he was more mature and more self-assured he was able to bridge the gap which still existed socially up to the Second World War. There were no student grants in those days, and the university received hardly any State aid until 1919.

Layton, although of athletic build, did not play team games or row while at Trinity, though this was a time when excellence in these pursuits was still held in high esteem, and the main division within colleges was between the intellectuals and the hearties. Bump suppers, except at Trinity and King's, still often ended with the hearties throwing the aesthetes into the college fountain or the Cam. Leonard Woolf wrote: 'Trinity was such a large college that one soon formed one's own circle of friends and acquaintances ... The hostility of the ordinary man to the scholar and the intellectual was therefore a good deal less important and less noticeable at Trinity than at some of the small colleges.'[5] While, as at present, the man who gained a first in his Tripos and a Blue was the most admired, many of the hearties read only for a pass degree, or went down with no degree at all. Only at King's from 1869 were all undergraduates required to take Honours, as soon became the custom in women's colleges, although women had to be content with a mere title to a degree until 1949. For a woman before 1914 to get to Cambridge at all required outstanding willpower, if only to overcome family opposition and social prejudice against blue stockings. So the women at Cambridge tended to be a bright lot.

In Layton's time only half the male undergraduates of the university were reading for Honours and, indeed, at Trinity the proportion was about 36 per cent Honours, 38 per cent pass degree.[6] The remaining 26 per cent took no degree at all, some because they never got over the first hurdle then presented by the 'little-go' exam needed for matriculation, but which could be taken after going into residence.[7]

For those reading Honours the most prestigious subjects were still mathematics (the only Cambridge Tripos until 1820) and classics. History and law were increasing in popularity (separate Triposes dating back to 1870) and natural sciences and engineering were well established. Economics, which Layton had come to read, had only started as a separate Tripos in 1903, having before formed part of the moral sciences and history Triposes. Its inception was largely due to the efforts of the Professor of Political Economy, Alfred Marshall.

While the university was much smaller in Layton's time, and socially was far more uniform than today, important changes were going on which make the Cambridge of 1904 recognizable to us today. The conventions and beliefs of late Victorian Cambridge were under strong attack. As Leonard Woolf put it: 'We found ourselves living in the springtime of a conscious revolt against the social, political, religious, moral, intellectual and artistic institutions, beliefs and standards of our fathers and grandfathers. The battle against Victorianism had not yet been won. Victory depended on us.'[8]

Society, in general, was becoming much more open and relations between men and women undergraduates simpler and more direct, even though chaperones were still required for women going to lectures or visiting men's colleges. Several developments in Layton's time helped towards the emancipation not only of women – although this was of the greatest importance in changing attitudes – but also of many of the more intelligent male undergraduates. The philosopher G.E. Moore had great influence. His ideas cut through the intellectual contortions of past philosophers and simply 'asked us to make quite certain that we knew what we meant when we made a statement, and to analyse and examine our beliefs in the light of common sense'.[9] Out of discussion of Moore's *Principia Ethica* came a neo-Platonism which gave prominence to the individual and his state of mind. It was a new form of rationalism which was immensely attractive to the young, since it seemed to give them a scientific basis for their beliefs.

This was also the time when Fabian socialism was making an impact on those with a social conscience, when Rupert Brooke and J.T. Sheppard were making the acting and witnessing of Greek tragedies exciting (even to those who did not understand ancient Greek), when the Marlowe Society gave great scope for undergraduate acting and when Bedales, the first of the coeducational schools, sent a small but particularly brilliant set of young men and women to Cambridge.

Layton at first made few close friends, but he was an intelligent, sensitive and conscientious young man and could not fail to be influenced by the new ideas all around him. Sometimes he reacted against them. He wrote in his Memoirs:

> I found myself among the Apostles, Lytton Strachey, Maynard Keynes, Bertie Russell and others of the circle with whom Charlie Sanger had consorted as a Fellow of Trinity. These highbrow discussions were not really my cup of tea.[10] Far more congenial to me was another group drawn from both Oxford and Cambridge, many of whose members later reached influential positions in practical affairs.

But Maynard Keynes was to become Walter's colleague from 1908 when both were to become lecturers in economics at Cambridge, and indeed they remained in close touch until Keynes's death in 1946. Moreover, Moore's rationalism must have appealed to Walter and he would have had sympathy for some of the new ideas being debated, even though he would have vigorously opposed others.

More to his taste was the talk that went on in King's at Lowes Dickinson's Discussion Society, to which some people from Trinity went. Lowes Dickinson, a lecturer in politics and political philosophy, and one of the main proponents of a separate Economics Tripos, was much admired by Walter's generation, both for the Socratic dialogues in his *Modern Symposium* and his *Letters from John Chinaman* and later for his advocacy of the League of Nations, at which Layton was himself to play an important part. Lowes Dickinson's combination of idealism, lightly carried though deeply felt, and his charm and interest in practical solutions to problems of peace and war had a great effect on Layton's contemporaries, including Rupert Brooke, Hugh Dalton and the author's father (F.W. Hubback).

Rather more radical than the Lowes Dickinson Society were the Fabians who had started a Cambridge town branch to discuss the ideas of Beatrice and Sydney Webb, H.G. Wells and others. Ben Keeling, a Wykehamist of the same year at Trinity as Layton, but reading history, took him to the town Fabian meeting in almost his first week, although he records:[11] 'Layton protested his fidelity to sound economic truth.' Keeling also records: 'The meeting was not enlivening. The five persons who were present (including Layton and myself) sat on disused grocery cases in an attic above a milk shop in Bridge Street. I remember that one of the members smoked a pipe which did not turn up into a bowl at the end, but opened out like a sort of megaphone and exuded a steady dribble of tobacco ash over its owner's trousers. I wondered if that was a specifically Fabian pipe.' Keeling was not deterred by this experience from founding a university branch in 1906. By the end of that year there were sixty members.

Although Layton liked him, Keeling's views were far from orthodox or 'sound'. He was in some ways the equivalent of his time to John Cornford, another Trinity historian (but a communist) in the 1930s. Both were to die young, Keeling as a sergeant-major, having refused a commission, leading his bombing platoon on the Western Front in 1917, Cornford in the International Brigade in Spain in 1936.

It may be that it was through his Fabian friends, such as Bill Hubback, that Layton got to know Rupert Brooke, and hence some of the young women of Newnham. Although Brooke, who was a keen member of the Fabians, found some Fabian ideas hard to take, proclaiming himself 'a William Morris sort of socialist', his good looks must have been a feature of Fabian meetings. These, unlike most University societies, were open to women and feminism was much discussed. Amber Reeves (the heroine of H.G. Wells's *Ann Veronica*) became treasurer and Katharine Cox, with whom Rupert Brooke fell unhappily in love, also held office. In the same circle, and all from Bedales, were Jacques Raverat (later to marry Gwen Darwin), and the four beautiful daughters of Sydney Olivier, a Fabian himself, who later moved from the Civil Service to become a Labour politician.

The Bedalians were, in part, responsible for the popularity of camping holidays and reading parties, which now filled part of the summer vacation of Layton's group of friends and later enabled them to keep in touch with each other after they had gone down. The previous generation would not have countenanced young men and women camping together, or sharing tumbledown country cottages. But now these reading parties came at Cambridge to be recognized as respectable enough and highly enjoyable whatever the weather. For some they led to love affairs and sometimes marriages, and for most these holidays helped cement friendships that lasted a lifetime. Even the fastidious Maynard Keynes joined in.[12] Walter Layton was then at the edge of a group of people of great vitality and intelligence, with some of whom he was later to become close friends and one of whom, Dorothy Osmaston, he was to marry. She attended his lectures and described him as the best looking young man in Cambridge after Rupert Brooke.

As an undergraduate Layton was, in many ways, self-sufficient, on his own, and very much taken up in his work. He was much influenced by his mother's ideals and by radical political ideas, though less so by the nonconformist faith in which he had been brought up. Perhaps his closest friend was his sister Margaret, to whom he expounded his philosophy of life in a letter which shows him moving away from his earlier conventional religious beliefs:

> Happiness only consists in the development and use in each man of his capabilities, and capabilities mental and physical when left unexercised decay and die ... If you take my philosophy of the ideal self, there is

> nothing for it but to find the ideal . . . I think I am getting out something of an ideal, finding out what I am capable of, what I wish to do, what balance to give to the various elements in life and in general slowly getting a firm footing in my outlook on life . . . The question to hammer out is this, what is there worth doing in life, how can I help?

Margaret must have questioned this simple faith, for he wrote again:

> So you don't think the Ideal Self very satisfactory. I'm not sure that I do either but I do think it is every whit as good as any other religion, for after all neither you nor I nor any other normal person guides their life in everyday matters by religion; we are almost entirely creatures of habit. I am afraid my Ideal Self idea is merely taking facts as I find them and putting on a covering from above without going to the root of the matter, but where is the root?

But, if Layton started his Cambridge life without many close friends, he does not seem to have suffered from loneliness. In a letter written in 1909 when he was working at Toynbee Hall, he tells Margaret:

> I well remember my first birthday at Cambridge. [This was his 21st birthday.] I was just beginning to feel what my new independence meant. I seem to remember having a special lot of lectures on that day and going home to a lonely lunch of bread and cheese, and realising what it meant to be a responsible person, a feeling which slowly grew from the time I went up. In the evening Keeling and Sandison came and feasted in my little room in Portugal Place in my honour.

Walter certainly worked hard – eight hours a day was his normal quota – but in a letter to Margaret of October 1905 he says he could easily fill in another eight hours with social engagements. But he did not mean parties, as he mentions playing music and singing at the Castle Inn Mission on Saturday nights, and at a Temperance meeting and a Harvest meeting. He also taught at an adult Sunday School. He went on to mention the cards on his mantelpiece about the activities of the Liberal Club, Missions in South East London, and the Social Discussion Society, which was a discussion group started by Professor Alfred Marshall. Then he mentions the Trinity Chess Club, of which he was secretary, the Field Club, the Athletic Club, the Non-Conformist Union, the Congregational Society and the Magpie and Stump (a light-hearted Trinity College debating society). In another letter to Margaret he wrote: 'I know these things run away with a tremendous amount of time but I can't help feeling it is not really time wasted and these are the things which keep me in touch with the outside world.'

He kept up his interest in politics and spoke occasionally at the Union. He attended Professor Marshall's Social Discussion Society whenever he could and played an active part in its discussions. He was sensible enough to go for a long bicycle ride before his Tripos exam in the summer of 1906 and wrote Margaret an ecstatic letter about bird song in the Cambridge countryside.

Cambridge Economics

Layton was fortunate in coming to Cambridge in 1904 with some knowledge of economic theory and statistics, thanks to Foxwell and Sanger at University College, London, just when Cambridge economics under Alfred Marshall was developing a blend of theory and practice for the solution of social problems, which suited Layton's mind and temperament.

The new Economics Tripos had started the year before, mainly as a result of argument and pressure over a long period by Marshall, supported by Lowes Dickinson, who became the first secretary of the Economics Board, and by Dr Ward, Master of Peterhouse. In his Plea of 7 April 1902 to the Senate, Marshall, after pointing out that there were economics faculties at London, Manchester and Birmingham Universities, argued that a separate Tripos was needed at Cambridge because 'Economic issues are growing in urgency and intricacy and economic causes exert an increasing control on the quality of human life'. Another reason was that:

> such studies offer abundant scope for the training and the exercise of those mental faculties and energies which it is the special province of the university to develop. The third is that those who are looking forward to a business career or to public life are likely to be preferentially attracted to a residentiary [sic] university which offers a good intellectual training and opportunities for distinction in subjects that will bear on their thoughts and actions in after life. It is not suggested that a technical preparation for

> business should be given here: nor that those looking forward to public life should leave Cambridge provided with ready-made opinions on controverted [sic] issues of the day. It is suggested merely that economists should be able to obtain here three years scientific training of the same character and on the same general lines as that given to physicists, to physiologists or engineers.

The main opposition came from Archdeacon Cunningham, the economic historian who was Layton's Director of Studies at Trinity during his first year,[13] and from M'Taggart, the philosopher. Cunningham said that the new Tripos would lead to overspecialization; a broadly based culture was needed for the study of economics, as was already provided by the history and moral sciences Triposes. M'Taggart found the demands of the economists arrogant.

Marshall and Lowes Dickinson won the debate in the Senate fairly easily, pointing out that the serious student of economics should not be required to learn a lot of medieval history, or to grapple with philosophy, which left him comparatively little time for his chosen subject. 'By the age of 22', wrote Marshall in his flysheet of 5 June 1903, 'examinations have done a man nearly all the good they can do him but not nearly all the harm.' Lowes Dickinson wrote in his flysheet at the same time:

> The Tripos it is said will be too narrow, too highly specialised. I am inclined, myself, to regret we have not at Cambridge any course of study so broad and so liberalising as Classical Greats at Oxford, but we have not; and a new proposal made at Cambridge should be judged by Cambridge standards. So judged, the new Tripos will, I believe, compare favourably with most of our established schools. It will be more humane than Mathematics or Natural Science, will provide a better intellectual discipline than History, and will, for many minds, be more stimulating than Classics.

Although Marshall and Lowes Dickinson won the debate, it is worth reflecting that until the 1920s most British economists of the front rank took their first degrees in other subjects. Pigou took history and moral sciences and won the Chancellor's prize for English Verse. His first fellowship thesis at King's was on Robert Browning as a religious teacher. When this thesis failed he turned, on Marshall's advice, to 'Variation on the price of tinned meat in the nineteenth century', which succeeded. Keynes read mathematics and, indeed, was only twelfth Wrangler.[14]

Layton soaked himself in Marshallian economics by attending Marshall's lectures for all his three undergraduate years. He wrote:

> It may be thought that this was overdoing it since his lectures were supposed to be for Part II of the Tripos, but I do not think I shall be exaggerating if I said he never once repeated himself. It was commonly said among the undergraduates that he took his text out of that morning's *Times* and talked about anything that had struck him in the day's news. It would be nearer the mark to say that he gave us the benefit of his current thinking on the book he was writing on industry and commerce.

Thus Marshall's lectures were always topical and informal, although to Keynes the informality of Marshall's lectures was such that 'in 1906 when I attended it was impossible to bring away coherent notes'. Walter Layton's notes, however, are clear and neat. Perhaps he wrote them up after each lecture, or perhaps he listened more carefully than Keynes, who studied economics under Marshall for only one term in the autumn of 1905 while making up his mind whether to go into the Civil Service or become a don – in the end he did both.

Pigou, whose lectures Walter also attended at this time, said in the course of a lecture given in 1939:

> For forty years down to 1914 economic thought in the UK was dominated by Marshall. For junior students the effect of this moral dictatorship was almost wholly good. The broader problems of economics being safe in Marshall's keeping, we were content in our early theses to attack narrow issues reasonably within our compass, but young men were put off tackling major issues because Marshall was so impressive.

The attraction of Marshallian economics to Layton was that it provided the general framework of ideas which satisfied a young man's desire for some certainty, while being closely related to the real world. In the Cambridge of the 1930s Marx and communism provided much greater certainty and more pervasive and demanding beliefs which attracted many young men and women then reading economics and history. But Layton would have almost certainly shied away from all that dogma and oversimplification. He approved, too, of Marshall's rejection of the arid *a priori* reasoning of the classical economists, based on the concept of economic man, and his insistence on the importance of economic history which showed the diversity of human behaviour. Theory had to be tested against the close study of the detailed facts of trade and industry. In his inaugural lecture in 1885 Marshall emphasized that economics was 'not a body of concrete truth but an engine for the discovery of concrete truth'.

Marshall, while reinforcing the liberal principles on which he had been brought up, helped Layton to feel that, provided the right facts and figures were assembled, it was possible to find solutions to many economic and social problems. Marshall thus strengthened the faith in reason which remained with Layton throughout his life. Marshall, too, had a great sense of social purpose and of the part Cambridge economics might play. The peroration of his inaugural lecture of 1885 was very much a clarion call:

> It will be my most cherished ambition . . . to increase the numbers of those whom Cambridge, the great mother of strong men, sends out into the world with cool heads but warm hearts willing to give some at least of their best powers to grappling with the social suffering around them; resolved not to rest content until they have done what in them lies to discover how far it is possible to open up to all the material means of a refined and noble life.

The new economics faculty had few undergraduates at first.[15] Only ten took Part I with Layton in 1905, of which five were women, and only three took Part II. In the early years there was a high proportion of women, perhaps because part of the Tripos was concerned with social problems and because teaching in most girls' schools meant that many women came up to Cambridge with a lower standard of achievement than men in mathematics, classics and science.[16] While the numbers of undergraduates were low at first, the number and standard of the dons lecturing on economics was high, with historians and moral scientists coming to share in some of the lectures. Layton kept his lecture notes neatly in hard-backed notebooks, some with marbled end papers. From these it is clear that, in addition to attending Marshall's lectures throughout his three years, for instance in Michaelmas term 1904 on Credit and Speculation and in the Lent term 1905 on the Structure and Problems of Modern Industry and the Interpretation of Modern Statistics, he went on to hear Lowes Dickinson on the British Constitution, and Pigou on the Principles of

Economics. He also went to hear Hugh Meredith, D.H. Macgregor and E.A. Benians on General and Economic History, H.Y. Oldham on Economic Geography and W.E. Johnson on Mathematical Economics. While Lowes Dickinson advised his pupils who found they could get more out of reading than out of lectures to stay away, Layton clearly found lectures useful. He also took pride in his essays, some of which he kept throughout his life with the rest of his papers. Read again now, they seem good solid stuff based on a real grasp of the subject. In May 1905 he was writing an essay for Archdeacon Cunningham on the good and evil of Joint Stock Companies from a strict economist's point of view. It is not possible to tell what the Archdeacon thought of his efforts, but Marshall always used to write his comments – which were normally copious – in red ink. He wrote on one of Layton's essays: 'You ought to do more papers. You could correct them yourself almost as well as anyone else could. Almost every answer you send me contains something that is high class. It would do you a great deal of good to make a precis of your answer getting at the gold and dumping the earth on the refuse heap.' He also wrote later: 'I hope you may grow up to be too good an economist for the Civil Service to content you. But, of course, a man at the Treasury has great opportunity, e.g. Llewellyn Davies.'[17]

Quite early on Layton began publishing his work. First an article in the *Economic Journal* in March 1905 on the Argentine and Food Supply, a remarkable feat for a first year economist. Then in October 1905, also in the *Economic Journal*, a review of the Report of the Royal Commission on the Supply of Food and Raw Materials in Time of War, a subject he knew well from the work he had done as assistant secretary to the Commission in the early part of 1904 while waiting to go up to Cambridge.

Layton got his First in the first part of the Tripos in 1906, though Marshall warned him he was rather lucky and he must restrict his outside activities if he was to do well in the second part. It seems doubtful whether, in fact, he did follow that advice. He certainly took part in the *Eumenides* in the autumn of 1906 and he was the runner-up for the Winchester Reading Prize, which is surprising for one who later was a poor public speaker. In any event, he duly got a First in the second part of the Tripos in 1907 and also won the Gresham

Studentship in Economics at Caius College, the first postgraduate endowment at Cambridge. He records that he moved down the road from Trinity with regret, but he went on to win the Cobden Prize with a very solid piece of work on changes in the relative wages of mining, textile, iron and steel, agriculture and domestic workers. There were no less than twenty appendices.

In the autumn of 1907, when he was finishing off his Cobden Prize essay, a major dispute was boiling up over the refusal of the railway companies to recognize trade union officials as negotiators for a wage claim. Layton was asked by Richard Bell, secretary of the Amalgamated Society of Railway Servants (predecessor of the present NUR), to analyse the replies received to a census of railway wages organized by Bell, who had claimed that 100,000 railwaymen earned less than £1 a week. Layton completed the job within a month with the help of Professor Bowley and twenty assistants. He showed that 38 per cent of railway workers were receiving only £1, or less, for hours far in excess of those worked in most industries. But Bell was disappointed since most of the low-paid were found to be on the £1 a week mark and not below. However, publication of the facts aroused public sympathy for the railwaymen and Lloyd George, then President of the Board of Trade, intervened to force the railway companies to negotiate with the unions.[18] Had it not been for this work on railway wages, Layton would have played the part of Mephistopheles in *Faust*, which the newly formed Marlowe Society was to perform in the autumn of 1907, but he could not get to rehearsals and eventually Rupert Brooke took his place.

In 1908 Layton started taking Workers' Educational Association tutorial classes, first at Battersea, later at Leicester and Portsmouth. These classes consumed a lot of his energy, but much more important from the point of his future career was a meeting with F.W. Hirst, editor of the *Economist*, who heard him speak in the spring of 1908 at Marshall's Discussion Society on the Licensing Bill, then going through the House, and asked him for an article. Layton provided a well written, thoroughly readable piece, arguing that a licence to sell liquor conferred a valuable monopoly for which the State at that time received a totally inadequate return. This was the beginning of an association with the *Economist* which lasted until his death fifty-eight years later. From 1908 onwards, up to the outbreak of war in 1914, Layton went to the *Economist* at least once a week and sometimes more often, to work as one of the assistant editors.

It was in the autumn of 1908 that Layton's career really took off, even though his attempt at a Trinity Fellowship failed.[19] By then Pigou, at the age of thirty, had succeeded Marshall as Professor of Political Economy and appointed Layton as one of his assistant lecturers, financing him with £100 from his own pocket, just as Marshall had previously financed Pigou. It seems that this arrangement went on until 1911 when Layton became a university lecturer. Marshall was delighted at his appointment, especially as he had feared that he might go into the Indian Civil Service. Keynes was appointed an assistant lecturer at the same time and on the same terms. Marshall wrote to him: 'I am delighted indeed that you are to join our economic staff. I think it is a brilliant compact group of eminent men, full of the highest promise for the future.' The group, apart from Pigou, Keynes and Layton, was made up of Lowes Dickinson, W.E. Johnson, J.H. Clapham, C.R. Fay, H.O. Meredith and L. Alson.

Layton lectured on the problems of industry and labour, and later on public finance. Lectures at Cambridge were not compulsory but his were well attended. He records that Hugh Dalton and Gerald Shove and his future wife, Dorothy Osmaston, were among his early students, who increased in number to twenty-nine in 1910. At that time he was also lecturing to Laurence Cadbury (with whom he was to be associated at the *Daily News* and *News Chronicle* for a great many years) and a number of young men who later became eminent economists, such as Dennis Robertson, F. Lavington, Claude Guillebaud and Harold Wright. In the same year was Philip Noel Baker, who became a lifelong friend and, together with Laurence Cadbury, a trustee of Dorothy Layton's marriage settlement. Among the women were Margery Olivier and Faith Bagenal, who was later to marry Hubert Henderson, another eminent economist whom Layton taught and who became a close colleague in later life. His lectures were also attended by engineering and other undergraduates not reading economics. But Keynes usually outshone him. Dr J.N. Keynes recorded in his diary in January 1910 that Maynard's lectures on the

Stock Exchange attracted an audience of fifty-two, 'and there wasn't even standing room'.

To supplement his small salary as a lecturer Layton supervised as many undergraduates as he could manage. One of these was Laurence Cadbury, whose literary style Layton thought he ought to try and improve. He confessed in a letter to Dorothy in November 1909: 'I have been telling him to read literature – I who know nothing about it myself!'

In the period leading up to the outbreak of war in 1914 Walter Layton turned himself into a first-class applied economist through his teaching and other activities. As he put it in his Memoirs: 'In the ten years preceding the First World War, I was soaked in economic theory, first under Marshall's direction, then as a teacher. But my chief interest was always in applied economics rather than in theory ... It almost seemed in retrospect that I was being trained to take part in the central planning of a World War.'

There was no hint of a world war in 1908 and, indeed, the future must have looked calm and assured. Layton settled into the course he followed throughout his life, which was to work up to the limit of his abilities, not principally for money, but because he was intensely interested. It was not just the nonconformist conscience at work, or his desire to help his parents financially, though those were important influences. It was probably more his determination to get on top of his chosen subject and to take every opportunity to play his part, both at the university and in public affairs.

CHAPTER TWO

Walter and Dorothy, 1909–14

No one at Cambridge at that time can have been surprised when, in September 1909, Walter Layton and Dorothy Osmaston announced their engagement. Both were very good-looking and highly intelligent. Shena Potter, a contemporary of Dorothy's who later married Ernest Simon, a lifelong colleague of Walter's, wrote in a letter to Walter after Dorothy's death: 'I always think of her as I first saw her – she was two years junior to me at Newnham. I had never seen before – nor since – such gloriously blue eyes in a fairytale pink and white complexion and a halo of really blonde hair.'

Dorothy had attended Walter's lectures and did well in Part II of the Economics Tripos after only one year's work instead of the normal two. She recorded later: 'I was coached by Mrs Marshall of whom I was very fond, and who was as fond of me as the Professor was of Walter.' She and Walter had many friends in common at the university. Both were serious-minded and interested in politics with a radical approach, though at that time Walter was a Liberal and Dorothy still a Conservative. Both had a deep sense of responsibility to their parents. Above all, both were overflowing with energy. Perhaps it was surprising that Walter did not fall in love with Dorothy earlier, when he rowed her back from the May Races in 1907, or when they met at a Fabian meeting or, rather more excitingly, skating that same winter on the frozen Fens.

Fifty years later Walter wrote an extraordinarily moving book about Dorothy,[1] soon after she had died of cancer, a serene death after a long drawn out and painful illness. Some people found the book, especially the detailed account of Dorothy's last few months, embarrassing, but many of those who knew both of them well were glad that Walter was able, on this occasion, to express his love fully and freely, so much in contrast to his normal reserve. Walter's book *Dorothy* amply repays reading in full. Here it suffices to give a brief account of Dorothy's background and early years, with a glance forward to the way in which her character and Walter's complemented each other – each playing a very different role in family, if not in public life, in which Dorothy too had her triumphs.

Dorothy was three years younger than Walter. She was born in 1887 of parents both of whom came from large families. Her father, Francis Osmaston, was descended from wealthy industrialists and her mother, Eleanor Field, from scholarly Anglican clergymen. Dorothy's paternal great grandfather, John Wright, built an enormous mansion at Osmaston for his ten children. 'Coal was distributed throughout the house [it was three hundred and thirty feet long] by means of a small railway moving through a tunnel in the basement. The smoke from the fifty or so coal fires of the mansion was discharged in a single factory-like chimney, built some distance from the house.' His son (who changed his name to Osmaston) and his grandson, Dorothy's father Francis, both turned away from industry to painting. Francis wrote a classic work on Tintoretto's gigantic picture *Il Paradiso*, and translated Hegel's *Philosophy of Fine Art*. He was also a good amateur musician.

On her mother's side, Dorothy had eleven uncles and aunts. Her maternal grandfather, Canon Field, to whom she was devoted, was a classical scholar who tutored Edward VII when, as Prince of Wales, he was up at Cambridge. Three of her Field uncles were Anglican clergymen.

Dorothy had a lonely childhood. She was an only child until the age of five, when her brother was born (another boy came later), and her mother was very delicate. She wrote later that she suffered from a sense of insecurity. She spent much of her time away from home, staying with grandparents or uncles and aunts. She became happier when the family moved to 16 Church Row, Hampstead, when she was seven and there were plenty of children with whom to make friends. At that time, too, she loved the walks on the Heath with her father. This all ended two years later when her father had a near-fatal bicycle accident and she was sent away to boarding school, which she hated. She was desperately homesick but did not complain because her aunts had impressed on her that she must never say anything to worry her mother. In the holidays she was sent to relations and never returned to Hampstead.

Fortunately, the hated school went bankrupt and Dorothy was sent to Mrs Julia Huxley's new school, Prior's Field at Godalming, at the age of fifteen. Here she had first-rate teaching, both of academic subjects and the piano. She could also play 'real games', such as hockey and cricket, at which she excelled. There were Easter walking holidays in her teens with her father on the mountains above Lucerne, which Dorothy loved, but looking back much later, after her parents had died, and reading the letters they had kept, she found, to her distress, criticism of her cocksureness, matter-of-factness and selfishness. Reflecting on this criticism she wrote to Walter: 'A lot of this in my youth was due not to certainty of my own powers, but to lack of assurance really at heart, which, to an overwhelming extent, you with your astonishing love and appreciation and faith in me, dissipated.'

As for so many others of her generation at Cambridge, the world opened up for Dorothy when she went to Newnham, which she took by storm, although she records that she was 'at first really rather fundamentally lonely though popular at college as "Osmy"'. Within a year or so she made many lifelong friends, several of whom either were already Walter's friends or become so soon after. In a brief memoir written towards the end of her life Dorothy records:

> One of my first friends was Katherine Cox, but she soon joined a very narrow clique, far too narrowly intellectual for me, whom they despised. We all went crazy over The Eumenides which was acted in the university theatre, Walter was one of the devils [presumably Dorothy meant Furies] and we went about in red cloaks. Meanwhile, I joined the Raleigh Musical Society and became its secretary in succession to Evelyn Radford, who became my first real friend at the end of my first year ... I made great friends with Eva Hubback in my second year – a friendship which never sagged through all the years to her unexpected death in 1949 ... all our work for womens' movements we pursued together to the end. Through Eva I came to know Lynda Grier,

who was an economics student. Through Eva, too, and Amber Reeves, I was brought into the Fabian Society and began to make many Fabian male friends at the James Wards' Sunday evening parties ... there I met Donald Robertson ... Rupert Brooke and Dudley Ward. In my last year my old friend Marjory Olivier came up to college. All four Oliviers, Marjory, Bryn, Daphne and Noel, were great friends of mine at Limpsfield.

Whilst both Dorothy and Walter had many friends in common, Walter was very much aware of their different backgrounds, which he described in *Dorothy*:

One of them brought up in well-to-do circumstances of material ease but in a home where there were internal anxieties that gave her in her early years a feeling of insecurity and the loneliness of an only child. The other brought up in relatively straitened circumstances and the day to day task of earning a living, personally shy, perhaps, but full of confidence and revelling in responsibility. The one born into conservatively-minded surroundings and the traditions of the established church, the other to an atmosphere of non-conformity and radicalism. The girl seeming young and unsophisticated even to her college contemporaries, exuberant and full of vitality, and keen to respond to the call of the re-awakening world that had succeeded the Victorian era. The man plunged into a political maelstrom before he was twenty and seizing with both hands the opportunities and responsibilities that fate was pushing with rapid succession within his reach.

But there were similarities also that were at least as important as the contrasts. In the political field they shared a common opinion in several important matters. Female suffrage and the equality of the sexes was one. The Peace Movement was another. Both had grown up in a musical home. Love of outdoor life and physical exercise was yet another link. Finally, the relationship of lecturer and student, though by no means a guarantee of a smooth journey to a golden wedding, could not fail to widen the area of common interests and so help to give a life partnership a good send off.

Walter proposed rather awkwardly and abruptly to Dorothy in early June 1909 in the garden of Newnham College. He was terrified that, with the university vacation just beginning, she would leave Cambridge and he might lose her. She was naturally too embarrassed to talk since the garden was full of her fellow Newnhamites. So they bicycled out along the Coton footpath and resumed their talk lying in a meadow. Dorothy recorded in her diary 'He was quite confident' but she would not commit herself. They agreed to meet again from time to time, without commitment, but Dorothy at least put a wild rose in Walter's buttonhole. Then they rode slowly back to Cambridge.

The first meeting at Dorothy's home at Limpsfield was agonizing for Walter, as there was no opportunity for the talk he longed for with Dorothy. She did, however, ask him to go on a camping holiday in Sussex to which she had been invited by David Garnett, together with a number of Cambridge friends. Heavy rain flooded the tents and they all took refuge in a barn. So again there was no chance of private talk. Dorothy's return visit to Walter's home in Chelsea was no success either, probably because Walter was away most of the time and Dorothy was subjected to what she described as 'a very nonconformist atmosphere'. But she came again a few weeks later to make arrangements to do Care Committee work several days a week. She was still hesitant and worried. She wrote in her diary: 'Walter talks again about what he told me at Cambridge. I see he would never consider me as a mere friend. I think I ought to go home.'

But she stayed and went to Whitechapel the next day, the Jewish New Year, where everybody wished her a happy New Year. Walter and she discussed their differences about religion which then seemed a barrier, but that and other barriers were, in fact, coming down fast. They arranged to meet for lunch the next day at Toynbee Hall. Walter wrote in *Dorothy*:

> Punctually at one o'clock we both turned up in Commercial Street coming from opposite directions, and as we caught sight of one another on the crowded pavement we waved. It was enough. I knew at once that it was the green light. What the Warden [Ted Harvey] talked about to his luncheon guests I have no idea. Immediately after lunch we both went off to work, she to her Care Committee and I to the *Economist*. Back at Stanley House for tea, my sister, Margaret, sang to us until it was time for Dorothy to set out for Victoria to catch her train back to Limpsfield. We set out – but 'three yards settled it,' says her diary.

They were deeply in love. Walter overcame all his inhibitions when he came to describe, more than fifty years later, the great bear hug Dorothy gave him. All the doubts of the last few months were swept away as by a tidal wave.

The next evening after dinner as we sat in Mrs Osmaston's little study something physical happened to Dorothy. Whether it is properly to be described as an aura I do not know, but she certainly glowed with a beauty that I had never seen before, and as she turned to go upstairs to her room I looked at Mrs Osmaston questioningly. 'Did you see that?' I said. She smiled and nodded her head. I added, 'She was transfigured.' Again she assented. From that moment Dorothy's mother shared the knowledge of our spiritual union as no one else did.

Next morning I sent a message to my own mother in Scotland: 'I have seen the Madonna. It is inexpressibly lovely.' Her intuition correctly interpreted this cryptic message.

Their engagement was welcomed by both their families but inevitably they had to come down to ordinary life again. Dorothy's father's letter enquiring about Walter's means was to be expected, though it was expressed in slightly odd terms: 'I shall be anxious to hear that you feel it in your power to give her within a reasonable time a house that both my wife and myself can regard with every satisfaction.'

Things were not made easier for Walter when Dorothy, very soon after they had become engaged, dutifully accompanied her parents on a long planned two months' motor tour of the galleries of Western Europe. Mr Osmaston was anxious to see a picture of *The Three Graces* in Italy recently ascribed to Tintoretto which he might possibly buy. During this time Walter wrote to Dorothy every day, and sometimes twice or even three times.

Walter's love letters show him as an adoring lover with Dorothy his 'Madonna and little mother'. They also contain many prayers to God for the life they are going to lead together, both for his sake and 'for the sake of the woman given to me'. But not all the letters are heavily serious. Walter says he cannot appreciate pictures, and asks how Dorothy can bear to see a new one every day. 'Nor have I ever seen an Old Master which gave me as much satisfaction as the best modern pictures.' He also mentions a major political meeting: 'Asquith is at the moment making the biggest speech of his life at the Albert Hall and this afternoon they found two suffragettes hidden in the organ, of all places. Mother was playing there for one of their meetings last night.' He records too how when his friend Dudley Ward won a Fellowship at St John's in November they went out to

Grantchester and bathed in the river with Rupert Brooke on the strength of it.

These letters were often written on trains as Walter carried out his many work commitments. He wrote later in *Dorothy*:

> Force of circumstances had landed me in the heaviest programme of work I have ever undertaken with the exception of some moments of wartime crisis. Tuesdays, Thursdays and Fridays at the *Economist* where I set to work to revise the fifty year old Price Index number, initiated a regular compilation of the profits for Joint Stock Companies, compiled the first Index number of the volume and value of our foreign trade, and made other statistical innovations in addition to ordinary leader writing. Two courses of lectures at Cambridge on Mondays and Wednesdays, as well as coaching private pupils; a weekly tutorial class of the WEA at Portsmouth every Saturday night, and another one at Leicester on Wednesday evenings, both of which involve long railway journeys, and the correction of students' essays on my slow Sunday trek back from Portsmouth via Brighton to London and Cambridge; and when Dorothy and her parents finally crossed over to Europe on 1st November, at least one letter a day to her was added to the routine.

Not surprisingly, he could not keep up this fierce pace. When at Christmas 1909 he went to meet Dorothy at Klosters, where she was chaperoned by an aunt, he found skiing was quite impossible. He virtually collapsed, as he did on a number of other occasions in his life when the nervous strain became too great. On this occasion the combination of a long separation from Dorothy, high altitude and the effects of overwork was too much for him. The breakdown was probably triggered by Dorothy going off on long excursions with an expert skier, a widower who had been much attracted to her on her previous visits to Klosters. Walter must have felt jealous as well as inferior to Dorothy's companion in social class, worldly goods and ability to ski. The excursions were quite blameless, and indeed Walter had pressed Dorothy to go and get some high-level skiing without being restricted by him. However, he became acutely anxious when snow began to fall after they had been gone a few hours on the first excursion. He struggled up by the side of the toboggan run in the direction of the route by which they expected to return by sunset. But they were not back by the time night fell and Walter slowly made his way down again in darkness, only to hear they had skied down by a different route and would be coming up the valley by train, arriving at midnight. This experience terrified him:

> In two or three days I was a nervous wreck. I was ordered to bed, and before the week was out the local doctor sent us down into the valley, where we put up at a deserted station hotel and played dominoes, bagatelle and read novels to one another for a month before the doctor would let me travel ... When we got home Mrs Osmaston took one look at us and remarked 'The sooner you two are married the better.'

Having discovered the limits of his strength, Walter cut some of his work outside Cambridge by giving up his Portsmouth lectures and only going to the *Economist* one day a week. There was much discussion, too, about whether it would be right to leave Cambridge and even the *Economist* in order to take up a job in Manchester, writing for the *Manchester Guardian*, or going as professor of economics to Sheffield. It was clear that a lot of possibilities were opening up for Walter and, perhaps, by then, after years of Cambridge life, he was wondering whether he would not be able to support a family better elsewhere. He worried too that he might run to seed in Cambridge, where it was so easy to live pleasantly without achieving anything worth while. He wrote to Dorothy in November 1909:

> It is difficult for Cambridge people to remain progressive – the atmosphere is simply permeated with snobbery. It is not exactly the snobbery of wealth. It is the snobbery of intellect – intellect that does not know the world outside – that does not realise the limitations of mere intellect, although I am bound to say I have been surprised to find how readily people there will listen to what one has to say about what is going on in the big world outside. I have noticed in both Keynes and Pigou a most unexpected interest in the feelings and opinions of the man in the street, though I don't feel quite sure how genuine it is.

He did, however, write in a letter to Dorothy that he would be very sorry to leave the *Economist*: 'I am learning to write English, to express myself rapidly. To concentrate first on one thing then on another. To exercise judgement and as time goes on will carry more weight and get to know the City and, of course, be in touch with people behind the Press.' Moreover, he mentions that Marshall was reported as having said that: 'If Layton deserts Cambridge I'll never forgive him.'

But Layton did not desert Cambridge in 1910. The marriage was brought forward to April and Walter and Dorothy had an idyllic honeymoon in Dorset near Studland in a small four-roomed cottage shared with a gardener and his wife. Dorothy recorded later that they lived on the plainest of food and spent their entire time wandering about and making love on the Downs and the sand dunes, then completely deserted.

They then returned to a newly built house on the Hills Road opposite the second milestone out of Cambridge. The author's mother wrote to Bill Hubback: 'These two children are most happily installed here in a little house far out on the Hills Road looking straight out on the Gogs and with fields all round. They have only just moved in and are in the throes of making curtains and digging up the garden. In fact I am their first visitor. They are a great joke and chortle all day long.'

Just before his marriage Walter wrote a letter praying on behalf of both for strength. Later, in 1911, after they had been married eighteen months and had a daughter, Walter wrote: 'We must have family worship round the fire, servants present, Margaret holding mother's hand hearing father reading the words of profound truth.' This may have been written with tongue in cheek, but I rather doubt it. I think it is more probable that it shows the Victorian paterfamilias in Walter which later developed into his enthusiasm for teaching his children to sing and play musical instruments.

Marshall, who was obviously still concerned about Walter overworking, gave him sound advice in a letter written late in 1910:

> If you could make the same thoughts answer for:
>
> 1 Part of your duty to the *Economist*,
>
> 2 Part of your lecture work and,
>
> 3 A few short books or rather a collection of essays, I think your work would have a high quality and the chance of your breaking down through overstrain would be diminished. If you try and ride three horses at once I fear for your health; strong men who overtax their strength often come to the ground with a bigger thump than others ... I think Bagehot worked somewhat on those lines and I am inclined, being a mere old fogey, to support as a motto, Live up to Bagehot!

Walter accepted this advice, which fitted in very well with his interest in applied economics. In the next few years he achieved much without overworking himself. His study of the history of wages and prices was useful at the *Economist* and in the lecture room both in Cambridge and at University College, London, where he gave the Newmarch lectures. He was also able to publish several articles which culminated in his best-known book, *An Introduction to the Study of Prices*, which appeared in 1912. Walter clearly had an early reputation as an expert on statistics. In the Caius College magazine, *The Caian*, of 1911, there is an account of an imaginary feast attended by famous past members of the college, dating back to Thomas Gresham, William Harvey and Judge Jeffreys. The only representative of the modern age taking part in this imaginary discussion was Walter Layton, who talks index numbers and trade returns.

But there was quite a lot of play too. Dorothy and Walter sang together in the Cambridge University Musical Society in Elgar's *The Apostles*, which was performed in King's College Chapel, and in *The Magic Flute*. Walter tried to get Dorothy to play golf, but she was happiest when they went walking along the Roman Road over the Gogmagog Hills with a picnic lunch. They went walking, too, over the Yorkshire Moors, the mountains of North Wales and once right round the Mont Blanc massif.

They wanted children, and had them quickly, Margaret in March 1911, Michael in September 1912 and David in July 1914. Though Margaret had poor health as a young child, Dorothy managed to fit in a certain amount of outside work, including campaigns for votes for women. By June 1912 Walter had again begun to look outside Cambridge for promotion. It may be that though he was only twenty-eight years old he felt more money was needed. Margaret had been ill and a second child was expected. In any event, he applied for the professorship of economics at the Armstrong College, Newcastle. Although Marshall's testimonial described him as 'unequalled among the younger British economists in realistic study' and 'in every sense an accomplished efficient man of the world' he did not get the job. In 1914 he applied for and won an Otto Kahn travelling fellowship, which would have financed a year's tour of the world for the study of international economic and political affairs. The formal document, asking the assistance of all concerned abroad who might help him in his work, was dated 5 August 1914.

CHAPTER THREE

An Economist at War, 1914–19

Up to 1914 Walter Layton was establishing himself as a good applied economist with a deepening knowledge of British industry and a gift for making effective use of statistics. While not a professional statistician, he saw the necessity for filling the then major gaps in economic statistics, to meet the needs both of the academics and the policymakers. Layton's book on the study of prices, published in 1912, helped fill some of these gaps. Revised twice after the war, the book was required reading well into the 1930s. The work Layton and others did in updating the *Economist*'s Index of Wholesale Prices, until then based largely on the mix of imports of the 1870s, and in calculating foreign trade figures in volume as well as value terms, was also of great importance. Had there been no war in 1914 Layton might well have stayed on at Cambridge lecturing to increasing numbers of budding economists and industrialists, and either producing himself, or stimulating others to produce, more of the statistical series which later the government came to compute and publish. He had many friends and interests at Cambridge and might have stayed there all his working life, perhaps ending as head of a college, though probably not as professor of economics. More likely he would have been appointed to a Chair in some other university where the economics of industry were held in higher esteem, and perhaps, in due course, he would have become a vice-chancellor. If he had been consulted by Whitehall it would probably have been on technical matters rather than on questions of high policy.

The war, however, was to transform Layton's career and he was never to go back to academic life, though pressed to do so by Professor

Marshall in 1918. He left the *Economist* on 6 August because he was entirely out of sympathy with the anti-war views of the editor, F.W. Hirst, who had been arguing that Britain should be strictly neutral. He left his university job shortly afterwards to work at the Local Government Board under Seebohm Rowntree. His job there was to chart the expected increase in unemployment following the outbreak of war. But when it became clear that shortages of skilled labour were going to be the main problem, William Beveridge asked him to move to the Board of Trade to take a weekly census of employment designed to find out where skilled labour was to be found and whether it was usefully employed.

Layton made his mark in Whitehall quickly. According to a letter Keynes wrote to Pigou he was to have a staff of sixty including Hubert Henderson and 'most of those who have taken the Economics Tripos'. Layton did not, in fact, acquire such a large staff, but the regular manpower statistics produced, at first by an untrained staff working very long hours, were essential for the running of the war since they provided the basis for the country's first manpower budget.[1] This was important work; yet no one would have forecast when Layton was transferred to the Ministry of Munitions, set up in May 1915, that he was to become one of the main people on whom Lloyd George, Winston Churchill and other munitions ministers relied. Others of Layton's contemporaries, Maynard Keynes, Arthur Salter and Josiah Stamp, were to have a similar meteoric rise to fame during the war. Indeed, this might have been foretold of Keynes with his growing prewar reputation, dating back to his membership of the Indian Finance Commission. But it was Layton who was made a Companion of Honour in 1919 while Keynes was awarded the more usual CB allotted to many senior civil servants, and then only after Lloyd George had personally deleted Keynes's name from the list the first time it was submitted. Salter and Stamp had to be content with CBEs.

It is not easy to discover why a reserved, quiet young Cambridge don who did not push himself forward should have risen to near the top of the ministry by 1917, but Lloyd George and Winston Churchill both played important parts. Layton had been impressed by Lloyd George's eloquence as early as 1904 when he spoke in a Cambridge

Union debate and got to know him slightly in 1912 through Seebohm Rowntree. But Lloyd George had no chance of judging Layton's capabilities until the spring of 1915. Then, as Chancellor of the Exchequer, he became involved in munitions when the country grew concerned about Kitchener's totally inadequate grasp of the army's requirements, once the fighting in France got bogged down in trench warfare. In April 1915 Lloyd George was made chairman of a new Munitions of War Committee, of which Beveridge was a member, and Layton joined the committee's secretariat as statistical expert on the supply of labour. Lloyd George must have spotted Layton's talents, since he asked for his advice on a number of other statistical questions, and when the Ministry of Munitions was set up in May 1915 as part of the new coalition government, he took Layton with him. Layton wrote in his Memoirs:

> Within a matter of hours I found myself in a large bare room at 7 Whitehall Gardens, with only a table and a couple of chairs as furniture, in company with Mr Lloyd George and his parliamentary secretary, Dr Christopher Addison, who were planning to get the new Ministry going. Lloyd George's first question to me was 'What plant have we in Britain capable of making munitions? We must find out.'

Layton set up the census of machinery and plant, but before it was finished he was made Director of Requirements and Statistics, through whose office all the War Office demands for munitions had to pass. From these demands, and the returns from the production departments showing how far they were being met, Layton produced weekly printed progress reports for Lloyd George. This was one of the principal means by which Lloyd George, a remarkably good administrator, ran his rapidly growing department. Layton recorded in his Memoirs:

> Week after week the Minister's copy of this forbidding-looking document came back to me on Monday morning scored all over with underlinings, question marks, marginal notes requiring action. It was the instrument through which Lloyd George controlled the rapidly growing and shapeless colossus that he had created.

These reports were not always deadly serious. In December 1915 it was recorded that:

Sir Watkins Wynn is successfully developing a considerable output of 18 pdr. shell at Wynnstay Park. A considerable number of antiquated lathes collected from local collieries and small works have been ingeniously adjusted for shell making which is carried out by old servants of the estate and women of the household under Sir Watkins' personal supervision. The Inspector reports excellent work.

In giving evidence to the House of Commons Select Committee on National Expenditure in October 1917, Layton said 'his own position became very much that of a personal assistant to Mr Lloyd George'. In these early days of the ministry the sky was the limit for munitions, and the businessmen who had been brought in to run the production departments were allowed to thrust ahead on their own. But someone had to keep a check on what was happening and give Lloyd George a reliable estimate of how far the desired programmes for guns, shells and other munitions could be achieved. Layton had exactly the right intellectual gifts and training to do this job and he was able to assemble a staff which could provide Lloyd George with the crucial figures he needed to run his ministry and to get his way in Cabinet. He soon became indispensable. When he got ill through overwork in August 1915, Lloyd George wrote in his own hand to Dorothy:

I am so sorry your husband has had a temporary breakdown. I know how hard he has worked during the past few weeks. I blame myself for not realising in time that he was overtaxing his strength but the demands of this terrible war upon the resources of everybody are so unconstrainable that we can only go on until nature declines to march any further. His absence is a real loss to me but he must not worry. He will come back to his duties all the more vigorous for this enforced rest. I think that I too got a chill at the Cabinet meeting. I am rather disposed to believe that the facts we disclosed gave our colleagues a chill.

The pressure of work went on growing that summer and autumn. Lloyd George was determined that artillery production should be such that 'high explosives would pour like rain on the enemy's trenches all along the front'.[2] On his own responsibility he doubled the number of guns asked for by the War Office, to be ready by March 1916, in order to make sure there was enough productive capacity in the munitions factories. There was considerable opposition from the Chancellor, Reginald McKenna, and other ministers on the grounds that Lloyd George was asking for too great a share of the nation's resources. But Lloyd George for the most part got his way in Cabinet, and the guns were produced, even though their late arrival led to the start of the battle of the Somme being delayed until July 1916.

Layton went with Lloyd George to Cabinet committees and also to France for periodic meetings with M. Thomas, the French minister of munitions, and the Commander in Chief, Sir Douglas Haig. Layton's rapid success must have been only in part due to Lloyd George's liking for him. In a fast-growing ministry, mainly staffed in the higher ranks by businessmen with direct access to Lloyd George, the comparatively few senior civil servants must have recognized Layton's abilities to impose some order on the munitions programme, to work out the priorities and to produce reliable progress reports. He knew enough about industry to gain the confidence of the businessmen and he got on well with the generals, because he swiftly made himself expert on munitions. Moreover, he posed no threat to career civil servants, though he was showing all the characteristics of a first-rate civil servant himself.

The war had a far more momentous effect on Walter Layton's career than on his home life. Admittedly, his income fell from the £1,200 he had earned at Cambridge to £700, which was his Ministry of Munitions salary, but he was fortunate in that he remained a civilian and thus was not separated for long periods from his family like most of his soldier contemporaries. However, the tranquil setting of his house, The Milestone, on the edge of Cambridge, soon went, initially because the house was used for Belgian refugees and then because the family moved first to Limpsfield and then to four different flats and houses in London. Dorothy had her fourth child, Jean, in 1916 and both Jean and Margaret, the eldest daughter, suffered from illness when very young. Without Alice Carter, who came to work for the family during the war, stayed on for a long time afterwards and became known as 'Old Nanny' by children and grandchildren, life for Dorothy would have been even more difficult than it was. Even so, Margaret, who had a tubercular leg, had to be taken to Leysin in Switzerland for a cure in 1916 and did not return home for a whole year, during which time she came to speak French rather than English. Jean, as an infant, had a severe attack of pneumonia in the same year. Both Walter and Dorothy suffered from the deaths in the fighting in France of many of their closest friends and relations, including the husband of Walter's sister Margaret, who was killed at Ypres in 1915, and Dorothy's younger brother, an Air Force observer, killed in 1916.

As the war went on Dorothy and the children spent a good deal of time in a cottage at Little Holland on the Essex coast. With Walter working long hours and often going abroad, he saw far less of his children than most fathers not in uniform, and this was a pattern which from force of circumstances rather than choice, persisted throughout most of his subsequent career.

When Lloyd George left the Ministry of Munitions in July 1916 to become Secretary of State for War (and at the end of that year Prime Minister), Layton continued to work very closely with his successors as munitions ministers (first Edwin Montagu and then Dr Addison). He had the key job of secretary of the ministers' fortnightly meetings of heads of departments of the still rapidly growing ministry, which grew in this time from 5,000 to 13,000 staff. It was in these years that he and his staff developed the statistical framework necessary to mobilize the economy in war to produce ever-growing amounts of munitions. This meant working out the priorities for the supply of raw materials and labour, and called for the ability to take a synoptic view of the whole economy at a time when ministers were trying to deal with completely new problems of world war. He did not have the brilliance of Maynard Keynes, who in the same years was beginning to dominate at an equally early age considerable areas of Treasury policy, but he was none the less effective.

Keynes himself was deeply suspicious of Lloyd George's 'great gun policy', and indeed of the whole war strategy of large British armies committed to trench warfare, and was at that time in agreement with the orthodox Treasury view which assumed that the British economy was at full stretch. Hence Keynes argued that 'without a policy for the confiscation of private income, a considerably increased army and a continuance of subsidies to allies are alternative'.[3] Keynes with his hatred of compulsory military service was for maintaining 'subsidies', that is providing the Allies with the loans or supplies they needed to keep their large armies in the field rather than increasing the size of the British army to seventy divisions. Layton seems to have been more aware of the scope for much greater munitions production, whatever the financial limitations might appear at a time before the United States looked like coming into the war. He knew that the British economy was not yet fully mobilized. So Keynes and Layton could well have come into conflict as they briefed their respective ministers for Cabinet. But though McKenna, who succeeded Lloyd George as Chancellor in 1915, normally lost in Cabinet when trying to curb Lloyd George's ever-increasing munitions programme, there is no record of any argument between Keynes and Layton, who until fifteen months before had shared lecture rooms in Cambridge. Perhaps they were too busy to record any such discussions. But the lack of evidence is tantalizing to the biographer. Layton himself seemed to have no doubts that Lloyd George's policy was the right one.

Although Layton had often been in Paris in 1915 and 1916 and had got to know the French and Italian ministers of munitions and their staffs, 1917 was the year when his horizons were considerably widened by his accompanying Lloyd George (now Prime Minister) and Lord Milner in January to the Rome Conference, which was mainly concerned with Allied supplies to Russia, by his membership of the Milner Mission to Petrograd in February, and then of the Balfour Mission to the United States in April and May. These journeys followed on closely. He was due to leave Rome by train on a Tuesday, do a day's work in Paris on a Thursday, and leave for Russia on the Saturday. This ended his hopes of travelling via Leysin and visiting the five-year-old Margaret, who was halfway through her cure.

Back in London he joined the Milner Mission, of which he was by far the youngest member. Milner himself was a member of the War Cabinet and his mission included Lord Revelstoke, the banker, and General Sir Henry Wilson, later to be CIGS. Layton and Major-General Headlam were in the lead on munitions questions. The French mission, which joined in the Petrograd talks, was led by Doumergue, an ex-prime minister.

Layton, in the day or two he had in London after coming back from Rome, got the finance officer at the Ministry of Munitions to write to the Treasury for a £10,000 indemnity in case of his death. The letter ended: 'We thus avoid the difficulties we had with the *Hampshire* cases. Layton is a Varsity professor and one of the most valuable servants of the Ministry.' Kitchener and his mission, from which Keynes was left off at the last moment, had been torpedoed and drowned in the *Hampshire* the previous summer on a similar trip.

The five-day voyage round the North Cape to Murmansk in an auxiliary cruiser, the *Kildonan Castle*, taken over from the Union Castle Line, greatly impressed Layton with the unexpected beauty and peace of the Arctic night. He wrote to Dorothy: 'Even at mid-day the stars were shining brightly as the ship approached the coast of Lapland from where the snow threw a slight twilight glow across the calm sea.'

As it turned out the voyage was uneventful, except for one submarine sighting, but a good deal was happening in Russia. Rasputin had been assassinated the month before and the Duma was due to confront the Tsarist regime in March. The whole economy was in danger of collapsing under the strain of war, with the Russian armies lacking the arms to hold back the Germans and Austrians. The main question was whether Russia was on the edge of violent revolution or whether some compromise could be found which would leave the Tsar in power, perhaps as a constitutional monarch, at least to the end of the war.

For Layton the five-day journey to Petrograd by the Murmansk railway in Grand Duke Serge's overheated special train, pulled by an enormous wood-burning engine with tiny wheels, was like a slow-motion film after his long period of intensive work. He recorded in his Memoirs:

> Those five days and five nights are filled with a series of mental pictures. The slow manhandling of piles of newly cut logs into the colossal tender of the wood-burning locomotive; a clamber along a roughly hewn track among the blocks of ice fringing the shores of the White Sea and leading apparently to nowhere except to more ice shimmering in the gloom of the Arctic light. The great train, looking so out of place in this empty winter-bound corner of the roof of the world, was greatly handicapped by freshly fallen snow that narrowed the trench through which we passed. On one gently rising slope the train was brought to a standstill and for a moment it seemed as though our journey would end there, but the clumsy giant gently rolled back a mile or so and, starting again, gathered speed and charged the obstruction of snow until it was able to reach the crown of the track. And so we ambled along through this never-ending field of snow in a temperature which grew colder and colder as we left the coastal regions (kept relatively mild even in that latitude by what is left of the Gulf Stream) and penetrated southward into

> the interior of Russia. Of the handful of inhabitants we could see little and learn nothing.

On arrival in Petrograd, in spite of the bad news from the front and unrest in the towns, the mission was received with full ceremonial. The whole mission was presented at Tsarkye Seloe to the Tsar, who looked like a small replica of King George V. The photograph taken on that occasion shows the Tsar flanked by the great in full-dress uniforms except M. Doumergue, who appears to be bursting out of his evening dress suit, and Layton in the back row peering out over the generals and ambassadors. Later there was an Imperial Banquet for which the invitation card decreed 'Habit à boutons métalliques', but Layton could only manage ordinary evening dress. He was, however, comforted by seeing his Russian neighbour at dinner openly shovelling the little sweetmeats from the table into his pocket.

After the ceremonies Layton had to endure interminable meetings of the Supply Commission, sometimes presided over by Grand Duke Serge. But the long speeches could not help solve the underlying problem. The Russians asked for 13½ million tons of imported munitions and, in fact, needed more if they were to hold the German army, but the most the Murmansk and Trans-Siberian railways together could carry in a year was 3½ million tons. There was a desperate need for barbed wire but Layton had to point out that there were 50,000 tons of it lying at Vladivostok, which could not be transported. So there was an air of unreality about all the discussions. Layton found this affected the statistics too. He wrote in his Memoirs:

> I was shown a wealth of statistical material, of documents, charts and every conceivable pictorial form of presentation which the Russians had prepared. I had the impression that between the date of the Kitchener Mission and February 1917 the whole of the Russian Civil Service must have been occupied in producing more and more handsomely bound volumes. But, alas, I came to the conclusion that if, as was often the case, the basic data was missing or faulty, they did not hesitate to guess. At all costs, the final product must be superb and better than that of the government department next door.

Lloyd George had been impressed at the Rome Conference with the case made by the Russians that even a modest amount of British artillery would have a much greater effect on the Eastern Front than the same number of guns on the Western Front. So the War Office finally agreed to sending even more batteries to Russia than the scaled-down Russian request agreed by the Grand Duke. Thus, when Layton announced that more batteries would be sent than had been originally agreed earlier in the conference, he was surprised that the news was received in stony silence. The explanation came from the Russian liaison officer:

> Of course it is a magnificent offer but you really must understand our people. This evening you are the most unpopular man in Petrograd. Three days ago after the exchange of ideas between the Grand Duke and General Headlam these boys all took it for granted that the matter was settled. They printed the Protocol of the Conference, bound up the copies, embossed our initials. Everything is in superb shape. They have now got to go home, throw them in the wastepaper basket, sit up all night and produce a new document for tomorrow.

So the unreality continued until the *Kildonan Castle* steamed through the thin film of ice out of the Kola inlet on the way home. Layton then drafted his report – a long one covering all the main aspects of the Russian war economy. In his own report Milner said of the Munitions Supply Commission: 'I attach very much greater importance to this work than to all the other Petrograd proceedings put together.' Milner's report to Cabinet accepted the views of Sir George Buchanan, the British Ambassador in Petrograd, that there would be no violent revolution. Layton had come to a different view, shared by David Davies, one of Lloyd George's private secretaries, who was also on the mission. Because of their constant contact with middle-grade Russian civil servants and with the British military attaché they both thought revolution was near.

Lloyd George, in his *War Memoirs*, written a long time after the event, expressed his astonishment that Milner should have been so blind:

> Lord Milner was by training and temperament a bureaucrat. He knew nothing of the populace that trod the streets outside the bureau. He did not despise them, he just left them out of his calculations. A study of the ways and thoughts of the crowd constituted no part of preparation for entering the Civil Service or for success afterwards. . . . It was for the politicians to deal with these things, and he was not and never became a politician. Henry Wilson was every inch of him – and he had many more inches than

> the average – a professional soldier. The soldiers were not supposed to take cognizance of people, except the specimens who joined the army. He judged these entirely by the canons of discipline. The supreme test of discipline was saluting the officers. He saw with his own eyes that the Russian soldiers passed that test superbly. Mutiny in the army was, therefore, remote and if the army could be depended on, 'the Frocks', as he always nicknamed politicians, who babbled in the Duma, did not matter. . . . All the same they came away fully convinced there would be no revolution until after the war. Sir Walter Layton was, perhaps, an exception. When asked on his return 'Are they keen on the war?' he replied 'No, they are much too busy thinking of the coming revolution.' His official report, however, dealt only with munitions – and properly so – and the War Cabinet were not, therefore, informed of the conclusion to which he personally had come.[4]

While Layton's views were not formally reported to Cabinet, Lloyd George was clearly well aware of them. Within a week of the mission returning to London the riots started on the streets of Petrograd, soldiers shot their officers and the Tsar abdicated.[5]

Very soon after Layton had got back from Russia and had had a glimpse of his family in their new home in Platts Lane, Hampstead, he had to pack again to go to the United States. He went as the chief representative of the Ministry of Munitions on the mission led by A.J. Balfour (then Foreign Secretary), following the outbreak of war between the United States and Germany, to try and coordinate Allied financial and supply policies. Other members of the mission included Lord Cunliffe, Governor of the Bank of England, and Sir Eric Drummond of the Foreign Office, later secretary general of the League of Nations. So once more Layton got to know the people in power.

The Admiralty went to great pains to conceal the fact that the Foreign Secretary and his mission were to travel on a sister ship of the *Titanic*, the *Olympic*, which was full of wounded Canadian soldiers and American families being repatriated. The rumour on the ship was that the official party, for whom they had been kept waiting several days, consisted of the Tsar and Tsarina and their suites fleeing from Russia.

After a foggy crossing of the Atlantic, Layton travelled to Washington via New York for discussions with J.P. Morgan and Co., the

British government's purchasing agents in the United States. The main concern was how British contracts for arms purchases in the United States were likely to be affected by the large orders the US War Department would now be placing. The prospects were far from clear, as the US government had not yet begun to gear itself for war, but Layton got to know J.P. Morgan himself, E.R. Stettinius (the father of the US Secretary of State in the Second World War), Dwight Morrow, Thomas Lamont and Bernard Baruch.

In Washington, Layton soon confirmed his impression that the mission had arrived too soon to be able to reach any firm agreements about how the Allies' munition programme should be coordinated. Moreover, the War Department was clearly convinced that their own weapon designs should be adopted to arm the US army, even though the Allies' guns were well proven, and that to produce US types would mean considerable delays. In the event, the US divisions sent to France had to be armed with British and French artillery. Indeed by the end of the war only 130 US-made guns were used in battle and only 8,400 US rounds of ammunition were fired. Layton did, however, manage to agree with the French mission the main lines by which the Allied arms programme, including that of the United States, might be coordinated by committees meeting in London, Paris and Washington – in effect a blueprint for the Combined Boards of the Second World War. This was a subject of direct interest to Layton since from April 1917 the section of the Ministry of Munitions dealing with supplies to the Allies became part of his directorate.

Little real progress was made, mainly because of opposition from the generals who wanted to control the allocation of weapons between the Allies, until June 1918 when the Inter-Allied Munitions Council, made up of ministers of munitions, was set up. Winston Churchill then represented the UK with Layton as one of the three British officials attending.

Layton's first experience of the United States was not all work. Indeed, as the US government was not ready for decisions the visit became more of a good will mission. A huge dinner for 1,000 people was held at the Waldorf Astoria in New York in honour of the British and French missions. Walter wrote to Dorothy:

It was the most remarkable gathering I have ever seen and I have seen some strange ones lately. Roosevelt, Taft – the only living ex-Presidents – and, except for Bryan, all the men who have ever stood for the Presidency were present. All three national anthems were played, but the food was wholly American, Cherrystone clams, planked Delaware shad and roast squab chicken.

Other honours followed. The entire mission were made members of the Phi Beta Kappa Fraternity of the College of William and Mary in Virginia. Layton was singled out in an article (sent to Dorothy as 'screamingly funny' but in fact very near the mark) about the mission in the *New Republic* of 19 May 1917:

The most impressive of these was the slight figure who reminded me externally of the Greek professor in Bernard Shaw's *Major Barbara.* Before the war he had been a don at Cambridge, a teacher of economics, and he retained this senior laboratory manner of an expert who counts on holding attention. . . . He devised the organizing of America for destructiveness as an engineer might deliberate lining a leaky tunnel with copper and there was as little pretension in his manner as there was sentiment or doubt. His accent was cultivated, he was obviously a university man, but he had come to the top by mental equipment. 'Mental equipment' means many things, but plainly he was not of those remote emissaries who go in for cerebral scroll-saw work. He managed his mind as a woodman manages his axe. The exact swing and drive and bite of it could escape no one, and for all his almost plaintively modest demeanor he had instant arresting power.

In July 1917, Winston Churchill was appointed Minister of Munitions and threw himself into the job with characteristic exuberance, starting with a complete reorganization of the ministry. Layton was one of many who were apprehensive about the reorganization, which included bringing in at the top Sir Graham Greene, the then permanent secretary at the Admiralty. There seemed a danger that Greene would come between Layton and Churchill. Moreover, Layton may well have felt some guilt that he had spent three years in the safety of Whitehall while most of his generation were fighting and dying in Flanders. He had taken an officers' training course in the first winter of the war, he was thirty-three years old and A1 physically, so he thought that he ought to join up. Whatever the motives, he wrote a letter of resignation to Churchill which concentrated on the reorganization of the ministry:

As it is evident that your schemes for re-organisation of the Ministry will involve radical changes in the Secretariat, it seems to me that it would give you a much clearer field for building according to your own plans if I were to place my resignation in your hands. My position here is, I believe, a rather unique one in Government departments and has depended very largely on my personal relations with the Minister on the one side and heads of departments on the other. For it has been largely left to me to follow up supply and co-ordinate the effort of the departments, except where the Minister has done this himself, or has specifically placed this in other hands.

He also made it clear to Churchill that he thought it was time for him to join up. Churchill, who recognized Layton's abilities, just as Lloyd George had done, returned his resignation letter with the words: 'If you want to go you can go. You will be followed by my curses and as soon as you are in uniform the War Office will order you back to your post, which is here.' So Layton stayed on and soon found himself a full member of the new Munitions Council which Churchill had set up, consisting of a dozen senior men, each of whom controlled a group of departments. From the very start Churchill bombarded Layton and other members of the council with characteristic minutes demanding rapid action. On 3 August 1917 he minuted Layton:

Let me have on a single sheet of paper the following broad facts about the Tank programme, actual and prospective. How many tanks, and of what patterns, are to be ready month by month for the next 12 months? By whom, and to what extent, have these programmes been approved? How much steel do they require? How much do they cost? How much labour skilled and unskilled do they require in these 12 months? What are the principal limiting factors in material and class of labour? . . . Let me know the number of people in the Tank Department, the principal salaries paid, and the aggregate of salaries paid per annum. Show particularly any part of Tank production which overlaps aeroplane production, i.e. any transferable margin, whether of skilled mechanics or of ball bearings, etc in which these two branches of production are clashing competitors.[6]

Then again on 23 August 1917:

I want the following facts for my meeting with the Cumberland miners tomorrow: 50,000 tons of iron ore have been lost in consequence of the fortnight's strike and holidays. This 50,000 tons of ore would have made 50,000 tons of steel. How many ships of the Board of Trade standard pattern could have been made from 50,000 tons of steel? How many tons of wheat could those ships have brought to this country in the year 1918? Again, during the last few months the German submarines have been

> devoting every effort to sinking iron ore cargo upon the seas and in the last 2, 3, or 4 months they have succeeded in sinking – how many tons? I believe I am right in supposing that the fortnight's cessation of work on the Cumberland field has inflicted more injury on our shipping and food supply next year than all the efforts of the German submarines have been able to inflict in 1, 2, or 3 months as the case may be.[7]

The verbatim record of Churchill's meeting with a deputation of Cumberland miners on 24 August shows that Churchill made good use of the figures that Layton managed to provide the night before. The 50,000 tons of ore lost by the strike could have been used to build a dozen standard ships, enough to carry half a million tons of wheat to the UK in a year. On an average of the preceding three months, German submarines had sunk ships carrying 49,000 tons of iron ore on passage from Spain. So the two-weeks strike did as much damage as one month's action by German submarines.

Churchill rubbed in these figures and also argued that the loss of carrying capacity for half a million tons of wheat meant dearer bread, which would hit those who could not strike for higher wages. In the end Churchill got the men back to work after a very long meeting by patiently finding out the precise nature of their grievances and then settling them fairly. The miners, worn down by Churchill's powerful mixture of solid arguments and appeals to patriotism, formally recorded their thanks at the end of the meeting.

Later that autumn Churchill found even the Munitions Council too large for rapid action, so most of its business was conducted through a coordinating committee known as the Clamping Committee, of which Layton was a member from the start and chairman by the following May. Layton wrote in his Memoirs: 'Thus at the age of 33 I found myself at the centre of the new and exciting task of planning the economy of the nation.'

For Layton experience of active warfare in France was limited to trips just behind the line with Churchill, most of which were done in style, complete with champagne and visits to Churchill's many army friends. Churchill also had his own château which he visited from time to time. But normally the destination was Paris, where there was much hard work for Layton at endless conferences with French, Italian, and later United States allies about coordinating munitions supplies.

At many of these conferences and similar meetings in London, the interpreter was Professor Paul Mantoux, a distinguished historian whom Layton knew from before the war through his work on British economic history. Layton and Mantoux's paths were to cross several times again after the war, for instance at Versailles, where Mantoux was interpreter for the Supreme Economic Council, and at Geneva, where both were members of the League of Nations Secretariat in 1920.

In the autumn of 1917 Layton must have seen a lot of Arthur Salter and Jean Monnet, when, after many attempts, a really effective inter-Allied organization was set up to control shipping. This was the Allied Maritime Transport Council, the groundwork for which had been done by these two young men. Arthur Salter was an Admiralty career civil servant; Jean Monnet belonged to the cognac firm of that name, and had used his experience of selling brandy in London and North America before the war to invigorate the French munitions delegation in London. Here again Layton formed friendships which were to last for the rest of his life and which were renewed through working together to repair the ravages of war.

Layton was fully stretched right up to the end of the war and after as chairman of the Clamping Committee, which met every week, as delegate to the Inter-Allied Munitions Council, and as chairman of the Reconstruction Committee on postwar iron and steel requirements. When peace came much of this work continued. He went to Paris in January 1919 to take part in the negotiations for the military and economic clauses of the Treaty of Versailles. In particular, he found himself working again with Sir Henry Wilson (now CIGS) on Marshall Foch's committee which was to draft the military clauses. He was the British representative on committees which dealt with limitation of armaments to enemy countries and which reported to the Council of Four in May on the supply of arms to Central Europe. Here there was great concern, particularly on the part of Lord Robert Cecil, that a damaging arms traffic was developing which would lead to war and unrest in Central Europe and the Balkans.

There was enough new work heaped on Layton to occupy him for many months. Nevertheless the main question in his mind at this time must have been the choosing of a permanent career.

CHAPTER FOUR

Walter Layton, the Man, 1919–39

Choosing a Career

In the months up to January 1919 Layton was considering the various options open to him now that he had proved himself, both as an economics don and as a civil servant highly regarded by politicians and officials in Whitehall, Paris and Washington. The world was at his feet. He knew that he was to be offered a knighthood but he refused because neither he nor Dorothy wanted a handle to their names. Moreover, Lloyd George's honours lists had become suspect because of the sale of political honours. However, shortly afterwards Layton became a Companion of Honour.[1]

If Layton did not want to stay in Whitehall or take some international job concerned with the reconstruction of Europe, he could return to university life, either as a lecturer at Cambridge or very likely a professor elsewhere. Or he could go into industry or the City or politics. While the choice must have been very wide he, in fact, took the first job offered him – that of director of the Iron and Steel Federation. Perhaps he was over-anxious about his prospects and did not realize at the time how much he was to be in demand. In any case, as a result of his prewar study of industry and his wartime Ministry of Munitions experience, he had become expert in the iron and steel industry, which was then of greatest importance to the economy. Moreover, the money was good – £3,000 a year rising to £5,000 by 1921. This was bound to be important, as Dorothy had had her fifth child and third daughter, Olive, in December 1918.

It is true that Layton hesitated when he was approached about the job that December, saying that Churchill had asked him not to commit himself before the end of January to leaving the government's service. Moreover, he had doubts about joining an organization which was, in effect, a price-fixing cartel. Keynes had always thought that Layton should return to Cambridge, as he was the only one in the front rank of younger economists who had first-hand knowledge of industrial and labour questions.

In the end he consulted Marshall, who wrote him two long letters. In the first, in December 1918, he urged Layton to accept the job provided he was free to express his views on protection and on wage levels. Layton took this advice, and in replying to the Federation's offer he made it clear that he was a firm believer in free trade, that he was convinced that labour should have a greater say in industry, and that any important industry should not follow sectional interests which might conflict with wider national economic policy.

Professor Marshall's second letter in January, however, shows that his views had swung round. He feared that because of his position as director Layton would always have to take the side of the masters. Instead Marshall urged Layton to return to Cambridge and by lecturing on industry and wages 'do more towards fashioning the life of Britain in the second and third quarters of this century than anybody else'.

In spite of Marshall's characteristic appeal to Layton's idealism, he did not hesitate further and formally accepted the Federation's offer at the end of January 1919. His five-year agreement, however, gave Layton the right to terminate if he found his views did not accord with those of the Federation.

If he decided finally this time that he did not want to go back to university life, politics were even less appealing, following the coupon election of 1918 and the major split in the Liberal Party. Layton had admired Lloyd George as a minister, and was to work for him again in producing the Liberal *Yellow Book* in 1928, but he was not attracted by the sterile politics of the postwar period. As he put it: 'For me, as for other young Liberals who had held key positions during the war, it was no longer possible to reconcile our loyalty to the Liberal Party and to Lloyd George.' When in 1920 Lloyd George asked Layton to take over the political management of domestic affairs in his private office (Philip Kerr was to take over foreign affairs), he refused.

So Walter Layton started the peace as director of the Iron and Steel Federation, some members of which congratulated themselves that they had acquired the full-time services of a bright young man who was well known to the Prime Minister and to most of those with influence in Whitehall, though some of them must have wondered whether he would turn out to be too radical in his beliefs for many of the iron and steel masters. With his abundant energy Layton was able to start his work at the Federation at the end of March 1919 while continuing with a great deal of his Ministry of Munitions work, both in London and Paris, up till June. Nobody seems to have raised the question whether there was any conflict of interest, and in the free-and-easy atmosphere of the time, Layton took away quite a number of official papers from the ministry which he considered of special interest.

The Layton family made a new start too by moving house from Hampstead to Weybridge, where there was a good mixed school for the elder children, and where the country air was thought to be better for Margaret and Jean, who had had so much illness during the war. But the move coincided with Dorothy herself contracting erysipelas, and having to spend the next six months convalescing in Cornwall. Walter describes in his book *Dorothy* how her absence brought him into closer daily contact with his own children than he had ever been before or, indeed, after:

> Though I went daily to London I tried to fill their mother's place as best I could as well as my own. I instituted a regular pre-breakfast parade. First, a few free exercises – breathing, arm and leg movements and muscular control – tense, relax, tense . . . and so on; second, standing in age order by the piano and singing descending scales, arpeggios, and familiar passages such as the runs in the chorus of The Messiah 'For unto us a child is born'. Then, to finish up with, a race round the garden – with appropriate handicaps – and so in to breakfast with cheeks aglow. Later the children began to play stringed instruments and I wrote a quartet which increased in difficulty with each fresh movement that was written. The cello part of the first movement, played by Michael, involved open strings only, second movement stopping with fore-finger only, third movement playing the scale of D in full.

Walter clearly had not forgotten his choir school training. If some find so much pre-breakfast activity unappealing, all who visited the

Layton family at that time – and indeed for the next two decades – came away with a vivid impression of the children's abounding energy and good looks. In a family where each child, as it grew up, tended to go its own way without Walter trying to impose his will, singing and playing music together was an important common bond.

When Layton took up his job as director of the Iron and Steel Federation in the summer of 1919 he came with the aura of familiarity with those in power. He made his first report to a general meeting of the Federation after attending his investiture as Companion of Honour at the Palace that morning. Characteristically, his report was a succinct account of how the economies of Britain's main steel-making competitors had emerged from the war. He wanted to put the troubles of the British industry in a broader setting. So there were visits to the Continent and further able reports. He also recruited two of the statisticians who had worked for him at the Ministry of Munitions to provide much fuller statistics about prices and the financial position of the steel industry.

Layton was liked and respected at the Federation but in January 1920, after being there full-time only six months, and in spite of his five-year contract, he seriously considered an invitation from Sir Eric Drummond (now secretary general of the League of Nations) that he should come permanently to the League Secretariat to organize its economic and financial work. Drummond's view was that the Secretariat should fill the void left by the moribund Supreme Economic Council that had met at Versailles.

This time Layton had great difficulty in making up his mind. He wrote to Dorothy:

> Sentimentally nothing would please me more (and I know you agree) than to work under and for the League . . . I have, therefore, to find out from the highest authorities I can tap in the next few days whether the British Government really means to push the League into effective operation and whether the USA is coming in. I think the answer is 'yes' to both questions. (Assuming 'yes', will the League be used on the economic as well as on the political side. . . . The Supreme Economic Council died with the peace. Will it have a permanent descendant under the League? . . . The job may be of enormous importance, but the other side of the shield is that it may dwindle to an academic affair like the Hague organisation as compared with my present practical job which, at best, may become a means of establishing a

really sound basis for industrial organisation in this country leading possibly to a political career. In fact, is the time right to burn one's boats and become an internationalist or is there still more urgent practical work to be done at home. ... I am going to see Keynes and if possible Lloyd George on it tomorrow or Thursday.

Later he wrote:

Keynes thought there was nothing to do in that particular job at present, but considered it impossible to foresee more than a few months ahead. On the whole he is pessimistic. Lord Robert Cecil on the other hand, though admittedly vague, felt confident that somehow, sooner or later, the big economic questions would come to be dealt with by the League. Keynes says the League will certainly come for you when the time comes. So at the moment the balance is slightly against.

His doubts, however, were resolved by Lloyd George, who said 'he attached great importance to this side of the League's work', and by the Federation agreeing to release him for a year to take over from Arthur Salter as director of the Economic and Financial section of the League while Salter spent that year as secretary to the Reparations Commission. Layton's main job was to organize the first international financial conference after the war, attended by the representatives of thirty-nine countries.

One attraction for Layton of working in the League Secretariat is that his colleagues included Jean Monnet, who was one of the deputy secretaries general, and Professor Paul Mantoux, the interpreter at the main wartime and postwar conferences, who was director of the Political Section. Layton's salary was 50,000 gold francs tax-free, equivalent to £3,800, about the same as from the Federation. This was good pay at a time when a permanent secretary in charge of a Whitehall department only earned £2,000.

When Layton took up his post with the League Secretariat in March 1920 the plan was for the financial conference to meet at Brussels towards the end of May. Fortunately for him the conference, which was 'to study the financial crisis and look for the means of remedying and of mitigating the dangerous consequences arising from it', was postponed twice and only finally met on 24 September. These postponements were to give time for the Council of the League to consider whether the current negotiations between the Allies and Germany on reparations should be discussed at the conference. In the end the Council decided against, which meant that the conference's discussions would be more in terms of generalities than about the solution of immediate problems.

Layton was able to carry out the preparatory work at the League Secretariat's offices in Curzon Street in London, as the League's headquarters were not established in Geneva until the winter of 1920. His staff included the young Swedish economist Per Jacobssen, who later was to run the Bank for International Settlements and the International Monetary Fund, and Alexander Loveday, one of Layton's Cambridge students who was to succeed Arthur Salter in 1930 as director of the League's Economic and Financial section. Per Jacobssen's impression of Layton at the time was that he was a brilliant man, more organizer than economist. As for Monnet, he was 'a very nervous silent man whose qualities he had to take on trust'.

The conference chairman was M. Ador, President of Switzerland, and R.H. Brand of Lazards was one of the vice-chairmen. The UK was represented by Lord Chalmers, a former permanent secretary of the Treasury, and by Lord Cullen, a former governor of the Bank of England. Dudley Ward, a Cambridge pupil and friend of Layton, now a banker, and Frederick Leith Ross of the Treasury were advisers. Other countries were represented by men of similar standing and experience.

In spite of all this talent and the high standard of the preparatory work, Layton was not surprised that the report of the conference was more in terms of getting back to the prewar economic and financial system than of tackling the urgent problems created by the war and its aftermath. So there was much about the need to balance national budgets, to get back to the gold standard as soon as possible and to restore 'at least the degree of freedom of commerce that obtained before the war'. This declaration of orthodox financial virtues pleased Montagu Norman, the governor of the Bank of England, but did not advance matters very far. The conference succeeded, however, in insisting on the need to cut expenditure on armaments and on a number of practical measures, such as the establishment of central banks of issue in countries without them and the unification of laws affecting trade and foreign exchange.

The conference and Layton himself came in for criticism, particularly in the United States, which was represented unofficially only because the Senate had turned down United States membership of the League. In October 1920, the *Chicago Tribune* accused Layton and Monnet of trying to bring reparations back into the conference discussions, even if the amounts of the payments were to be settled elsewhere:

> the Brussels Conference failed because Under Secretary Monnet and Mr Layton, Director of the Economic Section, as officials of the League, tried to force on its prospective members a form of international co-operation closer than some were willing to accept. They forgot that the executives of a co-operative concern must conduct its business according to the wills of its participating members, and not according to their own wishes.

Even if in that sense the conference was a failure, it was important for two reasons. It marked the return of the Germans and other defeated nations to international conferences on a par with other countries. It also set the pattern for a long series of economic and financial conferences at the League up to the Second World War.

After the conference, Layton, now working at the first Assembly of the League at Geneva, was in two minds whether to return to his job at the Iron and Steel Federation or stay on at the League. He was impressed by the standard of some of the Assembly debates. He wrote to Dorothy: 'The other day a debate (on the anti-typhus campaign) was opened by Barnes, ex-labour agitator, and other speakers were Nansen, ex-Arctic explorer, Ranjitsinhji – ex-cricketer and Paderewski, ex-pianist.' He considered a compromise suggested by Sir Eric Drummond by which, while working for the Iron and Steel Federation, he would become a member of the British delegation to the Financial Committee so he could keep in close touch with the League. But a talk with A.J. Balfour, during a walk along the lake side, convinced him he would do better to concentrate on Iron and Steel.

He went back to the Federation early in 1921 but became increasingly worried about the way in which his views were clashing with those adopted by his employers. At a time of worsening slump he wanted policy towards the unions to be more, rather than less, liberal. Employers should give their work people details of their costs and commercial results. Moreover, the government should not be pressed to abandon its scheme for the nationalization of mineral rights. He wanted to be able to express freely the strong opinions he held on these and other matters and to undertake work outside the office.

He had, in fact, already joined Keynes on the board of the National Mutual Life Assurance Company, but he wished to be free to take up more public work. The editorship of the *Economist* had become vacant in the summer of 1921 when Hartley Withers left to become financial editor of the *Saturday Review*. Layton, having worked on the *Economist* before the war, was in the running to succeed him. So in November 1921 Layton offered his resignation, secure in the knowledge that he was likely to be offered the editorship.

Layton's change of mind must have been infuriating for his employers, but Sir Frederick Mills's reply showed no sign of irritation. He simply wrote back promptly accepting Layton's resignation and saying he was not surprised because he had felt Layton needed much more public scope for his very great abilities.

At Home and at Work

The Iron and Steel Federation had proved a false start. Although he probably did not realize it at the time, Walter's heart was really in public life. While he was not seeking the limelight of publicity, he wanted to play an active part both in tackling the major financial and industrial problems of the time and in their public discussion. His own inclinations and the growing demand for his services led him to work for the League of Nations Secretariat in 1920, to become editor of the *Economist* in 1921 and chairman of the *News Chronicle* in 1930. Within the same span of years he worked for the League of Nations Financial Committee on a variety of economic problems, he advised successive British governments, whether Conservative, Labour or National, on international financial problems, and he attended many meetings abroad as a British delegate. He also made time to take the lead in working out new policies for the

Liberal Party from the start of the Liberal Summer Schools in 1921, and especially in drafting the 1928 Liberal *Yellow Book* on industrial policy.

Whether or not he made a conscious choice to do so he, in fact, took on so many responsibilities that he worked up to the limit of his powers, and occasionally beyond, for virtually the rest of his life. He had, of course, become used to working at great pressure in the Ministry of Munitions during the war. But, while most of his contemporaries went back to normal office hours, complete rest at weekends and generous holidays, Walter after some slight let-up in the winter of 1919 when Dorothy was ill, soon returned to the high-pressure working in which he seemed to find the most satisfaction.

It is not easy to determine why he worked so hard. He could have earned enough money to bring up his children (there were seven by 1929) and to lead a full and interesting life as editor of the *Economist* and later chairman, and in effect editor in chief, of the *News Chronicle*. Most men would have resigned the editorship of the *Economist* on moving to the *News Chronicle*. Very few men or women would have taken on so much other demanding unpaid work, whether for the Liberal Party or for the government of the day.

A partial explanation is that Layton excelled at this type of work and that by undertaking such a wide diversity his three major interests reinforced each other. As editor of the *Economist* and the *News Chronicle* he was at the centre of the exchange of ideas and opinions and could voice his own views on the major topics of the day. All doors in the City, Fleet Street and Whitehall and the universities were open to him. Through his work for the Liberal Summer Schools and the *Yellow Book* he was able to help the Liberal Party in putting to the electorate the new policies which might restore the party's fortunes. As adviser, and sometimes as negotiator for the government, he was well placed to try and get his preferred policies carried out. His wartime experience showed him the importance of being in the inner councils of government where decisions are taken.

It looks, however, as if Layton was very willing to take on all these additional responsibilities for reasons other than justifiable satisfaction in doing the job well. Although he sometimes complained he was not paid his market value at the *News Chronicle*, it was not riches he sought, nor did he value power as such, other than that it gave the holder the chance of getting the right things done. Although Dorothy thought he was undervalued and saw him as a future prime minister, he himself had no delusions of grandeur, nor did he think that, even after Lloyd George regained the leadership of the Liberal Party in 1926, there would be a Liberal government in which he might have been a minister. He stood for Parliament three times in the 1920s as a Liberal, but did not seem to mind being beaten. He would, in fact, have found life as a backbench member frustrating and largely a waste of time. He became a peer in 1946 but he was a most modest Press baron with none of the urge to be the power behind the throne or flamboyance of Beaverbrook, with whom he was always on good terms, or of Rothermere.

The most likely explanation of his readiness to sacrifice the usual pleasures and pursuits of a successful professional man lies in his upbringing. The puritan work ethic and desire for independence was instilled in him from his childhood by his strong-willed mother and by the discipline of the choir school. From the age of seven he won his own way by scholarships and once he started regular earning had helped support his parents. Having acquired the habit of hard work through necessity, he had little difficulty in maintaining it for the rest of his life. His willingness to take on such a wide variety of work derived from his keen desire to help whenever he thought he had a worthwhile contribution to make. He had remained convinced throughout his life that, as he had written from Cambridge to his sister Margaret, 'the question to hammer out is this, what is there worth doing in life, how can I help?'

His generous response to calls on his time allied with his strong sense of duty might have led to a worthy and laborious existence, but he was no prig, and his work from Cambridge onwards was by no means all hard grind. At Cambridge he studied and taught subjects of great interest to himself, and later in the First World War and after, right up to the 1950s, he was often doing work which he found satisfying and at which he excelled. So his work and pleasure to a large extent overlapped and his exerting himself right up to the limits of his physical strength certainly did not make him a dull man. But there were inevitably considerable costs to be paid by himself and by his family.

For himself the price was suppression of much of his natural emotional life, leading to difficulty in expressing his feelings to his immediate family. Although the high pressure at which he worked must have increased the intensity of his feelings, he seemed inhibited from expressing them freely and became a remote figure to his children and a reserved rather shy man to many who worked for him. His long hours of work meant that he saw little of his children, except in the early morning and during his often curtailed weekends. When he did join the family for holidays at Little Holland in Essex and later at Porthleven on the south coast of Cornwall, where Dorothy's father had a house on the cliff with a huge drawing-room window looking directly over the sea, he often spent part of the day working on his papers. The children knew from their mother that he was a wonderful man but they did not feel close to him. Perhaps relations were easiest with his youngest daughters, to whom he was known as Daddy Longlegs.

Although he went abroad often for long periods, throughout his life Walter hardly ever wrote letters to his children. He sent them his love through his letters to Dorothy and it was almost always Dorothy who bought his birthday present to them. If there were barriers between himself and his children it was not because he did not love them and take great pride in them. Even to Dorothy, who was very much the centre of the family and with whom he was very close, he could not express his love fully. He wrote her biography in order to record the extent of his love which he had failed to tell her in her lifetime. But perhaps it is significant that, although there is a lot about family life at the beginning and end of the book, the chapters in between are mostly about both parents' work rather than about the family.

His youngest son has called him a pragmatist, a rational beast, complementing Dorothy, whose emotions flowed over and who was perhaps the truer radical and the more accomplished musician of the two. If this was indeed the way things worked out in practice it was because Walter, preoccupied with public affairs, gave precedence to his great rational abilities over the intuitive artistic side of his nature. An indication of this is that in spite of his love of music he did not develop his undoubted talent or his range, but remained content with the music he had got to know as a boy.

On holiday he liked playing golf and tennis and tried to get his children, often against their will, to go swimming with him before breakfast. The family custom was for everyone to bathe naked. This was rare at the time and embarrassed some of the visitors included in the bathing parties, especially when the daughters were growing up. One daughter, however, has always maintained that the bathing parties were not at all sexy. Until late in life he had a cold bath in the morning and succeeded in keeping himself fit in spite of working excessive hours.[2] But even on holiday he needed a definite activity, such as golf, rather than walking along the cliffs or lying on the beach. Nor did he spend much time in reading unconnected with his work, although he built up a good library of biography and history. Only late at night did he relax by doing the *Times* crossword, which he completed daily, or by reading detective novels.

In spite of his upbringing he was not interested in organized religion, but he had a strong moral sense. He told his daughter Olive that she would always know when she was doing wrong – her conscience would tell her. It would be wrong to describe Walter as a puritan, even though he did not attach much importance to the usual pleasures of life pursued by many of his contemporaries, who may well have considered him as such. Compared, for instance, with his fellow economist Keynes, he was right at the other end of the hedonistic scale. Keynes devoted much of his abounding energy to the pursuit of pleasure, whether at the parties where he constantly met his numerous friends, or through his love affairs, homosexual for twenty years, but ending in an enduring, though childless, marriage. Keynes also derived great pleasure as a collector of modern French painting and rare books, and as a patron of the ballet and theatre. Layton enjoyed life too, but in a totally different way. He did not like parties except those for the family, nor was he interested in food and drink, although unlike Dorothy he was no teetotaller. He enjoyed singing and playing chamber music with his family, but did not go to concerts or the opera. The visual arts and the theatre played little part in his life. His satisfactions were largely to be found in his work, his family and in keeping to the ideals of his youth. Indeed, he became more of an idealist after the Second World War when he hoped to bring about, through the European Movement, the better international relations for which he had worked ever since going to Versailles in 1919.

He had always been a reserved man and as he became older he tended to become more inarticulate, so it was difficult for those around him to be fully aware of his thoughts and feelings. There were only two or three people, one of them his sister Margaret, to whom he could unburden his feelings. He must have had considerable self-control. His children do not remember his losing his temper at home. Only when driving did he get angry with Dorothy for her back-seat advice, and then his daughter Jean found his anger frightening, as it was so unexpected.

When things were going well there was sometimes a sparkle in his eyes which not only heightened his good looks, which he kept until late in life, but showed there was plenty of wit behind his cool exterior. His personal friends appreciated this, and indeed some of the younger men and women who worked for him found him likeable – even lovable. He was certainly attractive to women whose company he enjoyed, although remaining entirely faithful to Dorothy. It was a pity that this very human warmth did not come through more to his family and to his colleagues. Lady Violet Bonham-Carter, who had a real regard for Walter, showed her ambivalence when she described him, when in full evening dress, as 'the handsomest little grey mind in Europe'.

This may give too bleak a picture of Walter's personal life, as if it was all plain living and high thinking. With seven children born between 1911 and 1929 there were always young children and an abundance of animal spirits at home. This must have brightened his life, even if he was so often away. Above all was his constant love for Dorothy, which, although not always expressed, gave him great strength and stability. And looking back his children would recognize that their family life had been immensely rewarding. While Dorothy provided the colour and the warmth, Walter provided the support which, although rather remote, enabled each child to find out for itself the direction in which it wanted to go.

This outline of Layton's character so far does not explain why he was so universally trusted. Why was his advice so much in demand on so many occasions between the wars? Why, for instance, did it seem natural at the time that he should join with Seebohm Rowntree to try to persuade A.J. Cook, the miners' leader, to agree a settlement in July 1926 long before the strike actually ended? Here, despite his knowledge of industry, he was on entirely new ground, but his commonsense solution might have succeeded but for the well-meaning but muddled intervention by a group of eminent Anglicans and Free Churchmen described in a later chapter. Why, although he was a committed Liberal already running the Liberal Summer Schools and responsible for the Liberal *Yellow Book* on industrial policy, was he asked to advise the Conservative government in 1927, the Labour government in 1929–31 and the National government that followed?

Looking back it is extraordinary that the editor of the *Economist* should have been trusted with so much inside information. But there were no leaks in those days. It was even more extraordinary that the trust Layton built up should have survived in the more feverish 1930s when he kept a close eye on the leading articles each day in the *News Chronicle*. There were complaints from time to time from succeeding prime ministers that he had been unfair, but never that he had abused the trust placed in him. Admittedly, Ramsay Macdonald in a personal letter of February 1933 complained that the *News Chronicle* report that he might be invited to join the Carlton Club was 'beyond the bounds of ordinary decency'. According to Tom Jones in his diary entry for September 1936, Baldwin too criticized Layton as 'one of your intellectuals and Cambridge at that'.[3]

One reason for the trust Layton inspired lies in the qualities which took him near the top of the Ministry of Munitions, that is the ability to get to the heart of the problem and to give an objective view of the best practical solution. Although after the first war he had clearly become a member of the Establishment, in that he moved easily in high places both at home and abroad, he was a classless figure without any arrogance or self-importance.

Perhaps because he had been a don and a civil servant he had a cautious professional approach. He spoke little. He insisted first in obtaining the facts before giving his opinion, and in Fleet Street he felt he had to be highly responsible. There was no question of publish and be damned. It may be, too, that his reserved manner gave some guarantee that the last thing he would do was to gossip and give away confidences.

Another reason why Layton was so much in demand is to be found in his being a leading member of the group of Liberal radicals who exercised a major influence on public opinion in the interwar years. It is difficult to find a parallel in other times to this tightly knit group, members of which met each other constantly in Whitehall, in the Westminster lobbies, in clubs, in Fleet Street, the City and at the ancient universities. Layton, Keynes, Hubert Henderson and Dennis Robertson, all Cambridge economists, were at the centre of this network whose members included such remarkable ex-civil servants as William Beveridge, Josiah Stamp and Arthur Salter, businessmen with a strong social conscience such as Ernest Simon and Seebohm Rowntree, bankers such as R.H. Brand of Lazards, political thinkers such as Gilbert Murray, Graham Wallace and Ramsay Muir and idealistic politicians such as Philip Noel Baker, Charles Masterman and Philip Kerr.

The views of this remarkable group of people sometimes conflicted but more often they reinforced each other in their attempts to work out more rational and humane policies, both in home and overseas affairs. Nearly all its members played an active part in the Liberal Summer Schools – starting in 1921 – of which Layton became the director and the mainspring from 1922 onwards. Most were young at that time, but had not fought in the war, with the exceptions of Dennis Robertson, an infantryman, and of Philip Noel Baker, who had served in the Friends Ambulance Unit on the Italian Front. Most of them had gained their experience of government as civil servants in the First World War. They were amongst the outstanding survivors of a generation which had suffered terribly in that war.

Most of them had acquired in wartime Whitehall a conviction that government could and should intervene to deal with economic crises and to tackle social problems. The traditional suspicion of government had to some extent been replaced by a suspicion of private enterprise. Many had themselves had practical managerial experience of helping to mobilize the British economy for war, or of controlling shipping or running rationing schemes. Others had been immersed in the problems of how to finance the war and how to manage financial relations with the United States and the other Allies.

Many of their ideas and ideals were acquired before the war, whether from the reforming Liberal administration of 1906, from Quaker concern about poverty or from Fabian socialism. For some the war had pointed the way to a more egalitarian society, but for nearly all their war experience helped them to see how their policies might be realized in practice. The economists among them, while differing between themselves, felt they knew enough about how the economy worked in practice to be able to advise the government how to intervene. They became more interested in finding solutions to practical problems than in elaborating economic theory. Many had become knowledgeable in how to get things done in Whitehall and Parliament. They had become skilled operators as well as penetrating thinkers. Moreover, they were ready to spend a lot of time on public affairs so as to ensure that their ideas received full publicity and political support. They looked upon themselves as initiators with the advantage of being free of the restraints placed on the higher Civil Service.

Although they nearly all voted Liberal they were, for the most part, apolitical in the sense that they came together to work out practical policies rather than to write party manifestos, or concern themselves with the split between Asquith and Lloyd George. Some were very near to the intellectuals of the Labour Party, which, indeed, Noel Baker and Ernest Simon later joined.

Layton, Keynes and Henderson, together with Ernest Simon, had another common link in that they edited, controlled, or at least had a seat on the boards of the *Economist*, the *Nation*, and the *New Statesman*. Layton edited the *Economist* and was on the board of the *Nation*; Keynes influenced the policy of the *Nation* through his financial stake in the paper and through his weekly talks with Henderson, who became its editor in 1923.

Ernest Simon invested in both the *Nation* and the *New Statesman*. Indeed, he helped finance the *New Statesman* in 1912 to the tune of £1,000, as a result of his admiration of the Webbs. In 1931 the *New Statesman* and the *Nation* were to merge, while in 1927 Layton had taken charge of the editorial policy of the *Daily News* and in 1930 had become chairman of the newly merged *News Chronicle*.

Layton, his economist friends and Ernest Simon were thus able to express their views in the then rather staid *Economist*, as well as in the more lively *Nation*, where Keynes saw to it that the literary part of the paper was in the hands of his Bloomsbury friends, and there was also some useful influence in the leftwing *New Statesman*. From 1927 they had access to a daily paper in so far as the Cadbury family, which financed the *Daily News* and later the *News Chronicle*, allowed Layton his head. None of these papers were ever likely to undermine a government, but their long-term influence on opinion was considerable.

From the time he became editor of the *Economist* in 1921 Layton acquired a growing reputation in Fleet Street, although if he had simply been an editor, however distinguished, it is doubtful that he would have been consulted by such a range of governments and international organizations. But he was in fact one of the few available highly competent economists interested in practical problems rather than in abstract theory. Keynes was, of course, outstanding as an economist but his brilliance and willingness to change his mind puzzled and sometimes upset the politicians, civil servants and bankers, while Layton's more cautious approach, based on a careful analysis of the facts, was much more acceptable. Above all his advice was disinterested. There was no suspicion that he was forwarding his own fortunes or those of a particular political party.

I have in this chapter tried to outline the direction in which Layton developed as a man and as the father of a large family, as well as a highly successful and trusted leader of opinion. The chapters that follow are concerned with his actual achievements in the various tasks he set himself, whether in politics, in international affairs or in the newspaper world.

CHAPTER FIVE

New Policies for the Liberal Party, 1920–9

The Liberal Summer Schools

By 1920 the Liberal Party was in increasing disarray as the split between Lloyd George and Asquith widened. The radicals of the party no longer trusted Lloyd George and became convinced that new policies were needed if there was ever to be a Liberal government again capable of meeting the challenge of both the Tories and the growing Labour Party.

Ernest Simon, prominent as the chairman of a growing Manchester engineering firm and of the Manchester City Council Housing Committee, and soon to be Lord Mayor, had taken the lead in the summer of 1920 by inviting some of his Liberal friends to a discussion about industrial policy at his farm at Leadon Court in Herefordshire. His guests included Ramsay Muir, then professor of history at Manchester, E.T. Scott, son of C.P. Scott, editor of the *Manchester Guardian*, and Philip Guedalla, the historian. The new policies discussed were mainly those proposed in Ramsay Muir's book *Liberalism and Industry*. They included nationalization of mines and railways, control of trusts and cartels, more public spending on housing and social services, more progressive taxation, a minimum wage and profit sharing in industry. No conclusions were reached other than that the time had come for a complete reappraisal of Liberal policy to be carried out through annual Summer Schools at which leading experts would speak on the main industrial and economic problems of the day. The Summer Schools were to enquire into policy, not to hold political meetings. They were to enable people from industry, the universities, politics and business to discuss ideas in an academic setting. To some extent they were to follow the example of the pre-1914 Fabian Summer Schools, although on a much bigger scale. So that the discussion could be kept unofficial none of the leaders or officials of the Liberal Party, and no members of Parliament, were to be invited.

Layton accepted Simon's invitation to the first Summer School at Grasmere in 1921 with alacrity, but added that it was 'perfectly useless to discuss industrial or economic questions without touching foreign policy so far as it affects Reparations, War Debts and the European currency question'. He got his way and led the discussion on international affairs as well as on railways. He also gave the valedictory address. The meeting was a great success. Ninety-five people turned up instead of the expected fifty. The other main speakers were Beveridge, J.A. Hobson on Taxation, Muir on Coal and Eleanor Rathbone on Family Allowances.

By the following year Layton with Ramsay Muir was organizing a nine-day Summer School at Oxford with Ernest Simon as treasurer. Six hundred people came to Oxford and a thousand to the Summer School in Cambridge in 1923. There were weekend meetings on special subjects in between the Summer Schools. Even with the efficient Colonel Tweed (later Lloyd George's secretary) to help organize, a lot of work fell on Layton. Tweed wrote frequently about the programme, which covered leisure events as well as speakers. There was trouble over a river trip because Arthur Salter's father, who ran the river steamers at Oxford, was a Sabbatarian – 'Salter definitely refuses to arrange for steamers or boats of any kind on Sunday on grounds of principle.' There had to be a garden party instead, but it was clear that those attending the Summer School were meant to take the proceedings seriously. A book list was sent out with the programme so that those coming could prepare themselves. By 1922 the determination to keep away from politicians had been overcome. Asquith gave the inaugural address and Viscount Grey the valedictory address. Gilbert Murray spoke on the League of Nations and J.A. Spender on Imperial Policy, while Layton spoke both on the State and Industry and on Nationalization.

In 1922 there was no attempt to bring in the Lloyd George

had produced proposals – providing for reorganization of the coalmines to take place before any wage cuts were worked out – which were acceptable to the TUC but which were turned down by the miners, led by a stubborn president, Herbert Smith, and a left-wing secretary, A.J. Cook. Samuel's memorandum was published in full by the *Economist* on 15 May and the paper continued to criticize the owners' attitudes.

Layton got drawn into subsequent events that summer, not only as editor of the *Economist*, and knowledgeable about the coal industry, but as a Liberal and because his friend and colleague at the Liberal Summer School, Seebohm Rowntree, was also playing an active part. Layton and Rowntree joined forces and after their first talk with A.J. Cook on 30 June were fully occupied in seeking a way through a very tangled situation for the whole of July. At the same time they kept in close touch with the Ministry of Labour. Although Sir Horace Wilson, the Permanent Secretary, was discouraging, Layton and Rowntree drew up some proposals for a settlement which provided for a joint conference between owners and unions to negotiate on the basis of the Samuel Report, with Samuel himself to be called in as arbiter if needed.

It was clear that an attempt at mediation had to be made quickly, as the government had already introduced its Eight Hours Bill which extended permitted working hours in the coalmines. Cook was told that if he could agree to these proposals as a basis for negotiation, it should be possible to hold up the Eight Hours Bill. He insisted that there should be no reference in the proposals, which were to be kept private for the time being, to any increase in miners' hours. (Though later the suggestion was made that miners could choose, district by district, whether they worked longer hours or took less pay.) Cook finally signed but in the following terms which did not commit him at all: 'I am prepared, speaking for myself, on condition that the Government does not proceed with their Eight Hours Bill, to recommend my officials and committee to consider these proposals as a basis for discussion.'

As a result of this qualification the Minister of Labour said he could not persuade the Cabinet to hold up the Eight Hours Bill, which became law on 8 July. Nevertheless, both before the Bill had become law and afterwards, Layton and Rowntree persisted with their attempts, which were made difficult by the elusiveness of A.J. Cook, who at the critical moment flew to Berlin to collect money from Russia to help the striking miners. When Cook came back he promised to consult his union executive but it transpired later that he never did so.

To make matters more frustrating, the Churches' Committee, which included Anglicans and Free Churchmen, started trying their hand at mediation on 14 July, putting forward quite unrealistic proposals more favourable to the miners and totally unacceptable to the government and the owners. Layton and Rowntree had a far better chance of success in that, since they worked closely with the Minister of Labour, they knew the views of the government while the Churches' Committee proceeded in ignorance of them. As Asa Briggs in his *Life of Seebohm Rowntree* pointed out: 'This was the crucial point, and it drove Rowntree into believing that the intervention of the Churches' Committee was disastrous to the cause which they all shared, the desire to end the strike as quickly as possible. He maintained to the end of his life that if the Churches' Committee had not intervened in 1926 a settlement could have been reached on the basis of the Rowntree and Layton proposals.'[4] Whether this is true or not, Baldwin at a meeting at No. 10 on 19 July disillusioned the Churches' Committee, insisting that miners' working hours had to be lengthened.

Nevertheless, Layton and Rowntree still persisted. On 23 July, Layton (rather than Rowntree, who might have been suspect as an idealist) saw the owners and recorded the outcome: 'I was afraid the owners would be hopeless and I find they are absolutely hopeless. It seems to me that the only possibility is to get the Government to impose terms on the owners.' Rowntree tried hard to see the miners' executive but failed. With the Churches' intervention all was in confusion, and in any case it is probable that the miners were no longer interested in middle-class go-betweens, however well intentioned. Layton records in his Memoirs:

> After various efforts to get the Government to take the responsibility of imposing on the industry certain recommendations of the Commission, Rowntree and I abandoned our activities and watched the miners for the

next few months slowly drifting back on the terms dictated by the employers. I share Rowntree's view that but for the intervention of the churches there was a distinct possibility that the miners might have gone back to work on a carefully considered compromise settlement in the summer of 1926 instead of drifting back to work in mid winter at the end of their tether. The failure and the bitterness it left behind made nationalisation of the mines inevitable.

The Liberal Yellow Book

The need to inquire into the state of British industry had been discussed at a number of the annual Liberal Summer Schools, but this was a major task which would require a good deal of money. The way was not clear until 1926 when Lloyd George, having taken over from Asquith as Liberal leader, announced that he was prepared to finance, to the tune of £10,000, 'a thorough inquiry by the Summer School into industrial problems'. Lloyd George imposed no conditions in return for his money and undertook to respect the independence of the Summer School. All he asked was that he should be free to take part in their discussions. Fortunately by then his long-running quarrel with Keynes, dating back to 1915, had receded into the background.

Layton took the lead from the first in organizing this wide-ranging inquiry, for which the mass of papers looked like overwhelming some of the participants. At one time it seemed that Sir Herbert Samuel might be chairman of the Executive Committee organizing the inquiry, but in the end Layton was appointed. One reason, no doubt, was that he was already chairman of the Liberal Summer School Executive Committee. But more important, he had the expert knowledge and was prepared to do the hard work needed to produce a good report. Ernest Simon became vice-chairman. The other members of the Inquiry Executive Committee were nearly all members of the Liberal Summer School Council, to whom were added the politicians, Lloyd George, Charles Masterman, Sir Herbert Samuel and Sir John Simon.

The terms of reference of the inquiry were wide, including consideration of 'the economic and social problems of post-war British industry, with special reference to the possibility and means of changes in the organisation of industry which would encourage better use of national resources, increased employment, and closer cooperation between capital and labour' and of the action needed to secure these ends.

This huge task was to be tackled by seven subcommittees. Layton was chairman of the Statistics Committee which analysed the state of the British economy, helped by Hubert Henderson and Josiah Stamp. He also served under Keynes on the Finance and Industry Committee. Ernest Simon was chairman of the Trade Union Committee and Lloyd George himself chaired the Unemployment Committee. It was a mark of the times and, indeed, of the Liberals, that four women served on the subcommittees, including Dorothy Layton and Eva Hubback (the author's mother). A few people outside the Liberal Party were invited to help because of their special knowledge, but one of them, R.H. Brand, the banker, wrote to Layton in December 1926 explaining that he could not take part in a Lloyd George inquiry because he was 'absolutely convinced it would not be an inquiry into the truth but would be used for purely party purposes in the end'. Sir John Simon dissociated himself from the draft of the report on trade union law, and unfortunately Charles Masterman died in the autumn of 1927 after having made a major contribution. Otherwise the work of the various committees coordinated by Layton and Simon went on steadily.

As nearly all the members were extremely busy during the week, much of the work was done at Lloyd George's country house at Churt in the course of eleven weekends. Hubert Philips, the economic adviser to the inquiry, wrote:

> During that period, the Executive – and its officials – met, for eleven week-ends, at Ll. G's country house, Bron-y-De, Churt. We used to drive down on Friday night, in a couple of hired Daimlers, returning on Monday morning. There were thus about six sessions, each week-end.
>
> Ll. G. was an admirable host. At lunch and dinner, we sat round a long table – there were usually sixteen of us. Ll. G. presided, seated at one end of the table; at the other – until his untimely death, in November, 1927 – sat Charlie Masterman. Like the two corner-boys in a Minstrel Show, Ll. G. and Charlie kept the conversation going. The opening gambit was, usually, some question, put by Ll. G. to Charlie, as to whether he (Charlie)

> rememberd this or that incident of the palmy days when Ll. G. had been Prime Minister.
>
> Cheerful meals, those dinners and lunches were. Champagne was usually served. Ll. G. made every effort to involve all who were seated at table in the general conversation.
>
> One of his favouriate gimmicks was to think up some question of general interest, and then go round the table, asking each of us, in turn, to answer it.
>
> One such interrogatory concerned the number of hours which everyone slept. I recall that I appeared to spend less time in bed than anyone else, and that Maynard Keynes appeared to spend more. 'I snuff the candle' – said Maynard – 'at both ends.'

Some of the meals certainly induced sleep. On 17 September Lloyd George provided a dinner, all the food for which was grown at Churt. The menu was:

Bean Soup

Trout
Roast Loin of Lamb
Rabbit and Pork Pie
Roast Pork
Duckling
Gosling
Chicken
Partridge
Brawn

Apple Tart
Raspberry Fool

Greengages – Yellow Plums
Damsons – Apples – Green Almonds

To drink: Cider, Raspberry Wine, Mead, Buttermilk.

No doubt such a surfeit was exceptional as the pace set by Lloyd George was brisk. Seebohm Rowntree recorded his methods:

> He was a hard taskmaster. We would work from breakfast to lunch. Then he would ask us to work at some problem in the afternoon and he would meet us at tea time and then discuss what we had done. He, of course, rested in the afternoon. After tea he would be all fresh and ready to discuss the work we had done and he would work on until dinner time, which was

usually at 8 o'clock. After dinner he would meet with us again for a short time and then just before ten o'clock he would discuss the programme for the following day and the subject we would discuss. He would suggest that we might do some preliminary work on a particular problem and leave any documents we had prepared outside his bedroom door, which he would get when he woke at six o'clock in the morning and read in bed, so as to be prepared to discuss them with us at breakfast next morning.[5]

Layton succeeded in getting the various subcommittees to produce their reports in time and, where necessary, made the chairman provide redrafts. For instance, he wrote to Lloyd George on 6 August 1927 in an apparently rather peremptory way:

The following represents the net result of our discussions last Sunday and my talk with you on Monday evening:

You will furnish me with a re-draft of the following sections of the Unemployment Committee's Report:

(1) Roads.
(2) Housing and Garden Cities.
(3) Slum Clearance.
(4) Electricity.
(5) Afforestation.
(6) Agriculture.

As regards Roads, the section is to be fuller than in the last draft and with a little more information as to the situation.

Shortly afterwards Layton at last got away for a holiday, but it was typical that he used it to edit the various drafts. He wrote in *Dorothy*:

After collecting a great deal of evidence, constant discussions in the executive committee, preparation of reports by special committees and the circulation of countless memoranda, Ernest Simon with his wife and family, Mrs Hubback with her family, and Dorothy and I with ours, went together on a joint holiday to Devero in the High Alps above the Simplon Tunnel. There Ernest Simon and I worked on our documents and drafts. After about two weeks we moved down into northern Italy at the side of Lake Orta, where swimming and boating took the place of scrambling over the mountains and water polo alternated with political arguments. When we got back to England we brought with us a draft of the whole report which, after several discussions, mostly at Lloyd George's house at Churt, was taken down to Little Holland for a long week-end to be put into final shape by Hubert Henderson and myself.

The 500-page report, called the *Yellow Book*, to distinguish it from previous publications by the Liberal Summer Schools, namely, the *Green Book on Agriculture* and the *Brown Book on Urban Problems*, was published in February 1928. As the reviewers found, when they came to write their rather critical articles, the report is so packed with facts and ideas that it is difficult to summarize. In the main, however, it reflects the views of Keynes, who according to Layton was a principal intellectual driving force, of Ramsay Muir and of Lloyd George. So the section about national finance emphasizes the monetary causes of unemployment, the need to control credit, to bring the Bank of England under public regulation and to increase and channel public investment through a board of national investment. The government should be advised by an economic general staff and the national accounting system should be reformed so that Parliament had the relevant facts and thus would be properly equipped to control public expenditure. Private industry should publish full and accurate balance sheets.

The section on industrial relations, reflecting Ramsay Muir's ideas, argued for a minimum wage, profit-sharing, and family allowances. The section on national development followed Lloyd George's ideas of tackling unemployment and re-equipping the country for future prosperity by a large public works programme, of housing, roads, electrification and land drainage, financed by a board of national investment. The coal industry was to be reorganized and mineral royalities nationalized, but there was no proposal to nationalize any other industry. Instead, the State would intervene through regulation, credit control, and publicity.

The whole report made a coherent programme for which there was strong intellectual arguments, but made almost no political appeal. It offered no simple solutions and its ideas were too new and too complex to fit into the accepted political categories of the day. So it was not surprising that except for a favourable review in the *Economist*, the reception of all this hard work was disappointing. The *Nation* published a rueful article on 11 February 1928 recording that the Press were irritated by having to review such a solid work. Mr Garvin in the *Observer* complained that nothing in it stood out sufficiently. Some papers were unable to decide whether the *Yellow Book* was socialist or Conservative (by making capitalism work). Some reviewers found it outrageous; others platitudinous. The *Times* was dismissive: 'The report is useful as an incorporation of recent facts and current ideas in a compendious form.' Tom Jones wrote to Beatrice Webb on 10 February: 'I dined on Wednesday night with Keynes, Layton and other authors of the Yellow Peril. They seem rather flat at the reception of the book. It had clashed with the funeral of Lord Haig. I rather agree with you that it is a valuable Fabian document, a great deal of which will be taken over by the Unionist Government in 1929.'[6]

Tom Jones was wrong about the 1929 government but right in believing that other parties than the Liberals would put many of the *Yellow Book* proposals into effect. The time lag, however, was long. The *Yellow Book* ideas suffered from the polarization of politics in the 1931 crisis, but surfaced once more in 1935, when Harold Macmillan worked with Layton and Seebohm Rowntree to produce *The Next Five Years*, which was, in effect, a five-year plan for Britain. Harold Macmillan himself embodied much of the *Yellow Book* philosophy in his *The Middle Way*, published in 1938, and by that time the ideas Keynes had advanced in the *Yellow Book* had had their full intellectual justification through the publication of his *General Theory* in 1936.

However, it was not until the Second World War, when Keynes, Layton and Henderson were all back in Whitehall, that Keynes's thinking became largely accepted among all political parties. There was plenty of State intervention during the period after the war but no social revolution. So it was the Labour government which put into effect many of the ideas of the *Yellow Book*, in effect giving capitalism, within a mixed economy, a new lease of life. Unfortunately, that Labour government and subsequent governments have not made much progress towards implementing the *Yellow Book* proposals for improved industrial relations. Layton wrote in his Memoirs: 'Since 1945 full employment and Keynesian policies have been an assumption of our public life, at times to a damaging degree. The tragedy was that they won acceptance twenty years too late. Unemployment and slump left scars on the British working population that still cramp our ability to face the future.'

Although the *Yellow Book* did not help the Liberals to win the 1929 election, or, indeed, any subsequent election, by any reckoning its production was one of Layton's major successes, not at the time of its publication, but as the years passed and the force of its arguments became more and more persuasive. It is not surprising that the Liberal Party reissued the *Yellow Book* in 1977, when David Steel in his foreword wrote: 'Much of the Inquiry is still – alas – very relevant.'

CHAPTER SIX

The *Economist*

Apart from a few years during and just after the First World War, Layton was connected with the *Economist* throughout his life, from 1908 when he wrote his first article until 1966 when he died two weeks after attending his last board meeting as vice-chairman.

The *Economist* has proved to be Layton's most enduring achievement and most probably the one by which he himself would wish to be remembered. His work for the *Daily News* and the *News Chronicle* for thirty years was more demanding and, perhaps, gave him more political influence, but it ended with the collapse of the *News Chronicle* and much sadness. The peak of Layton's achievement was in the 1930s when, from offices on either side of Bouverie Street, he edited the *Economist* and managed the *News Chronicle* with great skill and financial success. Although addressed to very different audiences, each paper reinforced the other, not only in standpoint but through interchange of staff. Aylmer Vallance, who became editor of the *News Chronicle* in 1933, had worked on the *Economist* during the previous ten years, and Geoffrey Crowther, who succeeded Layton as editor of the *Economist* in 1938, had divided his time between the two papers ever since he was recruited in 1932.

The seventeen years Layton spent as editor of the *Economist* from the very end of 1921 until 1938 laid the foundation for its remarkable later success on both sides of the Atlantic. Geoffrey Crowther and his successor must be given the credit for bringing circulation up to its present level of about 250,000 a week, against which Layton's achievement in doubling the 1922 figure of 5,000 to 10,000 in 1938 seems unremarkable. But it was Layton who steadily over the years of his editorship made the *Economist* both more interesting to read and more authoritative. Layton wanted the paper to express his own highly responsible political views, while at the same time providing the facts and figures which were essential for any understanding of the British economy.

Layton recorded in a note on the editorship of the *Economist* he wrote in 1955:

> I had joined the paper soon after Hirst's appointment on a part time basis, my special contribution being on the economic and statistical aspects of the paper. I had walked out of the office on August 6th, 1914 owing to a sharp difference of opinion with the Editor on his attitude to the war and his prognosis of its economic consequences. My first years as Editor were packed with political issues. Three General Elections, the American Debt Settlement, the renewal of the Free Trade fight, the General Strike, the return to gold.

He might well have added to the list of political issues Reparations and the League of Nations. In his Memoirs he wrote that his first article as editor, which was about the 1921 Washington Naval Conference, 'set the tone for the *Economist*'s treatment of international affairs for the whole of my editorship'.

Running the *Economist* was Layton's most enjoyable activity as well as his most successful. He was well suited to the job. He had the wide range of interests and contacts, both at home and abroad, to be able to write, or get others to write, intelligently and responsibly on the main issues of the day. His great interest in statistics enabled him to develop the service the *Economist* had for a long time been providing by introducing new indices such as Shipping Freight Rates and Business Activity, to show how the economy was moving.

The permanent staff when he took over was small. Layton had his own room but the rest were housed in two rooms, even after the move from Arundel Street to Bouverie Street in 1928. So he could know everyone well. His brother Gilbert, who joined the *Economist* in 1911, did all the administrative work, thus relieving Walter of the routine jobs. Gilbert Layton also wrote some of the more straightforward parts of the paper in the 1920s. Walter's strength lay not in management but in bringing new ideas and encouraging the younger members of the staff to develop their own.

From the start Layton was determined to develop the tradition of editorial independence which had been so marked half a century earlier when Walter Bagehot was editor. The *Economist* had been founded in 1843 by James Wilson, supported by, but independent of, the Anti-Corn Law League. The paper, which Wilson edited himself, was profitable from the first and has remained so ever since. Wilson became a Liberal MP in 1847 and in the 1850s was financial secretary to the Treasury and paymaster-general. He seems to have continued as editor of the *Economist* while holding these offices, but when he went to India as financial secretary in 1859 he handed over to his son-in-law Walter Bagehot, who had married the eldest of his six daughters. It was Bagehot's editorship over the next eighteen years which, even though its circulation was only about 3,000, gave the *Economist* the authority and influence it has retained ever since, though to a degree varying with the ability of its succeeding editors.

After Bagehot's death the paper, still owned by the Wilson family trust, managed to increase its circulation to about 5,000 copies, although it became a considerably duller and more routine publication. It was F.W. Hirst, the editor under whom Layton served from 1909 to 1914, who followed Bagehot's example in broadening the scope of the paper once more and in recruiting an able staff such as Hilton Young (later Lord Kennet), Leonard Reid, later City editor of the *Daily Telegraph*, Oscar Hobson, later City editor of the *News Chronicle*, and Mary Agnes Hamilton, the first woman on the editorial staff of the *Economist* and later an MP.

When Walter Layton took up his post at the end of 1921 the permanent staff needed reinforcement, as did the overseas correspondents whose contributions became an increasingly important part of the paper. Layton kept the staff small but improved its quality. At that time (and indeed the practice has gone on) articles in the *Economist* were almost never signed. Unfortunately, all the paper's records were burnt in May 1941 as a result of an air raid, so it is often impossible to find out who wrote a particular article. However, surviving lists of contributors in the autumn of 1924 show that by then three of Layton's recruits, Arnold Toynbee, Hargreaves Parkinson and A.J. Cummings, were writing regularly. Aylmer Vallance was contributing his Shipping Freight index while secretary of the National Maritime Board, and his great ability as a writer led to his becoming assistant editor by 1929.

Even with new blood, to anyone now looking through the 1920s issues the *Economist* would seem staid both in content and appearance. The contents followed the old pattern, starting with developments in the money market, and continuing with five or six short leaders on political and financial subjects, short notes on recent events and letters from the main foreign correspondents, who were increased in number. These items together took up about twenty pages, while the remaining thirty pages of a normal fifty-page issue were devoted to the Stock Exchange, commodity markets, commercial news and statistics.

The paper's appearance was unchanged since Victorian times. In particular its title, partly in gothic script, was the same as from 1846, reading:

The Economist,

WEEKLY COMMERCIAL TIMES,

Bankers' Gazette and Railway Monitor

A POLITICAL, LITERARY, AND GENERAL NEWSPAPER.

Headings for articles were kept small. There was no attempt to please the eye. Each article followed closely on the last and the statistics were set out in uncompromising lumps.

Layton greatly improved the contents, both in the scope of the articles and the clarity of the writing. He always maintained that a few figures were needed in most articles, but only a few, and they must be the really significant ones. His own prose was clear, if not elegant, and indeed he wrote better than he spoke. But, having little aesthetic sense himself, he took twelve years before being persuaded by Graham Hutton that the typography and layout of the paper needed bringing into line with good modern practice. Keynes had seen to typography and design when he took over the *Nation* in 1923. Layton was closely connected with the *Nation* and yet resisted any similar changes in the *Economist* for a long time. Perhaps he thought he would lose sales among the conservatives in the City. He was right in so far as Montagu Norman was shocked by the new layout and, indeed, was never reconciled to it.

Layton does not seem to have been inhibited in the way he edited the *Economist* during his first five years when the paper was still owned by the Wilson family trust. He wrote a leader most weeks which, while not being in any way party political, was liberal and internationalist in tone. He restarted the monthly trade supplement which had been dropped in the war and greatly improved the statistical side of the paper. There were special supplements about international conferences and on individual countries' economies, including one on Russia in 1927. Maisky, whom Layton got to know well when he became the Russian Ambassador in London in 1932, wrote in *Novy Mir* in 1968:

> Layton tried to provide as objective material as possible about the Soviet Union and in March 1927 during one of the most difficult moments in Anglo-Soviet relations, two months before these were broken off, he published a special Russian supplement in which I also had an active hand. At that time this was an act of civic courage and political far-sightedness on Layton's part.

During this period circulation remained stable at about 6,000 copies a week and it became clear that more capital would be needed if the paper was to grow. From the time he became editor, Layton knew what he wanted to do. His objectives were to make sure that the editor of the *Economist* should be totally independent of the proprietors. The Wilson family trustees should therefore be persuaded, in due course, to sell to a group of people, sympathetic to Layton, who would be prepared to provide the money needed to improve the paper. The Wilson trust was naturally concerned to distribute the maximum dividends to the descendants of James Wilson and hence there were no financial reserves. As time went on the family was becoming more scattered and less disposed to take any real interest in the paper. By about 1927 the trustees had decided to sell the *Economist* as soon as a suitable purchaser, willing to carry on the traditions of the past, could be found. Layton saw his opportunity. He had in 1927, at the invitation of the Cadbury family, become adviser on finance and editorial policy to the *Daily News*. He was thus adding some expertise about newspaper finance to his general knowledge of the City derived from being editor of the *Economist*. The group he assembled to make a bid for the paper was made up of personal friends such as Ernest Simon and Laurence Cadbury, and acquaintances through work or the Liberal Party such as Sir Henry Strakosch, South African representative at the 1920 Brussels Conference and now chairman of the Union Corporation, Sir John Simon and Sir Walter Runciman, both of whom came to the Liberal Summer Schools.

The price discussed for buying the *Economist* was about £60,000 but Brendan Bracken, then a young man determined to make his fortune, was assembling a group of technical newspapers and periodicals under the name of Financial Newspapers and pushed the bidding up to £100,000. At that stage Layton did a deal with Bracken, helped by the Wilson trustees' refusal to sell the *Economist* outright to any newspaper group, or indeed to any purely commercial interest.

The Wilson trustees insisted that the tradition of editorial independence was the *Economist*'s most valuable asset and must be maintained. The bargain struck was that Layton's group and Financial Newspapers should put up £50,000 each, but that Layton's group should have three out of the five directors as well as the chairmanship and deputy chairmanship of the board. Bracken was to be managing director, but in practice he left the running of the business side of the paper entirely to Layton.

The editorial charter gave the editor complete power, to the exclusion of the board, to control editorial policy, to make staff appointments and to fix salaries. In Layton's words: 'It allowed the editor to run the paper as though it belonged to him.' To safeguard the editor's independence four trustees were appointed whose approval had to be sought before an editor was appointed or sacked, before there was any change in shareholdings in the *Economist* and before the chairman of the board was appointed. The original trustees were Sir Lionel Halsey, Sir William Beveridge, Sir Josiah Stamp and Sir Alan Anderson. The first chairman of the board was Sir Henry Strakosch, who stayed in this post until his death in 1944, when Layton himself took over. The other members of the board were Sir Walter Runciman, Layton himself, with Major-General Guy Dawnay and Brendan Bracken as the two Financial Newspapers directors.

This reconstruction of the *Economist* as a private company, which was completed by January 1929, gave Layton exactly what he wanted, both as to his own position and the means to build up the paper in the way he thought right. The permanent staff was kept small in number but the quality was improved, thanks to an influx of some outstanding young men. Layton had found he had little difficulty in persuading them to join the staff as the first step to careers in journalism, politics, the universities or the City. Lionel Robbins came for a short time in 1924 to report on the German Press. Humphrey Mynors (later deputy governor of the Bank of England) helped Layton in 1926 with the papers for the 1927 World Economic Conference. H.V. Hodson, a fellow of All Souls and later editor of the *Round Table* and the *Sunday Times*, came in 1928 because he could find at the *Economist* the statistics he needed to complete his thesis on overseas investment.

Aylmer Vallance became assistant editor in 1929 and often edited the paper in Layton's absence. Circulation rose steadily from 6,000 in 1930 to over 10,000 in 1938, thanks, Layton maintained, to the economic crisis in the early 1930s – which heightened public interest – and later thanks to the bright young men he recruited in 1933. Although Aylmer Vallance was left wing, and some people mistakenly thought he was a Communist Party member, or at least a fellow traveller, he wrote brilliantly and got on well with Sir Henry Strakosch. In 1932 Strakosch wanted Vallance to take over the editorship of the *Economist*, partly because Layton was away so much and partly because he feared that, with Layton running the *News Chronicle*, the *Economist* would be regarded as a Liberal Party paper.

Vallance turned down the proposal, pointing out that: 'The *Economist* has become no longer as it once was, a staid and colourless City weekly, made up largely of routine articles, but a very definite organ of opinion associated throughout the world with the name of an editor who is not so much a journalist as an international public man.' The loss to the *Economist* of Layton's name would be a grievous blow, he felt. As for Liberal Party politics, Vallance said he saw little danger of the *News Chronicle* ever being regarded again as a party organ, especially as 'You can hardly call Layton, its controller, a "party" man.'

Layton, who was aware of Strakosch's approach to Vallance through Vallance keeping him in touch, pressed on with recruiting more talent for the paper. At the beginning of 1933 Geoffrey Crowther, Douglas Jay and Graham Hutton joined the paper and, with Vallance moving on to become editor of the *News Chronicle* in 1933, became responsible for most of the more substantial articles. Crowther, who spent half his time on the *News Chronicle*, was to become editor of the *Economist* in 1938, Jay went to the *Daily Herald* as City editor in 1937 and Graham Hutton from 1938 onwards became a distinguished freelance journalist, specializing on Central and Eastern European affairs. Layton told Tom Jones, who had been deputy secretary to the Cabinet, that he found Oxford men better on the *Economist* than those from Cambridge. He was looking for good journalists, not professional economists.[1]

In these years Arnold Toynbee was still writing on foreign affairs and Nicholas Davenport continued writing about the Stock Exchange as he had in the 1920s. Roland Bird came in 1933 as Stock Exchange assistant and stayed with the paper all his career, to become one of the main architects of the present *Economist*. Among the part-timers was one of Keynes's postgraduate students, David Bensusan-Butt, who worked a day a week at the *Economist* before going into the Civil Service in 1937. Thomas Balogh and Nicholas Kaldor came into the office fairly often to discuss their own ideas and City gossip.

From talking with some of the above who have survived it is possible to put together a picture of Layton as editor of the *Economist*. To the new recruit Layton's habit of lapsing into silence was sometimes disconcerting. Roland Bird described what happened when he was first taken in to see Layton:

> Hargreaves Parkinson shepherded me into his office – Walter was always a great messer with paper. He was always fingering papers and rustling them about. We went in. I expected this great man, Walter Layton, to be

> a dynamic character. There he was taking no notice of anything and fidgeting about with these papers. It was most embarrassing. Nothing happened for three minutes or so. I began to think we ought to back out. Eventually Hargreaves Parkinson said, 'This is Bird who we would like to take on as Stock Exchange assistant.' This didn't make much impression and there was another awkward pause. At the end of it all he uttered the remarkable words 'Well, yes, I suppose so.'[2]

H.V. Hodson found Layton easy to get on with at work. He liked the way he treated all people the same, whether they were important or not. He liked, too, his lack of dogma and the way he impressed people because he obviously knew what he was talking about. Layton sometimes appeared to be boneless because of his indecision, but Hodson found that he had firm principles.

Perhaps it was because Layton sometimes had difficulty in explaining his ideas that Beachcomber, in his comic column in the *Daily Express*, reported in 1937: 'The knitted woollen statue of Walter Layton in Trafalgar Square is coming unravelled.' Even the experienced had some difficulty in understanding precisely what was in Layton's mind. Crowther used to say he edited the *Economist* when Layton was away by interpreting Layton's pregnant silences on the telephone.

Juniors such as Roland Bird regarded him as a headmaster. There was no use of Christian names until very much later. David Bensusan-Butt remembers the young men being in awe of Layton as a kind but reserved man with direct lines to those in high places. He had moral authority which all respected. Layton talked very little at the weekly editorial conferences but guided them firmly. It was quite clear at the end what line was to be taken and who was to do the writing. Douglas Jay remembers his laconic style as being rather similar to that of Attlee, for whom he was to work after the war. The staff, mainly made up of young men, found that Layton was perfectly willing to give rulings when there was a difference of opinion and this firm touch was appreciated and very much missed when, in 1936, he handed over many of his editorial responsibilities to Hargreaves Parkinson. Layton himself wrote infrequently in the 1930s, but then he was writing in the *News Chronicle* as well.

Layton's main efforts went into the actual editing of the paper, which was done with the greatest economy of time. Most issues were settled at the Monday editorial lunch, where he was at once diffident and kind, but quite firm in spite of his slight stammer. He would look in on Wednesday to see how the main articles were shaping up but always spent Thursday late afternoon and evening reading the proofs of those parts of the paper where opinions were expressed, as opposed to the purely factual material. Proof correcting could go on until late at night, Layton's corrections always being written in pencil and being directed to toning down phrases he found too extreme. He did not usually add new ideas but would knock out paragraphs and rewrite them in his own cautious style. When he had doubts about the conclusion of an article he inserted the words 'Time alone will show' at the end, thus avoiding commitment. He was a meticulous editor. Some of his staff found his redrafting difficult to accept, especially late at night. Graham Hutton's clerihew was clearly heartfelt:

Sir Walter Layton
Has a passion for alterat'on
Would to God someone could alter
Sir Walter.

In spite of these long proof-correcting sessions, the bright young men on the *Economist* were given greater freedom in what they wrote than on many papers. In fact, Layton used the long Thursday evening sessions as a safeguard against losing the City circulation. There were complaints that the *Economist* (and still more the *News Chronicle*) was too leftwing. Layton had to keep the balance. He believed in moderation and in avoiding extremes but on many occasions he by no means fitted in with the Establishment view.

Layton was a highly strung man, expending much nervous energy on his work, even in chairing a meeting at which he did not have to do much speaking. But he could be more relaxed at the *Economist* than at the *News Chronicle* because, having recruited a very good staff, he sensibly delegated most of the work and the paper virtually ran itself. The *Economist* always earned a profit, in part because it had a captive audience in Whitehall, the universities, the City and most financial centres of the world, but more so because Layton saw to it that the paper had a coherent policy on international affairs, on the need for removing obstacles for trade and for an expansionary policy once the 1931 financial crisis had been overcome. Graham Hutton is certain that Layton really enjoyed running the *Economist*: 'I remember his fiftieth birthday . . . he was still looking a rather young, if lined, man. At fifty he was still blond, blue-eyed, very tall, straight as a ramrod, had a beautiful voice, still in musical note, and I think he had all he wanted.'

Layton made sure that the *Economist* reflected his views on international affairs and, in particular, his belief that security could only be assured if the League of Nations was made effective. Between 1922 and 1935 he published nearly 150 articles on the need for reducing national armaments and for pooling the residue to make it possible to resist aggression through the League of Nations. It was for the British government to take the lead in invigorating the League and in making collective security work by promoting agreement on the limitation and pooling of armaments. With Hitler's rise to power the *Economist* continued to point out the danger of the government's failure either to build up the League or to win security through new alliances or rearmament. While some of the paper's young men in the 1930s thought that Layton should have been more outspoken, it was mainly his cautious nature they were criticizing. He was no appeaser. Layton had been to Berlin in April 1933 to learn something about the new Nazi government. On his return he wrote a cautious article in the *News Chronicle*, mainly reporting the interviews he had with Hitler, Goebbels and others, rather than passing final judgement.

Layton showed he detested Nazi methods when the *Economist* came under attack from the German Minister of Finance, Count Schwerin von Krosigk (whom Layton had got to know well during the Reparations talks of 1931), complaining of an article written by Douglas Jay on the *Brown Book of Hitler Terror*.[3] Von Krosigk demanded an apology for Jay's review, in which he wrote that Germany no longer had a civilized government and would have to be stopped by force. Jay maintained that the trial of the Dutchman van der Lubbe, and the other defendants accused of setting the Reichstag on fire in February 1933 would prove a travesty of justice. Layton did not apologize but replied that, as he assumed the Reichstag Fire Trial would be open and all the evidence would be in public, he himself would like to attend some sessions of the trial and he would see to it that the *Economist* reported the whole trial fully. Von Krosigk in his reply[4] did not invite Layton to attend the trial and, according to Jay – who was told by Layton to write a weekly report on the progress of the trial – the German authorities would not allow any representative of the *Economist* to go to the trial. Jay's weekly reports, which ran until Christmas, were critical of Nazi justice, even though the final verdict found only van der Lubbe to be guilty. Jay's reports got through Layton's editorship without much toning down and Layton's subsequent campaigns in the *News Chronicle*, as well as the leading articles in the *Economist*, showed how much he detested Nazi methods and objectives.

The bright young men at the *Economist* had fewer doubts about Layton's treatment of home economic policy. Throughout most of the Thirties the *Economist* stood for moderate reflation coupled with government intervention, where necessary, to stimulate economic growth. Layton, of course, retained his belief in the virtues of free trade and the evils of protection. The way to bring down unemployment was through increased world trade, which would follow from a general reduction in tariff barriers.

Broadly, Layton was in sympathy with Keynes except when, in the spring of 1931, he advocated a revenue tariff. But Layton, like Hubert Henderson, had doubts about the economic analysis Keynes was evolving later in the 1930s. Perhaps because of Layton's doubts about Keynes's theories – or perhaps because he no longer felt himself qualified to pass judgement on Keynes's major departures from Marshallian economics – Austin Robinson's review in the *Economist* of Keynes's *General Theory* was signed, contrary to normal practice in the *Economist*, where articles and book reviews were anonymous. This incident has continued to puzzle Austin Robinson, who recorded his feelings about Layton in a letter to the author:

> He was so able and in a way one of the early creators of quantitative economics. But he was at the same time curiously anti-intellectual. One of my most vivid memories of crossing swords with him was over the review in the *Economist* of Keynes's *General Theory*. He and Geoffrey Crowther (who was potentially more able but in practice very obstinate and anti-intellectual) were terrified of seeming to praise the *General Theory* or to say that it

was important. They not only made me sign the review when the *Economist* normally published unsigned reviews. They also cut out, without my agreement, the final paragraph in which I summed up the book. I never quite forgave Geoffrey Crowther and I still think that Layton ought to have had a little more perception and courage. He was a great man but he had rather severe limitations.

It may be, however, that this was but another example of Layton refusing to give a firm opinion when he had not got to grips with the subject – in this case the new Keynesian economics. His caution could be infuriating to others.

The *Economist* had been critical too of Harold Macmillan's book *Reconstruction*, which came out in favour of government economic planning and Keynes's financial policies in December 1933. But in 1935 Layton joined Lloyd George's Council of Action which was formed to enable Lloyd George to make a political comeback, with the help of Liberal *Yellow Book* policies brought up to date. At the same time he was a member of the Next Five Years Group, of which Macmillan, together with Lord Allen of Hurtwood, were the leading spirits. Macmillan had been trying to persuade the Conservative Party to tackle unemployment and industrial decay through government intervention. The *Economist* gave a general welcome to the ideas of the Next Five Years Group which, together with Lloyd George's Council of Action, continued to operate for the next two years. Layton had to take account of a critical and sceptical City, but the *Economist* in this period often provided a forum for progressive as well as conventional views.

It was no doubt criticism from the City which led to Strakosch writing to Layton and other members of the board on 28 June 1938:

It is felt that an undue amount of space has been devoted to foreign politics and the tendency has been to present these subjects in a manner which savours far too much of party politics. There can be no question about the *Economist*'s standing – as it has stood for 95 years – for the defence of Liberal principles in their widest sense; but in doing so it should never allow itself to descend to party politics. This means, in other words, that when dealing with political questions, the editor should have the fortitude to forget party lines, and deal with these questions in what might be called a judicial manner.

Strakosch then went on to raise the question of editorial independence, which under the articles of association conveyed 'dictatorial powers' on the editor. This letter must have annoyed Layton, who had tried to ensure that the *Economist*'s leaders were judicious and well balanced, even though his own staff sometimes thought they were too cautious. His reply to Strakosch and other members of the *Economist* board was measured. He was able to show that the amount of space devoted to politics had remained fairly constant over the years and denied that the paper had been in any way biased by party considerations:

> I should claim that its criticisms, though outspoken, have not been biased or actuated by any motive other than belief in the point of view put forward. If the criticism is that the views of the paper are too strongly expressed, my reply is that forceful and forthright comment follows the best traditions of the paper. The worst fault of a paper that seeks to carry weight and influence is to be neutral and dull. I maintain that the *Economist* should speak from conviction and put its views as forcefully as it can – provided always that its manner of expression does not overstep the boundaries – so impossible to define – of good taste.

Having made his view quite clear, Layton went on to agree that, given his own increasing preoccupation with the *News Chronicle*, which had not been foreseen when the constitution of the *Economist* was drawn up, there might be grounds for bringing the editor and the board of directors closer together to decide policy in the future. He therefore suggested that future editors should have the duty of discussing policy with the board when asked to do so, and that the editorship of the *Economist* should be regarded as a whole-time appointment or at all events the editor's sole important journalistic appointment.

Perhaps Layton did not mind giving up complete editorial independence since he was, in any event, about to resign the editorship of the *Economist*. In his letter of resignation of 20 July 1938 he wrote that he had in the previous three years been able to delegate a very great deal to Hargreaves Parkinson, the associate editor, but went on:

> Nevertheless, as I have retained full responsibility for the general tone, as well as for every judgement of a paper which is essentially a 'journal of opinion' it has still been necessary for me to give a great deal of time each week to planning the contents, to the actual work of editing the articles and notes, and to reading nearly everything in proof.

At the board meeting which discussed Strakosch's complaints, Layton's proposals for the directors being able at least to discuss policy were accepted and nothing more was said about the *Economist* becoming too party-political. Perhaps that was because Geoffrey Crowther, the new editor, though at thirty-two much younger than Layton, was to the right of him in his political views.

Many *Economist* readers were sorry he stopped being editor. One, a Yorkshire Liberal wrote:

> For years the *Economist* has said the things I wanted saying. It is the nearest thing to a 1938 Gladstonian voice we have; and I have been grateful this morning lying awake from 4 a.m. and feeling utterly sick at heart at the collapse of the Liberal (and liberal) things I felt a sudden sympathy for you. Free trade, the League, liberalism, from a position of eminence you have fought for them all. You have seen where evil lay and where it would come and how; and you have said so; and it is here notwithstanding. Now we can arm knowing the awful meaning of what we are arming for and we can pray for a miracle.

A Conservative, Sir Percy Bates of the Cunard Shipping Company, wrote:

> Under your guidance, your paper has handled figures with a rare honesty which I have appreciated and valued on very many occasions. In politics I have never fully shared the views of the political party to which I am supposed to belong. If, on many occasions, I have not felt quite so sure that the *Economist* was right, I have always understood and, I think, appreciated your paper's exposition.

Crowther, in effect, took over on 30 September 1938, the night of Munich. His leader that night, no doubt influenced by Layton, was cautious, as was Gerald Barry's leader in the *News Chronicle*, where edition after edition went out without a full leader on Munich while Layton made up his mind. Layton's farewell article in the *Economist* of 22 October – in fact the only one he signed – gave him a chance of summarizing the views he had been putting forward over the previous seventeen years. He showed that the *Economist* had always stood for free trade and the more rational attitude towards reparations and international monetary problems. He emphasized that in the period 1925–30 the world had lost a great chance of rebuilding prosperity on the sound basis of international economic collaboration. In politics the record of missed opportunities ever since he became editor was a sorry one, but there was still hope if the liberty-loving people of the world kept their nerve.

CHAPTER SEVEN

Economic Adviser in Europe and India, 1925–9

Layton ceased being an academic economist in 1914. At that time he was a good expounder of Marshallian economics with a special expertise in statistics. He was on his way to becoming one of the creators of quantitative economics. It was this bent which took him near the top of the Ministry of Munitions, an experience which developed his talent as an applied economist with the rare gift of being able to take a synoptic view of the problems to be solved.

After the war Layton published a revised edition of his *Study of Prices* and kept in close touch with his Cambridge economist friends – Keynes, Pigou, Dennis Robertson and Hubert Henderson – but he played no part in the postwar development of economic theory. Although influenced by Keynes in favour of more government intervention to tackle unemployment and against going back to the gold standard at too high a parity, he remained orthodox in most of his views on fiscal and monetary policy. He also remained faithful to his free trade beliefs, in spite of Keynes urging a measure of tariff protection in the early 1930s, and withdrew from being a member of the UK delegation to the 1933 World Economic Conference when government policy was in favour of tariff protection. He was very much a political economist with rather conventional views about how the economy worked, but endowed with strong Liberal ideals about the social and political system as well as about international relations. Keynes, too, was a political economist with strong views but he had rather fewer ideals and a great deal more intellectual genius.

Layton had great merits both as an economic adviser and as a delegate at international conferences. He never failed to make a positive contribution. He was a constructive thinker and a good negotiator, because he was in no way abrasive or difficult to follow. His advice was couched in conventional terms, but it nearly always advanced matters. He did not cloud the issue by discussing conflicting theories. He could – particularly on paper – express himself clearly. (It was only later that he had difficulty in expressing himself orally.) He had plenty of self-confidence based on his training in economics, which he believed had a real contribution to make to the art of government. He was much in favour of the proposal for an Economic General Staff which was foreshadowed in the Haldane Committee Report of 1918 on the Machinery of Government, and which was made explicit by Sir William Beveridge in an article in the *Nation* at the end of 1923. Later the proposal was worked out in detail in the Liberal *Yellow Book* and was adopted in a watered-down form by Ramsay Macdonald as Prime Minister when he set up the Economic Advisory Council in 1930. Layton joined in the discussions at No. 10 leading to the setting up of the Council and became a member of two of its committees.

Until the Second World War there were virtually no professional economists in the Civil Service. The academic economists recruited in the First World War left when peace came. There were financial experts at the Treasury, such as Niemeyer, Hawtrey and Blackett, but, with the exception of Hawtrey, they certainly did not consider themselves economists. The post of chief economic adviser to the Board of Trade existed between 1919 and 1939 but of its three incumbents only Sir Sydney Chapman was a professional economist (he had been Professor of Political Economy at Manchester) and all three were mainly concerned with international negotiations at the League of Nations and elsewhere rather than advising the government on economic strategy. The Economic Advisory Council, when set up in 1930, had only three professional economists on its staff, of whom Hubert Henderson was by far the most eminent.

So the government had to look outside the Civil Service for economic advice, and Walter Layton was a natural choice. He was well known as editor of the *Economist* at home and abroad, and just because he was not a controversial figure he was acceptable to a whole range of opinion, extending from Montagu Norman to Lloyd

George and Ramsay Macdonald. He himself became more and more interested as time went on in international affairs, and it was in dealing with international economic and financial problems that he made his biggest contribution.

A good test of Layton's ability was presented by the request in June 1925 from the Austrian Committee of the Council of the League of Nations that he and Professor Charles Rist, the French economist, should inquire into the state of the Austrian economy to discover whether 'the economic situation was such as to endanger the financial stability of the country'. Austria had had a League of Nations High Commissioner since 1922 (a Dutchman, Dr Zimmermann) to supervise foreign loans which had been made available through the League of Nations to reconstruct the economy. There had been hyperinflation and near breakdown immediately after the war.

The report Layton and Rist were to write was intended to be non-political, but politics were very much in the minds of the members of the League of Nations Austrian Committee. The main worry of the French was that Austria might form a customs union and eventually a political union (Anschluss) with Germany. The alternative of a customs union with Italy, where Mussolini had already taken over, or with the Czechs and Hungary, was almost equally worrying to a number of countries. But it was clear that if Austria was to become solvent she must be able to export to the successor States of the old Austro-Hungarian Empire in order to pay for essential imports from them. So the high tariff barriers, common in Central Europe, had to come down. Another cause for concern among those who had lent money to Austria was the socialist municipality of Vienna, whose housing and other social policies were expensive and well ahead of their time.

Layton and Rist managed to avoid these political pitfalls in a comprehensive and detailed report, produced with the help of Per Jacobssen, after only seven weeks of intensive work in Austria, during which they interviewed no less than 120 people. The work went on relentlessly right through July, and by early August Walter had to write to Dorothy to say that he could not get to the Liberal Summer School meeting in Cambridge:

> The real reason is that Rist – excellent colleague that he is – has no experience of working with a staff but can only work in his armchair writing with his own hand in his study. He is, moreover, not strong and has found it very tiring hearing evidence in Vienna, and has gone off to the Tyrol with stacks of books in German and with summaries of our evidence, to work quietly and to get his ideas into order. The result is I am left in charge with four excellent assistants plus five typists and two translators, and I must see that the machine works continuously and at full speed if we are to produce a report by mid-August. To come to Cambridge would have taken a week just at the critical time. In any case, I shall have to write most of the main report myself, and to be frank I was afraid to trust myself to write it in the train in sweltering heat and feeling a little tired. I have been keeping very fit by my half-hour of tennis every morning and I shall get better results in the report and get the survey of the evidence ready in time by staying in Austria and going for eight days to a hotel up in the Semmering, near Vienna.

By these methods he and his staff managed to digest the huge mass of evidence and produce a printed report of 213 pages by mid-August.

The Layton–Rist Report dealt firmly with the main problems. Its detailed investigation of Austrian industry and trade showed that the country was making a good recovery in spite of high unemployment. But if the recovery was to go on, the high tariff barriers of the Central European countries which used to make up the Austro-Hungarian Empire would have to be appreciably reduced. Austria could develop along the lines of the Swiss economy, another small country with even less in the way of natural resources and even more dependent on foreign trade. As for Red Vienna, the socialists had acted responsibly and their large housing programme was being soundly financed.

The Austrians were, for the most part, delighted with the report, and the League of Nations financial control of Austria was suspended. However, although the optimism of the report seemed justified at the time, the prosperity they saw possible for Austria if other countries cooperated did not materialize. The dictators of the 1930s in Germany, Italy and Hungary saw to it that Layton and Rist's good advice had no real chance of working in the long run. Austria had to wait until the 1960s before real prosperity came.

After the endorsement by the League Council of the report on Austria in late 1925, no year passed up to 1932 when Layton did not give a considerable amount of time, either to advising the government of the day or to negotiating on their behalf. This was all voluntary work and most of it abroad, for which he received his travelling expenses only. The constant travelling to Geneva, Paris, Berlin and Basle was nearly always by train, as air services were scant and unreliable. So, there must have been many nights in sleeping cars when sleep was difficult. The long sea voyage to India and back in the winter of 1928–29, when he went to advise the Simon Commission, was a pleasant exception. But the main incentive for Layton was that the work gave him an opportunity of having his say on some of the more important international issues of the day. As he put it in his Memoirs: 'I was asked in terms that were difficult to refuse, to serve on a number of international committees, most of them designed in one way or another to clear away road blocks deliberately erected to interfere, in the name of nationalism, with other country's efforts to recover.'

There were three main roadblocks. First, tariff barriers and other obstacles to the smooth flow of trade, which had sprung up since the war. Was it possible, either through the League or through wider discussions bringing in the United States (which never joined the League), to reduce tariffs mutually even if there was really no chance of getting back to the prewar situation? Second, there were the enormous war debts, and in particular German reparations, which looked like making German economic recovery, and hence European recovery, impossible and which, as Layton put it, 'had hung for ten years like a millstone round the neck of Europe'. Third, there was the international monetary system. The return to the gold standard by some countries was intended to pave the way to getting back to a world gold standard as before the war, but the Wall Street crash of 1929 and subsequent bank failures showed that it just was not possible to put the clock back.

As well as these roadblocks there was also the continuing problem of unemployment which cast a shadow over the whole interwar period. Was it possible to influence the economy in such a way as to abolish excessive unemployment?

The World Economic Conference of 1927 provided an opportunity to tackle tariff barriers, the first of the roadblocks. The countries invited to the conference extended beyond League members to include the United States, Russia, Turkey and Egypt. The individual delegates were appointed by governments, but they went as individuals, free to speak their own minds, rather than as representing their countries. In addition to Layton, the UK delegates were Sir Arthur Balfour, an industrialist and chairman of the government's committee on trade and industry, Sir Norman Hill, a shipowner, Sir Max Muspratt, an ex-president of the Federation of British Industries, and Mr Arthur Pugh, an ex-president of the TUC.

Layton put an enormous amount of work into writing papers for the conference, many of which were published in special supplements of the *Economist*. In Geneva he gave one of the main speeches about the need for lower tariffs and was hailed by the *Manchester Guardian* as the hero, or rather the pet, of the conference as opposed to M. Loucheur, well known to Layton because of his work during the war in the French ministry of armaments, whom the *Guardian* of 20 June 1927 deemed the villain. Loucheur suffered not only from his name, with its implication of being shady or shifty, but as the *Guardian* put it: 'He drives away in a larger more potent car than anyone else; he is always in a desperate hurry; he has a large mouthful of flashing teeth, big black moustaches, a seductive smile when he is speaking and an air of impatient anxiety when he is silent.'

Loucheur argued that free trade was unthinkable in the political circumstances of Europe and that the highly desirable international division of labour, the basis for the free trade doctrine, could be better achieved by international private agreements between national industries. 'In contrast,' said the *Guardian*, Layton:

> ruddy and of a cheerful countenance, his keen, youthful face suffused with enthusiasm, delivered at the opening of the conference the most weighty of a series of weighty utterances and has since been unable to escape the attentions of pressmen and portraitists. No suspicion of political ambition mars the purity of the motives of this disinterested theorist who seems to be at home with all the humbler duties of the producer and trader no less than with the more grandiose problems of economic evolution.

Layton was well satisfied with the conference's declaration that 'The time has come to put an end to the increase in tariffs and to move in the opposite direction'. He saw to it that the whole of the conference report, and of the individual reports of the three main committees, was printed verbatim in a second supplement to the *Economist*, published at the end of May. The circulation of the *Economist* at that time was only about 6,000 copies and the cost of this supplement must have been considerable. But clearly Layton thought it was worthwhile.

The recommendations of the conference were blessed by the Council of the League on 16 June, and it was agreed that the work of the conference should be carried forward by a new economic consultative committee, of which Layton was to be a member. This, alas, turned out to be the high point of Layton's vision of a better economic order, at least until after the Second World War when tariff barriers ceased to be the major problem. After some initial progress in freezing and even reducing some tariffs, and in the number of countries which signed a convention for abolishing import and export prohibitions, the whole movement lost its impetus. In practice it was only the UK which had a general belief in free trade as such and, having no tariffs, the UK had few concessions to offer. Most European countries were really convinced that to lower tariffs would increase unemployment. Congress saw to it that the United States was not even empowered to negotiate reductions, and indeed by 1929 the new higher Hawley Smoot tariffs were in force. It was a Frenchman, Briand, who put forward proposals in 1929 for a European customs union within the framework of the League of Nations, but this was mainly intended to deal with the agricultural problems of Central and Eastern Europe and to counter the constant pressure for an Austro-German customs union.

As 1929 wore on, the Wall Street crash and the ensuing slump pointed to more rather than less protection. Layton was certainly very much aware that it was not possible to go back to the trading arrangements of prewar Europe, but he stuck to his free trade convictions, which were shared by many of his contemporaries.

India

The time Layton spent in India in the winter of 1928–29 must have been a welcome relief from the series of international conferences which preceded and followed it. For some time the India Office had hoped to secure his services. In October 1927 Layton was invited by

Lord Birkenhead, then Secretary of State for India, to succeed Sir Basil Blackett as Finance Member of the Viceroy's Executive Council. Layton took some time to make up his mind. At that time there had been no real devolution of government into Indian hands, so he would have had considerable power in controlling central government expenditure and taxation, subject only to the Viceroy's Council and the India Office in London. It was an attractive, well paid job with a knighthood attached, which could lead on to even more important official appointments or, say, the vice-chairmanship of a major bank. Acceptance would have confirmed his entry into the higher reaches of the Establishment. Moreover India was a fascinating, if often infuriating, country and there was the challenge of trying to find a way of moving fast enough toward self-government to avoid repeating the mistakes the British had made in Ireland. The solution to the problem depended in part on strengthening India's public financial system.

But Layton turned the job down because he considered he had more interesting and worthwhile work to do at home and in Europe than would have been his lot in India. He did not want to leave the *Economist*. He had just joined the *Daily News*, he was deep in editing the Liberal *Yellow Book* and there were all the issues raised at the 1927 World Economic Conference. Moreover, he did not want to be separated from his family, since if the Laytons did as other British families at that time, the elder four out of their six children would have been left at school in England.

However, in the summer of 1928 came an offer which was much more attractive. Sir John Simon invited him to go to India for a few months as Financial Assessor to the Statutory Commission on India, which had been set up in 1927 and which had already spent a winter in India. The commission was to advise on the extent to which responsible democratic government should be introduced in India. Simon was the only Liberal, while the other members of the Commission were Conservative and Labour backbenchers from the Lords and Commons, who could be spared for a long absence abroad. They were not a very distinguished lot, so it was pure luck that one of the Labour members was Clement Attlee, who thus came to obtain a sound knowledge of India which stood him in good stead when, as

Prime Minister in 1947, he persuaded his Cabinet to agree to independence for India without a long-drawn out and damaging negotiation.

Since it was drawn entirely from the Houses of Parliament there were no Indians on the Commission. This gave great offence in India, especially to the Congress Party. The resulting boycott of the Commission's meetings made its task all the more difficult. Just before Layton arrived in January 1929 a pilot engine had to be run in advance of the Commission's special train because of a number of bomb threats. Protesting crowds were held back by numerous police, and sometimes there were baton charges to restore order. A veteran Congressman of the Punjab was killed in one of these charges.

Although the Commission was known to be having a difficult time in India, Layton did not hesitate this time before accepting a job which gave him the chance he wanted of seeing India at close quarters without having to give up his work at home. The offer came just at the time of the outcry aroused by Katherine Mayo's book *Mother India*, about the crudities of the caste system, the poverty and superstition of the masses, and above all the subjection of women that still continued in spite of 150 years of British rule.[1] Dorothy and her friends, such as Eleanor Rathbone, were deeply moved by this book. If Walter went to India, Dorothy would be able to accompany him some of the time.

With the British Raj still in the saddle, travel arrangements for the Simon Commission were superb, both at sea and in India, where official trains were capacious and beautifully furnished. Layton left Marseilles just after Christmas 1928 on the P & O liner *Ranchi* with a first-class cabin and a seat at the captain's table next to the Maharani of Cooch Behar, a rich young widow who lost a fortune at cards during the voyage. Layton kept to early morning swims, deck tennis and his briefs and books about India to prepare himself for the Commission. He also learnt from Lady Strathcona, who was going out to India to join her husband, a member of the Commission, that Sir John Simon had the reputation of treating the other commissioners as schoolboys. Perhaps this was because Simon was baffled by his task. He wrote to Dawson, the editor of *The Times*: 'I sometimes feel as though I had been asked to spend two years over a gigantic crossword puzzle with the tip whispered in my private ear that the puzzle had no solution.'[2]

At Bombay, Layton was met by his bearer, called Joseph, and by Benegal Rama Rau, an Indian civil servant who was to be his assistant. Members of the Commission did not have Indians as assistants, so Layton was perhaps a little adventurous, but not very, since Rama Rau, who became a great friend, had read mathematics at King's College, Cambridge, at the time when Layton was an economics don, and had entered the Indian Civil Service in 1913. Later, as Sir Benegal Rama Rau, he was to become Indian Ambassador to Washington and Governor of the Reserve Bank of India.

Layton wrote to his wife from Bombay that he would not be able to meet any of the Indians he wanted to see as 'they will be suspicious of meeting anyone connected with the Commission'. However, he was soon travelling with Rama Rau on a comfortable train to Delhi and Calcutta. At Delhi he stayed with Sir George Schuster, who had become Finance Member of the Viceroy's Council after Layton had turned the job down, and hence lived in the house he and Dorothy would have had: 'It is very expensive to run,' he wrote to Dorothy, 'but delightful and friendly. The situation is charming but the whole of New Delhi is a vast and appalling blunder.' Layton was no admirer of Lutyens's town planning. He had lunch with Lord Irwin, the Viceroy, 'a liberal-minded man, but it is not quite certain that he is strong enough for a most difficult job'.

He met the Commission at Calcutta, from where he wrote to Dorothy:

> The Commission are a wee bit stale after all these months and John Simon keeps his own counsel rather too much; so no-one knows what the Commission are likely to report. The Indian Central Committee who are travelling with us are rather a poor lot, for everyone agrees that the Swaragists[3] have got most of the brains. The evidence is also rather poor for the provincial officials don't really know what to make of the situation. The troubles are that no-one says the same in private as he says in public, the trouble between Muslim and Hindu pervades every aspect of life, bribery and still more nepotism – which is deep-rooted in the social system – pervade every aspect of life, Indianisation has admittedly reduced the efficiency of administration, the native Ministers are mostly

> backboneless and very few have been a success – and yet everyone, even the Europeans, agrees that things cannot go on as they are. A pretty tangle – much depends on finance but I cannot propound a financial scheme till the political constitution is more or less in shape.

Layton had his eyes opened to the extremes of Indian poverty in the Calcutta slums and then went on by sea to Burma with the Commission. The day's programme for each member of the Commission, and Layton, was set out in a printed list of engagements with a new edition produced each evening. The right dress for each occasion was stipulated. The whole day was by no means taken up by work. Time was made for golf and on 4 February there was an expedition starting at 7.45 am to see elephants piling teak.

After ten days in Burma which included a visit to Mandalay, Layton left the main party to talk with the finance departments in Calcutta and Madras, on his way to meet Dorothy at Colombo. To clear his mind while at Madras he sent Sir John Simon his views on India as he had formulated them after just one month in the country. He must have found that it is possible to see things more clearly after an initial short period than after a much longer time when the freshness of first impressions has faded. His paper would have made a first-rate special supplement on India if it had been published in the *Economist*. In forty pages of typescript he set out lucidly the impasse into which Indian politics had drifted. A gradual approach to the complete self-rule which articulate Indians were demanding would not work. The government of India, which had achieved so much for India in the past, seemed defeatist and without constructive ideas. There was, in fact, no satisfactory halfway house to self-rule. So although full Dominion status would not be possible for some years (there could be no question yet of India becoming entirely independent and walking out of the Empire the day after the treaty was signed) there must be a major move towards self-rule. Layton considered that India should become a loose federation of autonomous provinces with fully responsible governments. The central government would be elected by the provincial governments, and would have wide powers of taxation, much of whose proceeds would be distributed to the provinces.

It was hardly for a financial adviser to propose a new constitution for India, but with his wide political interests Layton was not prepared, on this occasion, to limit himself to strictly financial issues. There is no record of Sir John Simon's reactions, but the paper must have been like a breath of fresh air to the jaded commissioners.

Walter met Dorothy at Colombo early in March and they travelled together up the spine of India through Madras, Mysore, Hyderabad, Central Provinces, Delhi, the Punjab, North West Province and the Khyber Pass. Rama Rau came with them and they were often free of the rest of the Commission, so they felt they got a first-hand impression of how people lived in towns and villages. In one village Layton was, understandably, mistaken for a pukka sahib by the head man, who wanted him to order the untouchables living there to remove a dead cow from the village street. Layton, by explaining he was a mere tourist and not a government official, was able to keep his feelings about the caste system undisclosed.

At Mysore they were taken up a hill by one of the Maharaja's officials to see the sun set. When it got dark Dorothy was asked to press a switch on the table. Immediately, the whole palace and many buildings in the city were brilliantly lit up, much to their pleasure. Next day, Layton learnt from an Indian whom he had taught at Cambridge that every time the illuminations in Mysore were switched on the villages for many miles around had to do without electric light.

Both Walter and Dorothy had been prepared for the inhumanities of purdah by reading Katherine Mayo's book *Mother India*, but both were deeply shocked by seeing the wives of one of the Muslim members of the Central Indian Committee, which accompanied the Commission, being transferred from a motorcar to a heavily curtained reserved compartment of their train. 'The car was driven to the platform, funereal-looking screens were clipped together to form a black tunnel through which the woman or women were hurried like so much cattle from car to train – human beings not belonging to the world at all but just someone's private property.'[4] This and many other such sights in India led Dorothy to play a very active part in the British Women's Advisory Council on Indian questions for the rest of her life.

Walter, too, remained deeply interested in India. Immediately he got home he had the task of writing his report, the draft of which came under fire from Schuster and others in India as well as from the India Office. Layton's main theme was:

> ... there can be little doubt that, in conditions such as those which now obtain in India, it should be possible to stimulate production and to increase the welfare of the people by public expenditure designed to give greater economic security (by irrigation works, improved and more varied methods of cultivation, etc.), better physical well-being (sanitation, water supply, improved public health, etc.), and education. Indeed, taxation may be the only practicable means of creating a better and more secure livelihood.

To Layton it was clear that the central government should help to finance the provinces' expenditure on essential social services. This was good Liberal *Yellow Book* philosophy with a practical solution which, to Layton, seemed perfectly possible. The India Office and Schuster poured cold water on Layton's estimates of the surplus revenues the central government was likely to be able to provide to finance the provinces. What would happen if prices fell (as indeed they did in subsequent years during the world slump)? What would happen if the monsoon failed? Schuster also produced revised figures forecasting lower revenue on existing taxes. It would be impossible to reduce army expenditure, as Layton hoped. So there would be no adequate surplus without new taxation. If the provincial governments were to become more autonomous it would be for them to impose new taxes. There was no painless way. Schuster appealed to Layton not to say anything which would make it all look too easy.

Rama Rau, who had come to London with the Commission, was strong in Layton's defence. He argued that it would be perfectly possible for at least fifty per cent of the proceeds of income tax as well as those of the salt tax to go to the provinces, with the central government recouping itself by putting up income tax rates and having a new tax on such articles as matches.

The whole position was changed at the end of October 1929 when, with the encouragement of the new Labour government, the Viceroy issued a statement that Dominion status was a natural issue of India's constitutional progress, and that there should now be consultations with Indian leaders about possible constitutional changes. The Simon

Commission were not consulted about this statement, which was made against Baldwin's advice. Nevertheless, the Commission toiled on with the drafting of their report, which did not finally emerge until June 1930. By then it had been overtaken by events. Layton as financial assessor had nothing to do with the constitutional proposals, which while granting full autonomy to the provinces were hedged about with safeguards and made no mention of Dominion status. However, Layton's financial report, printed over his own name, survived untouched with its proposals broadly accepted by the Commission.

The Commission's report, though full of interesting and useful information, had little influence on events at the time and Simon was not even invited to the Round Table conferences at which the British government attempted in vain to find a solution through talks with the leading Indian politicians. But Layton kept in touch with Rama Rau and with Schuster, who by March 1933 was writing to say how he wished that Layton's proposals had been adopted more fully in India.

There was one other more immediate consequence of Layton's work for the Simon Commission – a knighthood in the 1930 Birthday Honours list. On this occasion, unlike 1919, he does not seem to have considered refusing. He accepted because a knighthood would help him in his work both at home – especially as he was becoming chairman of the *News Chronicle* – and abroad, and because his contemporaries such as Stamp, Beveridge, Salter and Ernest Simon had either already been knighted or would be soon. Dorothy certainly enjoyed the title more than he did, and he had, in fact, earned his knighthood several times over through all the work he had done for the Foreign Office and the Treasury.

CHAPTER EIGHT

The Crisis Years 1929–32

Not long after he had returned from India, and the second Labour government had taken office, Layton found himself in demand again, this time in seeking a way by which Germany's reparations payments for damage caused in the First World War could be fitted into the international monetary system. Between 1919 and 1932 reparations absorbed the energies of a great many able men as they tried to determine Germany's ability to pay. Another pressing question was the settlement of debts between the Allies, mostly payments due to France and the United States. The sums of money at stake seemed to contemporaries to be bound to have a major effect on the stability of the exchange market, on economic growth and hence on the extent of Europe's economic recovery. The bankers, economists and civil servants brought together from the countries principally concerned to try and find solutions to these problems were broadly of the same calibre as those who, after the Second World War, put the Marshall Plan into effect. The marked contrast is that the outcome of all this effort after the First World War was for the most part sterile, while the Marshall Plan was a great success in ensuring the economic recovery of Europe.

Layton himself did not take part in the earlier discussions on reparations but saw to it that the *Economist* published detailed accounts of any developments. For instance, he published the full reports of the Dawes and Young committees, which in 1924 and 1929 made considerable progress in getting reparations onto a sensible basis, more in accord with Germany's ability to pay. The Young Committee, in particular, put forward a proposal, for which Dr

Schacht claimed credit,[1] for a Bank of International Settlements (BIS) to act as a clearing house for reparations and war debt payments. The hope was that, by commercializing reparation payments to some extent, the whole question would be taken out of politics and become a matter for economists and bankers.

Layton already knew about a further proposal to turn the BIS into an embryo world central bank associated with the League of Nations, rather than being confined to reparation payments, because Arthur Salter sent him copies of letters he was writing to Sir Josiah Stamp, the leading British representative on the Young Committee. Layton took up these ideas in articles the *Economist* published on 15 June and 6 July 1929, soon after the Young Committee Report was published. He backed the proposed BIS as a step towards a world central bank, but insisted that there must be ultimate political control of central banks which should not be, and indeed could not be, sovereign powers within states. To link the BIS to the League of Nations would present difficulties, but these should not be insuperable in the long run. In any case, they should be considered when the constitution of the BIS was being drawn up.

To his surprise, in September Layton was asked by the Governor of the Bank of England, Montagu Norman, to serve with Sir Charles Addis (a director of the Bank and a member of the Young Committee) on the committee which was to organize the setting up of the BIS. Norman had got to know Layton well as editor of the *Economist* and was always accessible when Layton wanted to check rumours so as to keep the *Economist*'s reporting accurate and responsible. But it was remarkable that Norman should have chosen a man who was such an outspoken critic of his own beliefs that central banks should be independent of political control. Layton himself described what happened:

> Norman rang me up one day in the summer of 1929 in some excitement. He asked me to come and see him about something important. When I reached his office he mentioned the Young Plan and in particular the new Bank. He suggested that I should get in touch with Sir Charles Addis, who knew a lot about the subject, and that together we should work out some form of words that would place the Bank beyond the reach of Governments.
>
> 'That can't be done,' I said. 'Governments can't just be ignored and they won't be ignored.'
>
> 'Talk it over with Addis,' he insisted. 'Then let me know.'

As Addis was content to fall in with anything I decided, I struggled hopelessly with a draft and then called on the Governor again to report failure. He spoke with sharp annoyance.
'Why do you insist it can't be done?'
'Because,' I said, 'it's the right of every democratic government to reserve its freedom of action.'
I took my leave. There seemed nothing more to be said. But a day or two later I received an extraordinary letter from Norman. It began with a few courteous words of thanks to me for trying. It ended rather enigmatically and skittishly with a question: 'Was it not Cardinal Newman who said that the will of God is perfect freedom?'[2]

The other members of the Organization Committee included Dr Schacht, then president of the Reichsbank, of whom Layton was to see a good deal in the following few years. In the event, the Organization Committee was able to agree fairly easily on the structure and functions of the BIS. But Snowden, then Chancellor of the Exchequer, got his way in Cabinet, and in the League Assembly in September, when he insisted that there should be no question of the League providing political control over the BIS. Snowden argued that the idea was contrary to the main objective of the Young Committee, that reparations should be taken out of politics. While some link with the League might grow up naturally later, to provide for it from the start would scare off the United States bankers from cooperating with the BIS.

On the vexed question of the independence of the BIS the Organization Committee worked out a solution wholly in accord with Layton's views. The clauses in the BIS charter were divided into two categories – technical and constitutional. The first could be amended by the BIS itself, the second could only be altered with the agreement of the seven governments concerned.

Much time was spent on deciding the location of the BIS, the British wanting London, the Belgians in favour of Brussels, and indeed storming out of the conference room when they could not get their way. In the end Basle was chosen, an excellent choice then because it was the centre of Europe's railway system and on the neutral ground of Switzerland. So, although, as a result of Hitler's refusal in 1933 to go on paying reparations, the BIS soon lost its reparations functions, it became an easily accessible and attractive

Walter (aged 8) and his brother, Wilfred (aged 10).

Walter's parents at Stanley House, *c.* 1905.

The Layton family about 1905. Front row: Mary; Walter; Alfred. Back row: Gilbert; Margaret and Wilfred.

Dorothy, 1910

Walter at Cambridge, 1912

Reception by the Tsar, Petrograd, February 1917. The six in the front row (left to right) are: Lord Milner; The Italian Ambassador; the British Ambassador, Sir George Buchannan; Tsar Nicholas II; the French Ambassador, M. Paleologue; M. Doumergue. Walter Layton is standing behind the British Ambassador (see p. 42).

With Lloyd George at Churt, 1927. Left to right: Sir Herbert Samuel; Walter Layton; Hubert Henderson; David Lloyd George; Maynard Keynes.

The family home, Brett House, Putney, 1931 (see p. 149).

Plan of Brett House.

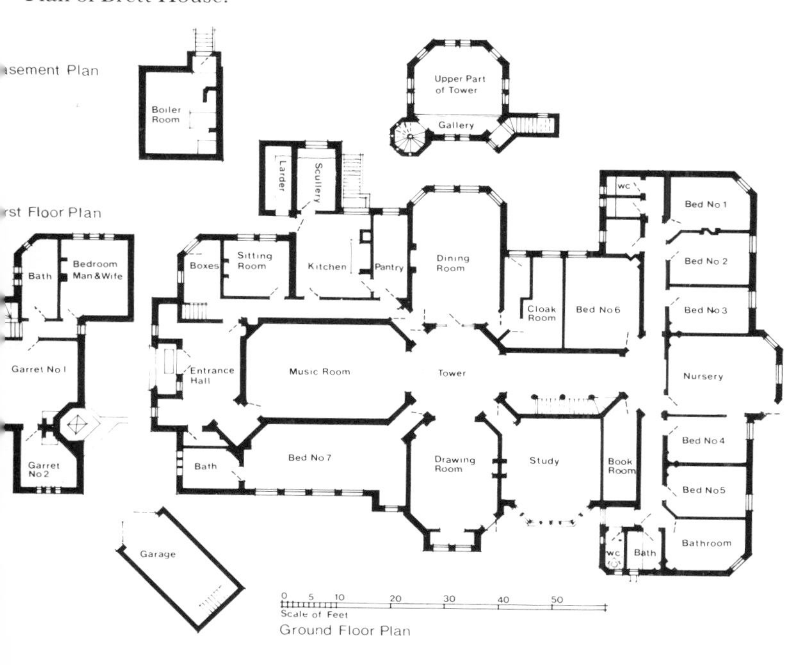

OUT FOR THE RECORD

Ministry of Production, 1942: a cartoon by Low referring to Churchill's problem of how to get Bevin and Lyttelton to work together.

Walter with scythe at Twittens, 1942.

Walter and Dorothy at Twittens, 1942.

Walter, with Churchill and Lady Violet Bonham-Carter, calling at 10 Downing Street, on their return from the Hague Congress on Europe, June 1948 (see p. 207).

Walter and Dorothy with their seven children, 1955.

all internal duties but it would be an important step towards freer trade in Europe from which Britain would benefit without abandoning her preference for goods from the Dominions.

Layton brought this proposal back to England but when he landed at Harwich the Labour government had already fallen and Neville Chamberlain was the new Chancellor and Lord Reading the new Foreign Secretary. Although the Committee of Experts circulated their report on 29 August, which stated that 'the ultimate goal must be to make Europe a single market for the products of any and every country in it', Britain went off the gold standard three weeks later and the general mood was in favour of more trade protection not less.

The Financial Crisis of Summer 1931 and the End of Reparations

While Layton's work on customs unions came to nothing at the time, the part he played in the winding up of reparations in the year between August 1931 and July 1932 had more influence on events. The financial crisis of 1931 provided the pressure which led to the general recognition that there was little point, given the depth of the world slump, in trying to get Germany to pay even on the reduced scale proposed by the Young Committee in 1929.

Layton was in Berlin on 20 June 1931, discussing a possible European Customs Union with Chancellor Brüning, when news was brought of President Hoover's suggestion that there should be a complete moratorium for a year on all reparations and war debt payments. Although this proposal was generally welcome in Europe, the French government only grudgingly accepted, since, apart from the United States, they were the one country receiving large sums in reparations. In July the financial crisis in Germany rapidly got worse as foreign short-term capital was withdrawn. Nearer home the mark threatened to carry sterling down with it. Layton attended the Seven-Power London Conference of 20–23 July, called to try and stabilize the situation. In a broadcast at the end of July to the United States about the conference he maintained that the key to the problem lay in relations between France and Germany. If France was 'ready to make a friend of her traditional enemy by freely helping her in time of need' the way to a solution would be open. In his typically cautious way Layton does not venture an opinion on what will happen; instead, as in many *Economist* leaders, he wrote: 'Time alone will show which road she [France] is prepared to take at this turning point in history.'

By August Layton found himself once more hard at work as the rapporteur of a committee of experts convened by the Bank of International Settlements to inquire into the immediate further credit needs of Germany and the possibility of converting her short-term credits into long-term credits. This committee, chaired by Mr Albert Wiggin of the Chase National Bank, New York, became known as the Wiggin–Layton Committee. It met in Basle on 8 August and signed a unanimous report on 18 August, which was printed in full with its statistical appendices in the *Economist* on 22 August. Layton's colleagues included Dr Carl Melchior, about whom Keynes wrote a moving memoir,[3] and Moreau, a former governor of the Bank of France, but Layton, as rapporteur, was largely responsible for the report. He decided early on that the report could not deal substantively with the reparations issues, which were bound to require another conference before the Hoover moratorium expired. Once the foreign lenders' confidence in Germany was shaken the whole house of cards was likely to collapse. But ministers were politely asked to face the political decisions that were needed to restore confidence. It was no good saying that once Germany took certain economic measures long-term finance would become available. More was required, namely to establish international relations on the basis of mutual confidence and to keep the scale of Germany's international payments to such a level as not to imperil her financial stability. This was only a diplomatic way of referring to the threat to confidence posed by the rising power of Hitler and to the need to end reparations.

The Wiggin–Layton Report was a good example of Layton's commonsense solution of the short-term problem while recognizing the need for longer-term action. It was backed by all the relevant statistics. Indeed, it was a remarkable document to draft and steer through a touchy international committee in the space of ten days. However, at that time the Labour government was too preoccupied by the run on sterling and Britain's own worsening financial crisis to worry greatly about Germany. Layton, as a good newspaper man fully aware of these preoccupations and being at the centre of the international financial community in Basle, did not hesitate to send Philip Snowden two long letters about the measures that were needed at home. He reported on the concern felt in Basle about prospects for sterling and the view of impartial observers such as the Swedes that 'the stability of sterling was the one sheet-anchor for Europe and that Great Britain was the only country that could help Europe to weather the storm'.

Most of Layton's proposed measures were highly orthodox, and his advice about expenditure cuts was similar to that given by Hubert Henderson to the Economic Advisory Council.[4] Both men, unlike Keynes,[5] were certain that drastic action was needed to restore confidence in sterling, so as to keep Britain on the gold standard. Layton, however, convinced that a balanced budget was not enough, went much further in calling for far more economic cooperation (including tariff reductions) between the main trading countries, which he believed offered the hope of a long-term solution rather than just dealing with the immediate crisis. He was setting Britain's problems in a world context.

Snowden must have been too busy to reply to Layton's letters as events moved swiftly with the fall of the Labour government on 24 August, and the attempt of the new National government to remain on the gold standard. In spite of a draconian budget and new foreign loans, this attempt proved unavailing once confidence abroad had been badly shaken again by the Invergordon mutiny on 16 September. Thanks to a rapid withdrawal of funds, Britain was forced off the gold standard on 21 September.

Layton was kept busy commenting on these dramatic events in the *Economist* and the *News Chronicle*, and by October (when the General Election in Britain was going on) Germany's financial position had weakened further. If another crisis was to be avoided, the standstill agreement of August covering Germany's commercial debts would have to be extended and the work on reparations begun in the Wiggin–Layton Committee, which had only pointed the way, would soon have to lead to action. Most of those who had long been concerned with the problem believed that the time was fast approaching either to end all reparations payments or to reduce them to a token.

In November the German government asked the BIS Special Advisory Committee, provided for in the Young Plan, to be convened. Layton was once more chosen by Montagu Norman to represent Britain and the other members included several who had been on the Wiggins–Layton Committee, except that Layton's old colleague, Professor Charles Rist, represented France instead of Moreau. In effect, the task of the committee was to advise whether the Hoover moratorium should be renewed for one or more years, or whether reparations payments should be resumed but on a much reduced scale. Layton himself had no doubt that the time had come to wind up reparations, and on his way to Basle at the end of November, he stopped in Paris to find out whether the French government was likely to continue to take a hard line against Germany. He and Rist went to see Laval, then French prime minister. Layton found that Laval – a shrewd man and an opportunist – was well aware that the committee might be forced to the conclusion that Germany could not pay anything, including the unconditional annuities, which, unlike the conditional annuities, were not supposed to depend on Germany's ability to pay. It was only to be expected, Laval thought, that the delegates would make suggestions privately to their governments about the unconditional annuities.

The Basle meeting went very much as Laval had forecast. The experts had no difficulty in deciding that the moratorium on payment of conditional annuities should continue until July 1934, but this left the real problem of the unconditional annuities unsolved. So, with Layton's encouragement, the experts drafted an unofficial aide-mémoire to supplement the published report. The aide-mémoire made it clear that the only way to restore confidence in Germany's financial status was a permanent settlement of reparations which would take account of the world depression and in the future automatically adjust Germany's payments to her ability to pay, without the need for any fresh negotiations. For the present all reparations should cease for several years, and it was difficult to see when it would be possible for payments to start again. But in the longer term fairly small sums – such as the surplus of about three billion gold marks earned by German railways in normal, as opposed to depressed, times – should be the only reparations payments made. These proposals were accepted in the end by all the experts except Rist, who acted on instructions from the French government. Layton sent copies of the aide-mémoire with a long explanatory letter to Ramsay Macdonald on 28 December.

Early in the New Year Walter at last took a holiday with Dorothy, having worked all through 1931. They managed to have two weeks in the sun at Amalfi while visiting the Greek temples of southern Italy. But he stopped in Rome on the way back in order to interview Mussolini for the *News Chronicle*, as described in the next chapter. He wanted to give more time to the *News Chronicle* and the *Economist*, which he had to some extent neglected since the previous May. He knew the official Treasury line was that the sensible course was to cancel reparations by common agreement, since the only alternative was unilateral default by Germany and acute political friction. He did not expect to play any further part himself. But at the start of the Lausanne Conference, convened in June 1932 to try to reach a lasting settlement of reparations, Herriot, the French Prime Minister, proposed that the Basle unofficial aide-mémoire should be taken as a basis for discussion. Ramsay Macdonald, who was in the chair, immediately asked Layton to come to Lausanne and used him as his go-between.

The conference began by agreeing to extend the Hoover moratorium from 1 July to the end of the conference to avoid appearing to put the members under pressure to reach agreement. But it proved very difficult to get the French and Germans to agree. Walter wrote to Dorothy from Lausanne:

> The French and Germans are at a deadlock on the amount of their final payment. It is largely a stage battle, for it is probable that much of it will never be paid. So I tried my hand privately (with the P.M.'s approval) at conciliation. Until a few moments ago I thought I'd pulled it off, particularly as I have succeeded in getting von Bülow who had been particularly difficult, to come round to my plan. But I have just failed to get the Heads of the Delegation who are taking their orders from Berlin. So we are back again at an impasse. It will, of course, have to be solved but it is very hard work to get agreement.[6]

Three days later Walter wrote again to Dorothy:

> Still no headway. Last night we were as near as could be. But the P.M. got a bad headache at teatime and rather lost his grip, and at the after-dinner meeting let slip his chance of clinching matters. Today Herriot has seen von Papen all the morning and has stiffened, so I am afraid we are in for some more hard argument. The truth is that the conference is badly organised by the Prime Minister. Good though he is in humouring his people when he sets his mind to it, he is not clear headed when you are on subtle points or complicated matters like reparations and the official staff round him *will* be so terribly blunt and *British* in their drafts of agreements etc. I think it possible that agreement may be reached tomorrow – even tonight – but not quite so good an arrangement as the P.M. could have got last night.

In the end, the conference, following the Basle experts' aide-mémoire proposals, cut down all future reparations payments to the interest on a three-billion gold mark bond issue to be marketed by the BIS without further reference to governments. The only other obligation on the Germans was to maintain the service of the Dawes and Young loans.

This eminently sensible agreement soon ran into difficulties, as the United States Congress stuck to the rigid view that the Allies' war debts must be honoured, whether reparations were paid or not. In 1933 it became clear that no future reparations would be paid, as Hitler, on coming to power, declared reparations at an end. The British nevertheless paid three more instalments to the Americans before they too stopped paying in 1934. Most other countries stopped by the end of 1932.

As was to be expected, the Lausanne Conference, having only dealt with the reparations problem, called for a second world economic conference to meet in 1933 to deal with 'the other economic and financial difficulties which are responsible for, and may prolong, the present world crisis'. Inevitably, it seemed, Layton was asked to serve on the preparatory committee for this new world conference and, indeed, started work. But with the National government's adoption of tariffs at the Ottawa Conference and the resignation of the Samuel Liberals from the government on this issue, Layton found himself in a difficult position. Although he had always been prepared to advise politicians whatever their party, he drew the line at becoming a member of a British delegation which would be inhibited from arguing for the abolition, or at least the reduction, of the trade barriers against which

CHAPTER NINE

The *News Chronicle*, 1927–35

It would have been difficult to forecast in 1927 when Henry Cadbury, the managing director of the *Daily News*, invited Layton to join the board as financial and policy adviser, that he would prove so effective in Fleet Street. He had certainly improved, but not transformed, the *Economist* (circulation had barely risen), which was more a learned journal than the high-circulation weekly expressing strong opinions that it became later. Clearly the Cadburys had spotted Layton's considerable ability, but most people would have regarded him more as a good, but rather inarticulate, chairman of committees, a clear expositor of ideas when writing rather than speaking, and without the ruthlessness that success in Fleet Street normally demanded. He did not look like being able to stand up to the Press barons of the day, who had few scruples about the way they gained advantage over their rivals. He was surely too gentle and reflective a character, too nice a man to push through the mergers that were required if a Liberal paper was to survive as the Liberal Party continued its long decline. But Laurence Cadbury had admired Layton since being tutored by him at Cambridge and realized that he had much to contribute to the *Daily News*.

The Cadburys concerned were the five sons by two marriages of the founder George Cadbury who between them managed the *Daily News*, the Bournville chocolate factory and the various philanthropic causes which their father had run in the early years of the century. Since 1912 Edward and Henry Cadbury had been the chairman and managing director respectively of the *Daily News*. In 1930 Laurence Cadbury, the eldest son of Dame Elizabeth, George Cadbury's second wife, became chairman of Daily News Ltd, the holding company for the *News Chronicle* and the evening paper the *Star*. Laurence had been managing director of Cadbury Brothers, the chocolate makers, since 1919. His brother Egbert, who had an outstanding war record, was the fourth Cadbury with an active interest in the newspapers.

Layton took as readily to the financial side of running newspapers as to the more obviously congenial aspects of determining editorial policy. Henry Cadbury's first idea was that Layton should become editor of the *Daily News*, but Layton refused the offer in 1926 because he would have to give up being editor of the *Economist* and his work for the League of Nations and the Liberal *Yellow Book*. He did, however, accept a seat on the *Daily News* board in April 1927 when Henry Cadbury told him that his responsibility would be control of editorial policy and investigation of the paper's financial position. He could go on being editor of the *Economist* and retain his other voluntary work. He was to be paid a starting salary of £1,000 a year with an additional sum related to the paper's profits.

Layton did, indeed, spend up to half an hour a day talking to the editor, Stuart Hodgson, and the leader writers. But he quickly played an active part in the merger with the *Westminster Gazette* which took place in January 1928, and in the negotiations which led up to the merger with the *Daily Chronicle* in 1930, thus bringing all three Liberal morning newspapers together.

All three papers had been losing money. The *Daily News*, founded in 1846 with Charles Dickens as its first editor, had been acquired by George Cadbury in 1901 when Lloyd George became one of its first directors. Cadbury's wealth–derived from chocolate–kept the paper going as a radical reforming journal backing the underdog. Soon after Cadbury took over, at a time when trade unions were weak, the *Daily News* opened a public fund and raised £30,000 to help the families of the slate workers of Bethesda in North Wales in their three year-long strike against their harsh employer, Lord Penrhyn.

Occasionally, George Cadbury compromised his Quaker principles. In 1912, when he acquired the *Star*, an evening paper, he allowed betting news to be published on the grounds that, as explained in a letter to his son Laurence, then at Cambridge: 'It was evident that the *Star* with betting news and pleading for social reform and for peace, was far better than the *Star* with betting news and opposing social reform and stirring up strife with neighbouring nations.'[1] He took comfort from reflecting that no ha'penny evening paper could exist without betting news.

George Cadbury's philosophy was set out in a letter he wrote to accompany the deeds of the Daily News Trust, founded in 1911 to control the papers through its holding of a majority of the ordinary shares of the Daily News Ltd:

> I desire, in forming the 'Daily News' Trust that it may be of service in bringing the ethical teaching of Jesus Christ to bear upon National Questions and in promoting National Righteousness; for example, that Arbitration should take the place of War, and that the spirit of the Sermon on the Mount, especially of the Beatitudes, should take the place of Imperialism and of the military spirit, which is contrary to Christ's teaching that love is the badge by which the Christian should be known.

Layton was to find the following extract from this letter of great use when the *News Chronicle* was accused of being too far to the left in the 1930s:

> I am an advocate of the taxation of land values, of the appropriation by the nation of unearned increment, and of such alteration in the land laws as would increase the number of small holdings; of cutting down military expenditure which presses so heavily on the poor of all countries; of relieving the labourer from all taxation for military purposes, and placing such taxation on the wealthy; of promoting such legislation as would tend to improve the lot of the poor and lessen the opportunities for the accumulation of wealth in a few hands; of the gradual acquisition by the State of all minerals below the surface, also of all monopolies that can be better administered by the community for the benefit of all.

Henry Cadbury had taken over the *Daily News* from his father in 1912, and by 1922 broke with Lloyd George after his refusal to join forces with Asquith. The *Daily Chronicle* had by that time been acquired by Lloyd George's political fund, but it later passed into the hands of Sir Thomas Catto of Morgan Grenfell and Lord Reading, after he had ceased being Viceroy of India. The *Westminster Gazette* had originally been an evening paper until it was bought by Lord Cowdray, who in 1921 turned it into a morning paper backing the

Liberal Party. By 1928 its sales were 300,000 and those of the *Daily News* 600,000.

The merger between the *Daily News* and the *Westminster Gazette* went through smoothly in January 1928, and the joint paper achieved a circulation of 900,000, thus retaining the readers of both papers. However, as the paper was now being printed in Manchester as well as London, profits from the *Star* did not quite offset losses on the morning paper, as had been the case with the *Daily News* before. The best solution was clearly a further merger with the *Daily Chronicle*, which should result in the circulation of well over a million, and thus enable the new paper to compete with the *Daily Express*, *Daily Mail* and *Daily Herald*.

Already in June 1928 Layton had heard from Catto that the *Daily Chronicle* was for sale and that the owners did not want the paper to pass out of Liberal hands. This looked promising. Catto came to see Layton, but soon afterwards decided to sell the *Daily Chronicle* to William Harrison of United Newspapers, who was trying to build up an empire of periodicals, printing works and a large holding in the Inveresk Paper Company. However, this empire collapsed in the 1929 Stock Exchange crash and the *Daily Chronicle* went into receivership. Layton was soon in touch with Catto, who was acting for United Newspapers, about a possible merger between the *Daily News* and the *Daily Chronicle*, but there were several obstacles to surmount. The Cadbury family had been divided as to whether or not to continue with popular newspapers. Indeed, Henry Cadbury wrote on 15 December to say that Cowdray and his friends would be acquiring full control of the *Daily News* and the *Star*, though the Cadbury family would still be represented on the board of directors. This idea got no further, but Laurence Cadbury was also vacillating and Layton threatened to withdraw from the negotiations with Catto unless he was allowed to go ahead with the scheme he had already worked out. He did not know at the time that Catto, without telling him, was also negotiating the sale of the *Daily Chronicle* to the Harmsworth family.

By early 1930, however, the *Daily Chronicle* was in even deeper financial trouble, thanks to the launching of a new-style *Daily Herald* by Odhams, and fortunately the Cadbury family managed to resolve their differences, agreeing to stay in the newspaper business provided that Layton became chairman of the proposed *News Chronicle*. With United Newspapers' financial position deteriorating further, Layton was able to drive a hard bargain in reaching agreement on the merger in 1930. Although the holding company, the Daily News Ltd, owned only 36½ per cent of the equity of the *News Chronicle* against the *Daily Chronicle*'s 50 per cent and the *Westminster Gazette*'s 13½ per cent, control, by a trustee agreement, was firmly in the hands of the Daily News trustees. It was laid down that there had to be preliminary agreement between Laurence Cadbury, as chairman of the trustees, Layton and Lord Cowdray representing the *Westminster Gazette*. These three votes provided a majority on the board of the *News Chronicle*.

The *News Chronicle* became profitable by 1931 and remained so for the following twenty-five years. Although the paper came into being in order to support the Liberal cause, if not the Liberal Party, which was split three ways between Herbert Samuel, Lloyd George and the National Liberals, Layton was the only dedicated Liberal among the five trustees. Laurence Cadbury was nominally a Liberal and paid great attention to family traditions, but his instincts were Tory and he moved a long way to the right as he grew older. Cowdray, unlike his father who had originally bought the *Westminster Gazette*, was primarily a businessman and the two United Newspaper trustees were Conservatives, interested in the paper only as an investment.

Henry Cadbury, who in 1930 gave up being managing director of the *Daily News* because of failing eyesight, wrote in a letter of advice to Layton:

> I should like to emphasise the fact that I think whereas the actual time given in a newspaper office should not be very great – say about 4 or 5 hours on any one day – I do feel it is essential that one's mind should be free to think things out, to see the tendency and trend of affairs, to be ready to switch off on to something quite new and fresh, and to sense quickly what the public is really thinking about. This kind of thing cannot be done by frequent attendances at the Reform Club. Indeed, I think that the Reform Club is the negation of any successful newspaper enterprise.

Layton never did join the Reform Club, then the home of old-style Liberals, but he usually spent much more than four to five hours a day at the *News Chronicle*, since he normally came into the office about

11 am and seldom left the building until after the leaders had all been written by 8 or 9 pm. He stuck to the policies he set out in a leading article in the first issue on 2 June 1930:

> The combined paper will stand, first and foremost for peace. It will seek by every means in its power to support and forward the ideals of the League of Nations. It will oppose both reaction and revolution with equal firmness. It will oppose waste, and fight steadily for real economy in public expenditure. Believing that tariffs are an attack upon the people's livelihood, it will resist both. It will champion, on the other hand, the social reforms which both papers have always insisted are demanded, both by common justice and common sense; and the liberties of speech, of thought and of religion for which both have always stood. And it will defend these causes for the future – at a time when many of them are gravely menaced – with the vigour and consistence which unity alone can assure.

The *News Chronicle* started publication in June 1930 with a circulation of about 1,400,000. In its early days, it was a serious paper compared with mass circulation papers now, rather like a Liberal version of today's *Daily Telegraph*. The paper had particularly good coverage of foreign news and of discussions at the League of Nations, together with well balanced leaders. Indeed, it paid more attention to international affairs than its contemporaries, reflecting Layton's own strong beliefs that the main issue of the day was how to evolve a sane international system based on collective security and economic cooperation. The parliamentary, economic and financial news was fully reported. If there was an important speech by the Prime Minister, or later by world figures, such as Hitler or Mussolini, long extracts were printed. The Budget speech received similar treatment, as did the more important White Papers. There seems to have been no difficulty in giving A.J. Cummings half a page every day in July 1931 for a survey of British industry, followed by an equally wide-ranging review of the United States economy all through August.

Layton himself often wrote a column headed 'Notes of the Day'. From the end of September 1931 until November (when he went off to the BIS Committee on Reparations) his column was usually devoted to explaining such economic and financial questions as the meaning of going off the gold standard and the case against tariff protection. The tone of Layton's column was that of an economics lecturer addressing first-year students. He never talked down to his readers –

indeed in his early days he may well have talked above the heads of the people for whom he maintained the paper was being written – that is in his own words 'the skilled artisans'. He instructed the leader writers that their articles should be intelligible to his gardener.

There were, of course, considerable concessions to the common man. The *News Chronicle*, like its rivals, gave prominence to railway disasters, air crashes, mountaineering accidents and abnormal weather. The numerous pioneering air journeys by Amy and Jim Mollison and others throughout the early Thirties were fully covered. So, too, were the Schneider Cup races for seaplanes which were later developed into the land-based Spitfires. The voyage of the submarine *Nautilus* under the ice to the North Pole was fully described. Photographs improved as time went on but there were no nudes, only very well covered bathing belles. Indeed, bathing girls appeared often from July 1931 onwards, when the *News Chronicle* launched a campaign to teach people to swim at the George Lansbury Lido on the Serpentine in Hyde Park.

Robert Lynd, the literary editor, wrote an elegant and lighthearted essay every Saturday. Some readers thought the paper too middle-class because of Lynd's essays and the space given to bridge and golf. Clearly many of the paper's features were not addressed only to skilled artisans. The competition for circulation through these years was intense. All the main papers sent round canvassers to induce people to change newspapers through the offer of free gifts. At one time, the *News Chronicle* was spending £200,000 a year in the hope of being able to recoup its money through higher advertising rates once circulation rose.

Of its rivals, the *Daily Herald* did particularly well, but the *News Chronicle* managed to hold its own. In 1933 when the *Herald* offered its readers the complete works of Charles Dickens for 11/–, the *Chronicle* retaliated with the same offer for 10/– for all sixteen volumes with a deluxe edition at 18/– the set.

There was no doubt that Layton was in command at the *News Chronicle* as chairman and, in effect, editor-in-chief from the very beginning. But as the Cadbury family owned the newspapers, all four brothers felt it their duty to express their strong views on policy and management. The correspondence was usually friendly enough, but throughout there is a current of unease because of the Cadbury's unhappiness that even though they were the proprietors, and as such responsible for the newspapers, they did not seem able to prevent Layton (and the editor of the day) going his own way. They had financial responsibility but little power.

Laurence Cadbury, in particular, sent Layton two or three letters a week even though he spent the middle of the week in the *News Chronicle* offices. Most of these letters were on points of financial detail, on staff appointments, on Cadbury's worries that Layton was taking too much outside work (which he certainly was in 1931) and on concern that Layton's Notes of the Day might be too long and too weighty (a justifiable criticism). He also commented frequently on the tone of the leader and on the make-up of the paper, and some of the criticism was to the point. For instance, Cadbury argued in March 1932 that as complete free trade had now become a lost cause with little appeal to the younger generation, the *News Chronicle* should, in future, argue in favour of low tariffs. But some of the criticism was trivial. In June 1930, just after Layton had taken over, Laurence Cadbury wrote a long letter about how important it was to use the *Daily News* traditional colour of yellow for the contents bills rather than the *Daily Chronicle* orange. In October 1932 he wrote another long letter about *News Chronicle* posters.

Laurence Cadbury, the son of two outstanding parents, George Cadbury and Dame Elizabeth, had inherited many of their good qualities. He was conscientious, physically courageous and devoted to his family and to his father's ideals. But he did not have the special talents needed to discharge his dual responsibilities as both managing director of Bournville and chairman of Daily News Ltd. Whatever his achievements at Bournville, he was not suited to running a major Liberal newspaper during a period when all mass circulation papers were going through difficult times. He was, in fact, in the wrong job, but out of family loyalty he persisted in it for thirty years, without acquiring enough journalistic sense to see what changes were necessary for survival. He tried hard and had the best intentions but was never really happy at the *News Chronicle*. His self-confidence in his dealings with Layton was to some extent undermined by having been his pupil at Cambridge. In November 1937, in a letter he described as 'frankly egotistical', Cadbury wrote: 'I want to take a major part in the paper and not to be just a nagging outsider.' Although the two men remained on friendly terms, Layton could not help at times being irritated by Cadbury and Cadbury felt jealous of Layton.

There were no real financial worries up to 1950, but even when the *News Chronicle* was doing really well, as it was throughout the 1930s, there was often an uneasy triangular relationship between Laurence Cadbury and Layton, and between both and the editor of the day. Cadbury was well to the right of Layton politically and hence they were bound to differ on major issues. The editor suffered further because both Cadbury and Layton had difficulty in taking decisions at the speed necessary in a newspaper office with its constant deadlines. The editor was thus left not knowing quite where he stood. So tensions arose. Layton had the outstanding intellectual power and quite enough journalistic flair to run the paper on his own, although he was a very different character from his fellow Fleet Street magnates. But because of Laurence Cadbury's different political views and his determination to share in the details of management he did not have complete charge without constant argument. Nor in his own sphere could the editor expect always to have the last word, since Layton was equally determined to decide the line to be taken by the leader writers.

At first Laurence Cadbury's main worry was about the political stance of the paper, particularly after Aylmer Vallance became editor in 1933, much to the disappointment of A.J. Cummings. The paper from 1930 onward had tended to attract leftwing journalists, and as time went on complaints increased, both from the trustees and Liberal Party members, that the *News Chronicle* was going socialist. While many journalists on the paper were, indeed, sympathetic to Labour and in the later Thirties they included some Communists, Layton himself was steadfast in his Liberal faith. But with the Liberal Party itself deeply divided, he saw that the best hope for the future lay in policies such as those worked out in the Liberal *Yellow Book*, being presented in such a way as to capture the Labour Party intellectually. After the 1931 debacle the Labour Party looked like being fertile ground for new ideas. In a policy statement in 1934 he wrote: 'The *News Chronicle* must keep before the public the points of difference between it and Labour policy without in any way obscuring the view that the carrying out of any programme will certainly require the cooperation of moderate elements in the Labour Party.'

To some of the more old-fashioned Liberals the *News Chronicle* seemed too ready to support the Labour Party. Laurence Cadbury was particularly sensitive to jibes to that effect from the National Liberal Club and some of the *News Chronicle*'s rivals in Fleet Street. Matters came to a head in 1934, when Clive Pearson of the Cowdray family, representing the Westminster Press, asked Layton for a statement of the *News Chronicle*'s policy and of the instructions given to the editor and staff. Pearson had been talking to Lord Lothian, who had turned down a proposal that he should join the Daily News and Westminster Board to advise on policy because he was convinced that the *News Chronicle* was too leftwing. At the same time, J.A. Spender, the distinguished Liberal journalist, was having difficulty in getting his articles published by the *News Chronicle*, in contrast to the treatment he had received from the *Daily News*, and he alleged that the space was being given instead to Labour MPs such as Ellen Wilkinson.

Layton replied on 7 March by sending a forthright statement: 'Our attitude towards the Labour Party should be one of sympathy and support in matters where they are in agreement with Liberal ideas and generally we shall endeavour to strengthen the reasonable elements in that Party. But this does not mean that we should give the impression of supporting the Labour Party as it at present exists.'

Lloyd George apparently was also concerned that the *News Chronicle* was going socialist. Frances Stephenson in her diary about life with Lloyd George has the following entry for 10 March 1934:

> Sir Walter and Lady Layton came in the evening and stayed to dinner – a long talk on the political situation. Agreement that Liberalism (or rather the Liberal party) had missed the boat and was a complete washout. D. [Lloyd George] said: 'We ran away at the last election, surrendering everything, and leaving all the bag and baggage behind.' He thinks there is no hope at the next election. Layton and indeed all the management of The News Chronicle are inclined to go Labour. D. had already told me of a talk he had had with Vallance, in which the latter gave a hint of a combination and understanding with the Herald on a progressive policy. And a young friend of ours who has got a job as leader writer on the Chronicle was told

that his line was to be 'half-way between Maxton and Samuel'. This evening after dinner Layton went still further and outlined a scheme for extending the News Chronicle–Star group into a much larger group of papers. (This included the purchasing of the Starmer group or the controlling interest in them, and the founding of a Sunday paper on the lines of The Observer.) These would operate on an advanced progressive policy, and Layton suggested that Elias (proprietor of the Herald) should have a large share in the management. Indeed he had evidently broached the subject to Elias. Then Layton put the question, which was obviously the reason of his visit: Would D. put money into the scheme? D. said he would.[2]

Pearson at the end of March asked Layton for a declaration against nationalization of industry and in favour of private enterprise. There were many complaints from dedicated Liberals, including one that the *News Chronicle* had become 'the persistent courtier of a contemptuous Labour Party'. Layton tried again in June by sending Pearson a new draft expressing his view that 'the line between state ownership and control or unfettered private enterprise is a matter of expediency rather than principle'. The test should be which method 'raised the material standard of living of the nation as a whole'. Such a plea for the mixed economy would be wholeheartedly endorsed by the Social Democrat–Liberal Alliance of today but was not accepted by orthodox Liberals in the 1930s.

Pearson, indeed, regarded Layton's new draft as a declaration of socialism rather than of liberalism. The *Evening Standard* had a tart comment suggesting that Layton was riding two horses at once:

If Sir Walter Layton has taken the decision that the 'News Chronicle' shall turn Socialist, then his own position becomes extremely interesting, for he is also editor of the 'Economist'. The 'Economist' is owned half by Financial Newspaper Proprietors Limited, and half by leading financiers, including Sir Henry Strakosch, and, it is believed, Rothschild and Cowdray interests. There can be, therefore, no prospect of the 'Economist' turning Socialist, so Sir Walter Layton will have to ride two horses. It is a feat to which he is accustomed.

No newspaper has attacked the National Government more fiercely than the 'News Chronicle', but no man has been happier than Sir Walter Layton on occasions when the Prime Minister happened to consult him.

Layton shrugged this off, but Pearson wanted Vallance disciplined. At this stage Layton, tired of Pearson's sniping, pointed out forcibly that under the merger arrangements the Daily News directors had ultimate control over policy and that anyway Pearson was not in a position to judge, since unlike his brother the first Lord Cowdray, who had died the previous year, he had not got to know the *News Chronicle* staff.

One solution very much in Layton's mind was that the Westminster Press and United Newspapers should sell out their interests in the *News Chronicle* to the Daily News Ltd, but that did not happen for two years. In the meantime, Layton backed Aylmer Vallance against his critics, and an uneasy truce was reached early in 1935 when he said that while he had not time to exercise continuous control over policy, he would be spending more of his day at the *News Chronicle* offices and would tighten control.

Layton emerged from this argument without having to change his policy for the *News Chronicle* and determined to buy out the other shareholders as soon as possible. It was ironic that in this confrontation, which arose ostensibly about whether the *News Chronicle* was Liberal enough, at a time when there were at least three versions of Liberalism, he was the only genuine Liberal. In dealing with opposition from the Cadbury family he found it useful to quote George Cadbury's testament calling for 'taxing the rich for the benefit of the poor and the nationalisation of monopolies better administered by the community for the benefit of all'.

Aylmer Vallance continued as a brilliant editor but difficult to control. One proposal later in 1935 was to make him managing editor of both the *News Chronicle* and the *Star*, while appointing a new editor at the *News Chronicle*. This idea was being considered when Vallance's unfortunate habit of making love in the office became widely known. On coming out of Vallance's office when he had surprised him with a girl in flagrante delicto, Layton remarked ruefully: 'And they did not even stop when I came in.' In a less permissive age than the present, this led to complaints from the staff. Vallance had also disgraced himself at Layton's election night party at Bouverie Street in November 1935 by applauding lost Liberal deposits and cheering at Herbert Samuel's defeat. Once Vallance had lost authority in the office, Layton decided he could not keep him on however able he might have proved himself. So Vallance was sacked before Christmas and given generous financial compensation before moving to the *New Statesman and Nation* as deputy to Kingsley Martin.

In spite of these troubles and worries about the *Star*, which was losing money right up to the war, the *News Chronicle* itself made good profits, quite sufficient for the Daily News Ltd to buy out the Westminster and United Papers interests at the beginning of 1937. The bank loans and mortgages needed to finance this deal were repaid a few years later.

The way Layton defended the radical policy of the *News Chronicle* and went on to achieve financial independence for the paper showed that he was a much more determined and, perhaps, ruthless man than he seemed on first acqaintance. While, in personal dealings, he was kind and often appeared gentle, he was tough enough to sack Aylmer Vallance, who in earlier years was very much his man, and he did so even against the judgement of Laurence Cadbury.

Layton was also tough enough, once it was clear that the Daily News Ltd trustees would be able to buy out the other partners in the *News Chronicle*, to propose a completely new organization for the Daily News and *News Chronicle* boards, together with a considerable improvement in his own financial position. In September 1936, with Geofffrey Crowther's help, Layton put forward a proposal by which he would have become governing director with an improved salary, a share in the profits and the chance of building up a capital holding in the company amounting to about £100,000 at the end of seven years. There was understandably some demur from the Cadbury brothers, who themselves wanted to have more say in editorial policy, while Layton's proposals seemed designed to reinforce his own position against those of the proprietors. Layton replied in a forthright manner:

> 1. The N.C. in its present form is from the financial point of view my creation; politically, I have kept its head above water at a time when the appeal of the Liberal party was almost nil; I have reconstructed its editorial staff.
>
> When I joined the Board, the weekly newsprint consumption of the Daily News was under 400 tons a week. This year the N.C. is consuming 1400 tons a week. Average loss of D.N. four years 1923/6 – £38,000; Average profit of N.C. four years 1933/6 – £95,000. Net capital made available from external sources since I became Chairman –

nil. The News Chronicle has now accumulated sufficient resources to make possible the present consolidation in the interests of the Star and of the continued control by the Daily News Ltd.

2. Since 1930, I have been in full charge of the N.C. The Board under my chairmanship has made all appointments (except that I have consulted the N.C. Trustees in regard to the Editorship); mine has been the deciding voice as to policy, subject only to being pulled up by the Trustees if in their opinion I wrongly interpreted the policy clause in the Fusion Agreement.
3. I cannot agree to a scheme of reorganisation under which this authority is in any way curtailed. There cannot be two kings in Brentford.
4. I am, however, not only willing, but am most anxious to collaborate with L.J.C. who has been a tower of strength. This collaboration should continue to apply to all aspects of the business including policy. Consultation and advice on political and economic matters is most welcome; but clearly I could not continue at the head of the N.C. unless its policy represents my point of view.

After this broadside negotiations went on for fifteen months. Although he did not say so at the time, it was clear that Laurence Cadbury was unwilling for Layton to hold any more Daily News Ltd ordinary shares and thus acquire a greater share of the equity.

This still left the question of Layton's pay unsettled. He raised it again in September 1937 in the following terms:

I have, as you know, the utmost reluctance to discuss my personal affairs, but I realise that I must put something on paper before this week's meetings, and if we are to make headway I must try and put down exactly what is in my mind.

Here is the background:

1) The market price of my job is at least £10,000 a year, plus a share of profits, plus a chance of acquiring shares in the business on favourable terms. ... I have never asked for this and I am much more anxious to pursue the ideas of profit sharing and to get an 'ideal' method of control of the press than to make money. But it is assumed by newspaper proprietors and, I find, by my own staff, that I am 'making a good thing out of it'. I must therefore say a word about my personal position.

2) My total income from all sources is very little more than it was in 1921 when I was working for the Steel Federation. It has enabled me to save practically nothing which would allow me either to retire or indulge in such expensive luxuries as going in for politics. I have some seven years left in which to make adequate provision for my family.

A settlement was finally reached in December by which Layton's salary was increased from £4,000 to £7,500 a year, and he was to receive preference shares to enable him to build up a sizeable capital sum. This was not quite what he wanted, as he still had hopes that he might eventually be able to buy the *News Chronicle* and hence needed a larger share of the equity. However, he records in his Memoirs that when, after the war, he was in a position to make an offer to Laurence Cadbury, Cadbury refused to sell. So Layton was never able to add the role of newspaper proprietor to his many other achievements.

The Threat to Peace and Democracy

Layton's great concern with international affairs had a major impact on the *News Chronicle*. In July 1931 the paper organized an Albert Hall meeting with Ramsay Macdonald, Baldwin and Lloyd George as speakers on disarmament and world peace. Layton was on the platform. In the mid-1930s the threats from Hitler and Mussolini abroad and from Oswald Mosley's brand of fascism at home were highlighted in both the *News Chronicle* and the *Star*. Layton himself interviewed Mussolini in February 1932 and Hitler in 1933.

In his notes of his talk with Mussolini, Layton describes the series of ante-rooms leading up to the enormous marble hall in which Mussolini held his interviews. From a distance, Mussolini seemed a mild and middle-aged gentleman growing bald and getting stout. Closer up Layton was impressed that he was a man with a mask, with his full round face and dark eyes which stared out under lifting eyebrows. He recorded in *Dorothy* his interview with Mussolini:

> On reflection, however, there is a doubt which of us did the interviewing. Mussolini started the conversation by asking me what I thought of 'the crisis'. I naturally asked to which of the many current crises (the devaluation of the pound, the reparations moratorium, disarmament, the Manchurian deadlock) he referred. So he made his question more specific and asked whether the *Economist* (of which he claimed to have been a regular reader) would support the disarmament plan which Signor Grandi had laid before the Disarmament Conference in Geneva two or three days previously. It was an interesting opening gambit which represented Mussolini

himself as Europe's number one peace-loving statesman. The pose was a caricature, though our long talk was both frank and friendly.

The visit to Berlin at the end of March 1933 was at the invitation of the German Ambassador in London. It was the time of the first boycott of Jewish shops and of the dismissal of all Jewish judges. On this occasion the expected beating up of Jewish shop-owners and sacking of their shops did not take place. The Brownshirts were held back to show that Hitler was more moderate than the foreign Press were alleging, and had full control over the thugs in the Nazi Party. Layton, no doubt, was invited that weekend to persuade him to moderate *News Chronicle* criticism of Nazi methods. If so, he was not taken in, as he had enough contacts to know that the Nazi terror was real enough. He described in his Memoirs his talk with Hitler:

I have never seen Hitler on the platform, but in his own office he was not impressive. Short, thickset and clad in a russet-coloured suit, his face had lost the sharpness of outline which is noticeable in his early photographs; but the famous lock of hair over the forehead was in its place, and I had the impression of a familiar personality, from seeing innumerable photographs of him in the Press. I came away feeling that I had not discovered the source of his power. He rarely looked straight at me (I was sitting on his right) but closely followed Schacht who was on his left and doing most of the interpreting. The only sign of the familiar Hitler was that from time to time he raised his voice – and it was a fine resonant voice – as though addressing a public meeting for he answered most of my questions with little more than the ordinary phrases that he had been using for years on the platform, and claptrap is nothing if it is not delivered fortissimo.

I asked him questions under three heads:

(1) economic questions and the Nazi idea of autarchy.
(2) the boycott and internal repression.
(3) international affairs.

On the first he refused to be drawn: I was given to understand that I might refer to Schacht, though whether Schacht interpolated or whether Hitler actually said it, I do not know. On the boycott Hitler, in effect, politely warned me off with the statement that it was an internal matter for Germany. He claimed – with justice – that the Nazi forces were well under control. This conclusion was prefaced by a short lecture on the history of the Nazi movement, and the struggle between two Germanys, one which had knuckled under the peace treaties, the other determined to uphold her pride. But the Nazi fight was not merely a German fight, it was also a war against communism. It was therefore a battle for other countries, England included. If we in England understood the true meaning of the communist movement we would be whole-heartedly supporting him.

Schacht subsequently told me that he had been present at a number of Hitler's interviews with various people from abroad, and that my interview had gone better than any of the others. But he had the feeling that Hitler always had difficulty in finding common ground with people familiar with international affairs and that he took refuge in his speeches. Time would show whether he would come to understand us better.

The Hitler I met, in short, was not the daemonic leader, inspiring millions by his oratory, destroying millions by his madness. It was the tame version of the schizophrenic personality, the man who gave bars of chocolate to children, the politician as yet uncertain in international matters, polite to foreigners, cloaking the increasingly ruthless actions of his Nazi followers in legalism as he tightened his grip on the controls of power.

Layton went on to see Goebbels, who reminded him, rather unfairly, of Philip Snowden, and who stated that the boycott of the Jews had been abandoned and would not be resumed unless foreign propaganda went on. He also had a talk with Brüning, who was in fear of arrest or being attacked. Brüning saw no way back for Germany to the previous parliamentary regime. Probably the only way to restore liberty was through a constitutional monarchy.

Layton had two talks with Dr Schacht, now president of the Reichsbank again. Schacht was entirely confident that Hitler, having taken complete powers, would be able to get Germany back into financial balance and to deal with unemployment. Schacht, though claiming not to be a Nazi, followed a strict Nazi line, arguing that Hitler's dictatorship was justified because he represented the national will. Democracy could disappear because the Nazi Party and the nation would become one.

Layton asked Schacht whether Hitler understood financial questions. To this Schacht characteristically replied: 'Yes, certainly. He has at least one idea and a very good one. It is to leave it to Schacht.' Layton obviously passed this story on, as a week later he got a letter from a nervous Schacht:

> I have been told in Basle about our Berlin conversation that when asked what Hitler would do financially, my answer had been, that he would do what I wanted him to do. This certainly is a misunderstanding. My answer was and certainly meant that he would do, what I would do. That is to say, that he has as sound ideas about finance as I pretend to have.

Layton's visit finished in very different company, that of Kurt Hahn, head of the progressive school of Salem, who later moved to Scotland to found Gordonstoun School on the same lines. Hahn had just finished a prison sentence for protesting against Nazi atrocities. Geoffrey Winthrop Young, who had been a war correspondent for the *Daily News* in the First World War and was an old friend of Layton's, was present, having come over to Germany to help save Salem School. Hahn was at that time convinced that Hitler could be controlled (perhaps ousted) by the Reichswehr, and wanted Layton to hear the views of General von Schleicher (who had been chancellor just before Hitler seized power and was to be shot on Hitler's orders in the Röhm purge of June 1934) and General von Hammerstein, who was then Commander in Chief. They met over dinner, when the generals expressed impeccable Liberal sentiments, insisting that the Reichswehr was above party politics. According to Hahn's record of the conversation, written much later in a letter to Layton:

> You and Geoffrey Young spoke freely about England's attitude towards the Nazi regime and the loathing which their system of oppression stirred. Hammerstein and Schleicher assured you that there were large sections of the German population which abhorred the Nazis and their methods of government. Hammerstein, although he was still in office at that time, had no hesitation in telling you that on the 31st January he had done all he could to prevent Hitler coming to power. He did, however, not go into details and did not reveal that he had offered to lead the Reichswehr against the Nazis. The Reichstag fire was discussed and there could have been left no doubt in your mind that Hammerstein and Schleicher believed that the Nazis were the incendiaries.
>
> I supported what you and Geoffrey Young had said by quoting from *The Times* and *Morning Post*. Both papers at that time gave expression to the indignation which was universally felt in England. The question then was raised, who could inform Hindenburg.

Neither general seemed willing to make any approach to President Hindenburg, and Hahn soon gave up trying this way of bringing some restraint to bear on Hitler.

Layton returned to London with a pretty fair idea of the evil nature of the Nazi regime and wrote three articles in the *News Chronicle*. They described the drastic action being taken against the Jews and others, but did not mention atrocities. He reported Goebbels as saying the influence of the Jews would be reduced gradually and that every effort would be made to prevent the recurrence of the outrages he admitted had occurred. Layton did not go on to condemn Hitler outright – perhaps because he had only just taken power, and perhaps because he said he was willing to accept the MacDonald Plan for disarmament, and that he desired peace, indeed, ten years of peace were an absolute necessity for Germany. But Layton ended by pointing out that, as long as Germany remained a dictatorship, the German government could not expect to command the sympathy of democratic governments.

Layton's distrust of Hitler was to grow the following autumn at the time of the Reichstag Fire Trial when von Krosigk protested against Douglas Jay's article in the *Economist*, as described in a previous chapter.

Oswald Mosley seemed in 1933 a more dangerous threat to democracy than he turned out to be later. When the *Daily Mail* gave its public support to Mosley in that year there were strong leaders written in the *News Chronicle*, the *Star* and the *Economist*. The *Star*, indeed, got into trouble by attacking Mosley in February 1933 in terms which led to a libel case. The paper had to pay out £5,000 in damages. Layton was deeply disappointed at the result, having been led to believe by his counsel, Norman Birkett, that the *Star* was likely to win.

Layton used the *News Chronicle* to great effect to get full publicity for the Peace Ballot, launched by the League of Nations Union, in which Dorothy Layton played a leading part, in October 1934. The results came out in summer 1935 in good time to influence the general election in November of that year. The *News Chronicle* vigorously campaigned for the project, which won the support of the Liberal and Labour parties and many leading Conservatives. The churches, peace societies, women's organizations and trade unions all joined in. It was as formidable an operation as any run by the Campaign for Nuclear Disarmament after the Second World War. The *News Chronicle* repeatedly published the ballot forms so as to make sure that as many people as possible could vote. Layton even persuaded Lord Southwood of the *Daily Herald* to put the resources of a large bill-posting company he owned at the disposal of the League of Nations Union.

Half a million volunteers were enrolled to canvass the questions, which were answered by 12 million voters. The key question on the ballot form was:

> Do you consider that, if a nation insists on attacking another, the other nations should combine to compel it to stop by:
> (a) economic and non-military measures?
> (b) if necessary, military measures?

Layton analysed the results in his book *Dorothy*:

> By far the most important question, however, was question number five, which went to the heart of the matter. Was the public prepared to take action to resist aggression? Here two possibilities were suggested, one being economic and other non-military sanctions, – the other force of arms. Nearly 87 per cent were prepared to support economic and non-military measures. On the crucial question of supporting collective security by force of arms, 58.6 per cent voted Yes. Half of the balance (21 per cent) said No, the other half (20 per cent) abstained from voting. In other words, nearly three out of every four who expressed an opinion were prepared to support Great Britain in joining with other nations to take 'military sanctions' against an aggressor. This is overwhelming approval on any open vote.
>
> A more serious criticism was that many of those who most strongly supported the League of Nations were opposed to the Government's rearmament plans and therefore it might be claimed that the ballot merely showed the irresponsibility of the public, who were ready to interfere in other people's quarrels but were unwilling to give the Government the weapons to do it effectively. But this reasoning overlooks the fact that the case for the League assumed that there would be agreement on the contributions to be made by the various members of the League for the enforcement of collective security. What the ballot implied was that any government would have had overwhelming support for an armament programme that represented our proper share of a League of Nations security force.

Layton may have been unduly optimistic in the prospects for building up a League security force, but Baldwin paid considerable attention to the ballot results in the period just before the General Election of 1935 undertaking to support the League and collective security. It was these considerations that compelled Baldwin to sack his Foreign Secretary, Sir Samuel Hoare, when a few weeks later it transpired that he had agreed with the French Prime Minister Laval to do a deal with Italy over Abyssinia, completely at variance with the policy the government had ostensibly been following at Geneva.

These events gave Layton ample scope to press for collective security through the use of sanctions, even though the first half of 1936 was to see Abyssinia overrun by Mussolini's armies, Hitler's march into the Rhineland, and in July the outbreak of the Spanish Civil War. Some critics thought that the Peace Ballot strengthened pacifism in Britain, but Layton always believed that by stimulating public discussion on major issues of peace and war it had prepared the way for common acceptance in Britain (however belatedly) of the need to resist Hitler.

While Layton did not share the views of those friends, such as Lothian, who were in favour of appeasing the dictators, some of his staff on both the *News Chronicle* and the *Economist* wanted him to follow a much stronger line in the leader columns of both papers. It can certainly be argued that Layton and many other publicists and politicians should have spoken out louder and clearer from the start, and should even have advocated the use of force to nip the growing threat in the bud, especially when Hitler reoccupied the Rhineland in 1936. That Layton did not do so until war seemed inevitable is not at all surprising. His views were very much in keeping with the progressive thinkers of his generation. Layton and his friends, many of whose contemporaries had been slaughtered in the First World War, were convinced that there must never be another such war. They held that all nations should disarm and the League of Nations should be the means of providing collective security. Even as late as May 1935 Attlee was saying: 'We stand for collective security through the League of Nations. We reject the use of force as an instrument of policy. . . . Our policy is not one of seeking security through rearmament but through disarmament.'[3]

People like Layton saw that Hitler was a threat but conceded that the Germans had been unfairly treated at Versailles, for which many in Britain had a guilty conscience. France seemed to be narrowly nationalistic. Our own defences were weak and we were in no state to risk a war, especially as there could be no certainty that the United States would come in on our side. Any sanctions to be used against Germany and Italy must be agreed through the League of Nations. Layton, like most of his friends, may have clung too long to the hope that the dictators could be restrained by the League, but from the mid-Thirties onwards he certainly did not oppose British rearmament, provided that the weapons were used for collective action through the League.

While there were bound to be tensions among the management and arguments among the staff, the *News Chronicle* continued to improve as a radical but popular paper in the years before the war. This was mainly due to an exceptionally able staff of journalists with a strong loyalty to the paper. Pay at the *News Chronicle* was lower than on most major Fleet Street papers but it was a good paper to work for. The staff were given their heads provided their views did not clash too much with Layton's outlook. They felt that if they had something important to say they could say it.

Fortunately for the *News Chronicle* circulation, both Aylmer Vallance and Gerald Barry, his successor as editor, saw to it that the paper became more readable as time went on. In Vallance's time Vernon Bartlett and Oscar Hobson had joined the paper, the first as diplomatic correspondent and the second as City editor. Barry made good use of the Gallup opinion polls which had just started up, and in this was far ahead of other newspapers. Barry, in particular, had a light touch which no doubt was needed to offset the grave news to which Layton saw prominence was given. Layton always considered that the *News Chronicle* should lead rather than follow public opinion, but Barry lightened the paper by making good use both of photographs and of cartoonists. In particular, Horrabin continued with his comic strip The Arkubs, which had started in the 1920s, and there were other cartoons. Vicky was not to come to the paper until 1941, but by that time he was needed all the more. Some of the editorial staff found Barry great fun to work for at this time and considered him the best editor the *News Chronicle* ever had.

CHAPTER TEN

The Coming War, 1936–9

But for the shadow cast, first by the threat and then by the virtual certainty of war, the years 1936–9 could have been a good period in Walter Layton's life. In his mid-fifties he was at the peak of his powers and both his work and his family were flourishing. His marriage stood up well to the strains of his excessively long working hours, which Dorothy could not help resenting. But she was immensely proud of the work he was doing, in much of which she was active too. And she knew she was essential to his way of life. He, for his part, was entirely content that Dorothy should be the centre of the family and the marriage was never really shaken. Dorothy herself was still in good health.

In 1931 the family had moved to Brett House, on West Hill in Putney, which looked like a large Indian bungalow with a tower. It had been built by John Brett, the artist, to house his seven children. By a curious chance another family with seven children then occupied it until, after a short interval, the Laytons arrived also with seven children, the youngest, Christopher, having been born in 1929. As the sketch within the illustrated section shows, it was a spacious open-plan house with an octagonal hall at the centre from which the major rooms were curtained off. There was a large music room, with two grand pianos, and the drawing room had a William Morris wallpaper on which pink peacocks were embossed. The parquet flooring throughout made the house ideal for parties and dances but also rather chilly. Though the house was one of the first in London to have central heating in all rooms, the heat seldom reached the far end of the building. Walter particularly liked his study in the tower, originally built as a platform for John Brett's telescope, where he could retire for peace and quiet and to sunbathe, and where he often slept at night. There he had a view right across London. When he wanted exercise he would go off and swim in a friend's pool nearby.

Although it was a big establishment to run, Dorothy enjoyed living at Brett House too and it suited the rest of the family well since they could do what they liked without getting in each other's way. The house was usually full of activity and there were many visitors, but Walter could get on with his work without being disturbed by the talk, the music, the committee meetings or the games which might be going on in different rooms. And when he wanted family life it was there in abundance.

Although both parents were strong personalities they did not attempt to dominate their children. Each child was allowed to go its own way. It was not a really close-knit family but any visitor to the house was bound to be impressed by the music playing and singing in which all the family joined. Of the seven children the three eldest had already done well at Cambridge, Michael as an engineer, Margaret and David as economists, and David had captained the University Hockey XI. Margaret was beginning to prove that she had inherited much of Walter's ability; Jean, after studying music in Vienna, showed much promise as a violinist and a pianist. Of the younger daughters, Olive was outstandingly beautiful and showed signs of becoming a good actress and singer. Ruth, then more of a tomboy, was good-looking too, and full of vitality. The whole family took great delight in Christopher, the youngest child, who was then a bright small boy with much of Dorothy's artistic talent.

The author knows of one young man who fell in love with Margaret, Jean and Olive in turn and suspects there were others who were bowled over by more than one of the daughters. Walter Layton was immensely proud of his children, though at that stage of life he was not very close to them. His easiest relationships were with Olive and Ruth, perhaps because they were young and, unlike his elder sons and Jean, did not have their own opinions, at any rate on public affairs. He showed great understanding and kindness to Michael's fiancée, Dot, who did not come from the Cambridge upper-middle-class circles in which his sons might have been expected to find their wives. He was certainly no snob and he broke the ice at once at his first meeting with Dot by taking her off to the cinema. The gloom of November 1938, when the international situation was deteriorating fast, was brightened for him by the birth of the first of his twenty-four grandchildren, Michael and Dot's daughter Deanna.

In the previous month Dorothy and he had given up the Osmaston house, Beacon Crag, on the cliffs at Porthleven in Cornwall and acquired Twittens, a family house in Sussex, set in woods and with a pond for swimming, which was accessible for weekends and was to be invaluable in the war. Here he could work on his papers out of doors and get exercise by bathing and scything the long grass in the meadow.

If his own children sometimes found him remote it may have been largely due to preoccupation with his work. He was never prepared just to chatter to other people, even his own children. As one of his sons has put it, his mind was working hard all the time but on a different wavelength to that of his children, and indeed of most other people. Because of his preoccupation with his work he often seemed unaware of other people, and of the niceties of social behaviour which he gratefully left to Dorothy. His renowned long silences on the telephone, which worried his staff until they got used to them, suggest some insensitivity to other people's feelings. But he was in no way arrogant and the silences were probably due to his search for the right word or phrase. He might easily have said something to show the caller still had his attention, but his failure to do so may again have been due to his lack of concern with the niceties.

Even so he was never unapproachable, although his second daughter, Jean, still remembers her disappointment at his failure to respond to her exciting news that she had won a scholarship to St Paul's School. He did not comment on Jean's piano and violin playing, which in the years before the war reached a very high standard, or come and listen to her while she was practising. But he occasionally said, when the family sang together on Sunday mornings, that he wished he had kept to music.

It must be more than a coincidence that during the war all four daughters were to marry highly extrovert foreign husbands, three of them Jewish refugees, from Germany, Austria and Czechoslovakia, the other an Anglo-Egyptian with a Mediterranean background. It seems that the daughters were seeking in their husbands the warmth that their father wanted to give them but too often was inhibited from doing.

In these prewar years Layton's work was going well too. Both the *Economist* and the *News Chronicle* were making money and he had won his battle to control policy. But for the threat of war, the prospect of building the *News Chronicle* into a still more successful and influential paper was promising. It was already the mainstay of the mass of people with Liberal views at a time when there was little chance of the Liberal Party recovering its former strength.

At the *News Chronicle* Layton was liked by some of the younger journalists, and in particular by Gwyneth McCleary, the daughter of a family friend. She was his personal assistant who helped him with all his activities, and went with him into the Ministry of Supply and the Ministry of Production during the Second World War. She remembers him as totally unselfseeking. He was prepared to work long hours, not for his own aggrandizement but in order to get things right – in particular the *News Chronicle* leaders. He seldom left the office until 8 or 9 pm.

In busy periods, Layton would ring up Gwyneth on Sundays and ask if she was thinking of going into the office. Normally she replied 'No', to which he answered he would pick her up and drive her to Bouverie Street. Although Layton always assumed that running a paper was a seven day a week job, and that the paper must take precedence over personal life, Gwyneth did not find herself resenting his assumption that she would fall in with his requests. Although no doubt irritated at times, she liked him too much to consider leaving. She also had to get used to Layton's famous silences and failure to answer her questions. Instead his mind seemed to go off on a tangent and he would ask her to get someone on the telephone, totally unrelated to the question she had asked. This habit must have been disconcerting at first, but she got used to it and in other ways he was open and friendly.

Although Layton normally assembled the leader writers in his room every day to give them his views, he would also visit the junior staff in their own rooms. He went to the staff canteen for supper at 8 or

9 pm rather than to a restaurant or a club. He still had plenty of nervous energy and a twinkle in his eye in his mid-fifties. He would always run up the five flights of stairs to his office rather than take the lift. He was still a handsome man and attractive to women.

Layton was horrified by the prevalent Fleet Street habit of heavy drinking. Drink, he thought, was one of the main causes of Aylmer Vallance's downfall. Although not a teetotaller himself, and indeed after the war he got to be reasonably knowledgeable about wines, there was virtually no alcohol at Brett House thanks to Dorothy's firm views. Visiting journalists found that when they accepted the offer of a drink, they got lemonade rather than the stiff whisky they longed for.

While much of life seemed good from 1936 onwards, Layton became more and more preoccupied with the growing threat of war. The same, of course, was true of any intelligent man or woman aware of what was going on, but Layton was even more involved from the very nature of his work in Fleet Street and with the Liberal Party. He heard the news sooner than most and had to give his views that night. The failure of the League of Nations economic sanctions to stop Mussolini in Abyssinia, Hitler's march into the Rhineland, the long agony of the Spanish Civil War, Hitler's occupation of Austria, Munich and finally the German occupation of Prague in March 1939 meant that Layton spent much of his time and energy trying to mobilize public opinion against the government's ineffectual policies.

His main instruments were the *News Chronicle* and the *Economist*. The *News Chronicle* took the lead in campaigning against Franco's bombing of open cities, especially Guernica, and in raising money to help the Basque children who came to England as refugees. Largely through the initiative of the most outstanding woman member of Parliament of the time, Eleanor Rathbone, and with the support of the TUC, a plan was made to bring 2,000 Basque children to England. In the event, the ship, sent with the help of the *News Chronicle*, brought over 4,000, only some of whom returned home when the Spanish Civil War ended. Dorothy Layton played a large part on the committee which helped these children, and continued to look after those who remained in England until after the Second World War.

The *News Chronicle* gave full coverage to the Spanish Civil War. The fact that two of its main correspondents in the early stages of the war,

Willie Forrest and Arthur Koestler, were Communists did not worry Layton when he came to hear of it later. Forrest was an exceptionally able war correspondent, not only in Spain but later in Poland, Finland and the Middle East. It was quite by chance that it was Forrest who went to Madrid in January 1937 while Koestler went to cover the fighting on the southern Mediterranean coast and was captured at Malaga by Franco's troops. It could have been the other way around, but Koestler's three months' imprisonment by Franco gave rise later to his brilliant and moving book *A Spanish Testament*. At the time, Layton used the *News Chronicle* to agitate for Koestler's release and enlisted the help of MPs of all parties. Koestler was finally released by Franco in exchange for a woman hostage held by the Republicans and recovered from his ordeal when staying with the Laytons at Brett House. Three years later Layton did his best to get Koestler into England after he had been detained in France as politically dangerous in the autumn of 1939.

Layton later wrote in *Dorothy*:

> In writing subsequently of these events, Koestler was clearly disturbed in his mind that he did not openly disclose that he was a Communist Party member. He need not have worried as far as Dorothy and I were concerned. In the thirties Communism did not mean in England and America what it has subsequently come to mean. It made a great idealist appeal to many young people at the universities, in the professions and elsewhere. In most cases this was a passing phase, as indeed it was with Koestler himself, whose writings show that it was in the months of imprisonment in Seville that the hold of Communism on him began to weaken. I was well aware that some members of the staff in Bouverie Street had been or at that time were still party members, a fact that was true also of the staff of several if not all of the national newspapers.

Layton, who quite apart from not knowing at the time that Koestler was a member of the Communist Party, was equally unaware that he had acted in Spain as a Comintern agent, and wanted to send him to Moscow as a *News Chronicle* correspondent. Gerald Barry, however, who knew of Koestler's background and connections, stopped this happening. It was agreed that instead he should do a tour of Greece and the Middle East and write a series of articles for the paper.[1]

Layton's main efforts in these years were directed to building all-party support for policies to resist the dictators through the League of

Nations, as long as that seemed a feasible policy, and later in alliance with Russia. As for home policy, he hoped it would be possible for the Liberal and Labour parties to co-operate by way of electoral pacts, where a progressive candidate had a good chance of a by-election. Very much the same arguments as are now advanced by the SDP-Liberal Alliance were used by Layton then. He tried to show that it was in the Labour Party's interest as well as the Liberals' that proportional representation should be introduced. Labour representation in the Commons was then relatively low, and with the party's habit of fighting its own left wing, then in the persons of Stafford Cripps and Aneurin Bevan, the prospects for the future were not good. Layton had only partial success. Pethick Lawrence wrote in June 1937 that it was not possible to do a deal but: 'You will observe, however, that we are leaving certain places alone and one or more of these places might prove suitable to your friends.'

The *Daily Worker* the previous year published a cartoon captioned 'The new sample of political gerrybuilding' with Layton as a bowing shopkeeper in tailcoat outside the Popular Shop Front Company with space to let for Labour candidates (Liberally furnished) and a notice saying 'Communists keep out. This is a refained front.' This ridicule did not deter Layton from taking part in both leftwing and rightwing attempts to form a Popular Front which would bring pressure to bear on the government to give up appeasement. He attended Popular Front meetings organized by Victor Gollancz, who was then running the Left Book Club, but the *News Chronicle* editor was told to use the term 'Peace Alliance' rather than 'Popular Front' with its leftwing undertones. To correct the balance he attended Winston Churchill's lunches, at which major foreign policy and defence issues were discussed.

Running the *News Chronicle* suited Layton because he had at least a foothold in the political world, without being exposed to all the knocks and unpleasantness of a politician's life. In his quieter more moderate way he carried on the tradition of C.P. Scott, who had dominated the *Manchester Guardian* up to 1929. The result was that the *News Chronicle* too became an outstanding Liberal newspaper, thanks to the quality of its staff and the sense of direction Layton gave it.

The Czech Crisis

Austria's fall in March 1938 concentrated attention on the threat to Czechoslovakia. The Czechs did what they could to mobilize Western public opinion. A number of sympathizers, including Walter and Dorothy Layton, Dr Wickham Steed and the Duchess of Atholl, were invited to attend the Sokol Festival in Prague in June 1938. The British Ambassador was apprehensive about the effect the visitors might have on the Czech government. He told the Foreign Office that their visit might help to stiffen Czech resistance to Hitler, rather than convincing the Czech government of the importance of making far-reaching concessions.

The Laytons were greatly moved by the mass gymnastics in the huge Masaryk Stadium and by much else they saw and heard in Prague, but it was clear that the crisis was near. Henlein, the Sudeten German leader, was making impossible demands and the Czech army had already mobilized. Litvinov's proposals, whether genuine or not, for staff talks to concert action by the West and Russia if Hitler attacked Czechoslovakia, seemed to be being ignored by the West. Layton had a long talk with President Beněs about the details of concessions which might be made to Henlein without the Sudeten Germans coming virtually under Nazi domination.

As a result of these and other talks in Prague, Layton acquired a detailed first-hand knowledge of Czech thinking and plans. The visit also left a lasting impression on him which was reinforced as the years passed. Immediately it led to a talk with Maisky, the Russian Ambassador in London, who said there was growing resentment in Russia towards Britain and France because the British seemed ready to buy peace at any price and France was subservient to Britain. Maisky insisted that if Czechoslovakia was invaded, Russia would come to her assistance provided France did likewise.

As matters got worse in September, Layton tried to keep in close touch with the thinking of British ministers through several talks with Sir Samuel Hoare, then Home Secretary, with the job of special liaison with the Press. After the first talk on 17 September, following Chamberlain's visit to Hitler in Berchtesgaden, Layton wrote to

Hoare arguing that the Allies' hand was stronger and the Germans' weaker than the government supposed. To give way now would be to hand over Central Europe to Germany: 'A victory for Hitler now would make it less likely that Russia would be on our side if acute trouble occurred. She would be more likely to come to a *modus vivendi* with Germany. It is at least doubtful whether the balance will ever be more favourable to us.' Layton saw Hoare again three times between 19 and 23 September. He was told that the French were weakening and that it was now up to the Czechs to agree to self-determination for the Sudeten Germans.

Chamberlain's second meeting with Hitler (at Bad Godesberg) was a failure, as Hitler demanded immediate annexation of the Sudetenland. In the small hours of 29 September, the day on which Chamberlain was due to leave for his third meeting with Hitler in Munich, where Daladier and Mussolini were also to be present, a leaflet was brought to the *News Chronicle* office by a young man just arrived from Prague. The leaflet had been issued by Henlein and showed the timetable for Germany's conquest of Europe. Czechoslovakia was to be absorbed in autumn 1938, Hungary in spring 1939, Poland in autumn 1939, Yugoslavia in the spring of 1940, Romania and Bulgaria in autumn 1940. Northern France was to come under German domination in the spring of 1941 and Russia in the autumn of the same year. By 1948 Germany was to control all Europe, including the British Isles and the Middle East, except for the Mediterranean basin, which presumably was to be Italian.

The leaflet could be political dynamite if published that day, since it would demonstrate that Hitler's word was not to be trusted. Layton came into the office after midnight to discuss with Barry what should be done. He recorded in his Memoirs:

> We had neither the means nor the time to discover what degree of official authority the leaflet possessed at propaganda headquarters in Berlin. But there was no real doubt, for its thesis was substantially the sequence of events that had been clearly expressed in Hitler's *Mein Kampf* a decade and a half ago. It was important that the Prime Minister should be fully aware of the propaganda that was being used to foster in central and south-east Europe an impression of immense and remorseless expansion of Germany's hegemony.

As so often happens when great issues are at stake some practical consideration settles the matter. Several editions without a word about the pamphlet had gone to press and were already on their way to Europe and to the more distant parts of the country. Not half of the next day's issue would contain a word of this startling proof of the reborn truculence – not of the ordinary German citizen, who like most other Europeans were terrified of the idea of a second world war, but of the Nazi Party. It was too late for any copies of the next day's paper containing the sensational leaflet to reach the European continent, or for its impact to make itself felt. But there was one man in whose hands the leaflet might affect the course of the negotiations. That was the Prime Minister himself. At 3 o'clock in the morning as I drove home I pushed through the letter box at No. 10 Downing Street, an envelope containing two or three copies of the leaflet and a letter in which I said that I would hold up publication for 24 hours as it clearly might cause him embarrassment at a critical moment; but that he was, of course, free to use it or not at his discretion during the conference with Hitler. For my part I reserved the right to publish it after 24 hours whenever I might think fit.

I was rung up next day by Sir Samuel Hoare at breakfast time, (I think from the airport, where almost the whole Cabinet had gone to see the Prime Minister off,) to say that Neville Chamberlain had received my letter with its enclosures and that he had asked Hoare, who was being used by Neville as liaison man with the Press, to thank me for the contents of my letter. While he would not attempt to influence my decision he would be very grateful, if I thought of publishing it in the immediate future, if I would let Hoare know.

I did not in fact publish the leaflet at that time. But it appeared in the issue of March 16 1939 – the day on which Hitler's troops were already moving into Prague.

Holding up publication was typical of Layton's highly developed sense of responsibility. For him the criterion was what would help Neville Chamberlain at a critical time, not whether the *News Chronicle* had a real scoop. He behaved more in his old role of government adviser than as a newspaper man. For the same reason he did not publish a hard-hitting article by Willie Forrest about the government's failure of foreign policy from Mukden in 1931 to Munich in 1938.

The *News Chronicle* had been arguing against the acceptance of Hitler's demands up to 28 September. Then came Layton's reluctance to publish the Henlein leaflet and, in Gerald Barry's view, a weak indecisive leader written by Layton, when Chamberlain claimed he had brought back peace with honour from Munich. Layton was, however, swift and decisive in setting up the Czech Refugee Fund, the appeal for which was launched in the *News Chronicle* on 3 October. The refugees were both Czechs from the Sudetenland and Germans, often Jews, who had taken refuge from the Nazis in Czechoslovakia.

The response from the public was generous, £7,200 (say £150,000 in present currency) arriving on the first day, and £44,000 by the end of October. From the letters which accompanied many subscriptions to the fund, it was clear that they were 'conscience money' because of the shame felt in letting down the Czechs, which quickly succeeded the relief that the Munich settlement had avoided war, at any rate for the time being. No doubt support for the fund was all the greater because the *News Chronicle* published a moving letter from a well known Czech feminist, Dr Irena Malinska, written to Laurence Cadbury's mother Dame Elizabeth Cadbury, reproaching the British government for giving way at Munich. Although a number of ironic and cutting remarks about Chamberlain were edited out, the letter was a formidable and moving indictment as the following extracts show:

Prague, October 1, 1938.

Dear Dame Elizabeth,

I am writing to you to say goodbye. I have loved you and held you in esteem – and I was happy to have been able to work with you and the other women of all nationalities in the understanding of the nations. I can do no more.

I have been innocent enough to take seriously all such fine words as justice, liberty, collective security and arbitration, and I have sworn to peaceful ideology. Today, when seeing my nation sacrificed, I have come to the conclusion that this was the motive employed by the Powers of our world to enfeeble the weak and make them a more certain prey.

Those who have done this have assured only one thing: the reign of the most brutal force on earth. If people understand international arbitration of the kind which has been practised at Munich, then I prefer that international disputes be settled by war. I have considered war as the most hateful and stupid of human inventions whereby only savages determine their differences. Another means has been invented: to tie down a free and independent nation, and one honest almost to ingenuousness, and when it remains surprised and powerless before forces among which are found its most cherished friends then the world mutilates and dishonours it and does not even allow it to defend itself.

Dear Dame Elizabeth, we, who have hated war, have come to the conclusion that war is far more moral than what your statesmen have done with Czechoslovakia. ... You have hoped to save your colonies, the Mediterranean, your Empire. But do not deceive yourselves, our nation in its grievous frenzy does not cry 'Gott strafe England,' because it knows that it will be neither the first nor the last nation which will be crucified as you have crucified us today.

France and you, who from the very first have forced us to adopt the policy we have adopted, and who have deserted us when your promise to us was 'peace' – all you, who have betrayed us, will know soon what the show of feebleness against brutality signifies.

Although totally overthrown and altogether humiliated, my nation is an honest one! I am more proud than ever to be a Czechoslovak, and I am ashamed to be a European. You have mortally wounded the heart of Europe – the whole of Europe will soon suffer for it.

The public's readiness to give conscience money affected the government too. A £10 million credit was made available to the Czech government later in October to help refugees. Of the £10 million, £4 million was an outright gift. Layton went to considerable lengths to ensure that the money was well spent, going to Prague three times before Christmas. On the first visit in October he tried to find out the dimensions of the problem and to make certain that those dealing with the refugees in Czechoslovakia knew who to get in touch with in England. There were many voluntary bodies concerned in England, including the Society of Friends and the TUC. Layton brought these together as the British Committee for Czech Refugees, with his daughter Margaret as secretary.

In November he went again to Prague with the Lord Mayor, Sir Harry Twyford, and visited the new frontier with Germany. He recorded in his Memoirs the appalling conditions in which Jewish refugees – some old and ill – were living in crude shelters, improvised from tarpaulins, in no-man's-land, as they were refused admittance into Czechoslovakia. On his return to Prague, Layton saw President Hacha, who had taken over after Beneš had resigned, to press strongly that the refugees in no-man's-land must be allowed to enter Czechoslovakia. After some delay, permission was given.

By that time the scale of the problem was clearer. There were about

15,000 Sudeten Germans in danger because they had been anti-Nazi and about 1,000 other refugees (mostly Jewish from Nazi Germany). There were also about 700 Jewish refugees from Sudetenland marooned in great distress in no-man's-land between the new frontiers. But a further 20,000 Jewish refugees were trying to get out of the Sudetenland.

On his third visit in December, Layton found that there was great fear among the refugees that they would be sent back to the Sudetenland, now German territory. The foreign minister reassured him that the Czech government did not intend using their right under the Munich Agreement to return refugees to Germany at the end of December. But later he told the British Ambassador that he had meant to say that the Czech government would not send back those refugees who were in danger. As the Czech government were the sole judges about which individuals were in danger, this did nothing to calm the fears of refugees, who found the period of waiting – often without any real help from the authorities – an agonizing experience.

Emigration started in the autumn but at a very slow rate, since few visas were made available by recipient countries except for the United Kingdom. Layton received many appeals for help and did his best to speed things up, but the Czech government was weak, frightened of the Germans and inefficient. The refugees knew that the British government and others had put up a lot of money and could not understand why more could not be done quickly. The need to get individual sponsors in Western countries before a visa could be granted made for very slow progress and the British Legation in Prague did not help by denying that the situation was serious.

Layton knew that progress that winter would be slow, though plans were being made for large-scale emigration in the spring, particularly if the outflow through Poland, which had started, could be maintained. It was this route that the British Committee used effectively up to the outbreak of war in 1939, when many hundreds of refugees were trapped between the German and Russian armies. In the end many refugees failed to escape, but Layton's ability to act as go-between for the Czech and British governments, while also being able to mobilize British public opinion, meant that many more were saved than would otherwise have happened. The Czech government used the British £4 million gift to help 1,500 refugees to emigrate.

A new situation arose after the German entry into Prague on 15 March. Many additional anti-Nazi or Jewish Czechs were then in danger. But the work went on although the Czech authorities were then completely dominated by the Germans. The British Committee had exhausted its voluntary funds by March 1939 but then used official funds until the Czech Refugee Trust Fund, a Treasury-financed body under Sir Henry Bunbury, was set up in July 1939. By that time the British Committee, which had grown into a complex and efficient organization of over 100 paid staff and a considerable number of volunteers, had brought 7,000 refugees to the UK, some several hundred of whom had been sent on to Canada. The committee had also run a special scheme for children which managed to bring 669 to England between March and August 1939.

Although Layton spent a lot of time in the last quarter of 1938 on Czech refugees, his normal busy life went on very much as usual. He ceased being editor of the *Economist* in October but the *News Chronicle* absorbed any time so freed. The *News Chronicle* policy conferences which he had started earlier that year became more frequent, attended by Laurence Cadbury, Gerald Barry, Robin Cruickshank (editor of the *Star*), A.J. Cummings, Vernon Bartlett and Ivor Bulmer-Thomas (later to become first a Labour then a Conservative MP). Layton was thus in a better position to control policy.

Some of the staff resented this control but most recognized that Layton was a good man to work for. Vernon Bartlett, who spent most of his time from 1934 onwards working abroad, agreed with the general view that such weaknesses as Layton had were derived from his basic 'goodness':

> I remember one day, and one day only – we were both in Berlin and he wanted to see Ribbentrop. He was supposed to telephone to fix a date, and I happened to notice the time when first he went to the telephone. It took him just over 46 minutes before he actually lifted the receiver.

> I'd got very impatient, but what a small complaint to keep in one's mind.... On that dreadful day in Munich, when Chamberlain and others had informed the Czechs the terms imposed upon them, I finally got to bed in my hotel at about 2 a.m. I had telephoned my very depressing story to the N.C. (the article which, I suppose, led Sir Richard Acland and others to suggest that I should stand as an Independent candidate in the forthcoming Bridgwater election). The effect of this article was so depressing that Walter said it couldn't be used in the N.C., but Gerald Barry and other important members of the N.C. staff said the paper would not be printed without the article from its special correspondent. Walter gave way, and my article was printed in full. I, of course, knew nothing of all this. After one of the most tiring, physically and mentally, days of my life, I got to sleep, and almost immediately I was brought back to reality by a telephone call from Walter who said 'Well, Vernon, now what do you think about it all?' Apparently my only answer was 'Fuck You' – not at all my normal reply, least of all to a man like Walter. He felt no resentment.[2]

Layton liked Gerald Barry as a man and their professional relations were good enough for Barry to remain editor for twelve years. But Barry himself was far more critical of Layton than were most of his staff. Barry, as editor, resented Layton supervising the leader writers and for overruling him on several occasions, particularly at the time of Munich. To some people on the paper Barry was a political lightweight and too much of a parlour socialist who was prepared to follow the fashionable leftwing line, both on home and overseas policy. He tended, too, to take up causes such as the lack of strategic roads and the need for windscreen wipers on trains, and then run them to death.

Barry's resentment against Layton did not erupt until near the end of the war, when in December 1944 he wrote Layton a letter maintaining that Layton had been wrong in forcing the *News Chronicle*, against Barry's judgement, to pull its punches. He had been wrong, for instance, in not printing the Henlein leaflet about Hitler's future plans on the eve of the Munich Agreement. He had been wrong, too, in stopping Willie Forrest's article 'From Mukden to Munich' just because the Prime Minister had received a great national welcome and the *News Chronicle* must be careful. Barry went on:

> There was also the night of the Munich news itself, when the Bartlett story came in and you questioned its accuracy, wishing me to whittle it down till I suggested to you that it would thus lose all its validity, that we ought to trust our man on the spot specially sent and that rather than garble it we had

better cut it out altogether. Our leaders following Munich bear witness to my contention. V.B. said the agreement was regarded as an almost complete capitulation to Hitler. Our leader that morning started off by saying the whole world would 'heave a deep sigh of relief', and that the first thought of millions would be one of 'profound thankfulness'. Lower down we talked of 'grave defects' and 'severe criticism', though we ended by saying 'the agreement had saved great numbers of innocent Czechs from war'. It is very difficult at this distance of time to recall with exactitude the events of those days, but I have to confess that my recollection and that of my colleagues is that during the critical days of that humiliating period we were obliged to hold in our horses and – if I may mix my metaphors – back-pedal.

Ivor Bulmer-Thomas, a leader writer just before the war, agreed that Layton was not a good journalist in the sense that he could not take decisions quickly on inadequate evidence by hunch rather than by reasoned argument. Layton's problem was that he could see every side of a question and his own contributions reflected this uncertainty, which was particularly evident on the night of Munich:

That night, exceptionally, Layton thought it was his duty to come into the office and settle the leader with us. We discussed and discussed from every angle, while edition after edition went out without any leader on the subject and when it did appear, in the latest editions, it was too indecisive to have any value. What was needed at that moment from the *News Chronicle* was a blast like Churchill's in the debate in the House of Commons a few days later, 'A total and unmitigated defeat'.[3]

The younger men on the editorial staff seem to have liked Layton. Mervyn Herbert found he had no difficulty in spanning the generation gap. While like others Herbert was at first disconcerted by Layton's silences, he put the habit down to Layton wishing to concentrate while his mind turned over fast. Donald Hodson, who was on the *News Chronicle* just before the war, remembers Layton's determination to get things right. He recollects that once at the time of the Munich crisis Layton:

came into the office and told me he wanted to write a long special article leader of 2/3,000 words – that is the whole page. However, the head printer, not an easy man, exploded when I told him. ... Layton seemed quite unaffected by the printer's rage and indifferent to the technical problems he was creating. He produced a mass of alterations and corrections through the evening, and the page was replated for every edition. I (and

Layton) finally left the office at about 3.30 am. Throughout he was polite and friendly, and tacitly assumed that we would understand that technical difficulties and printing schedules were of no importance compared with what he was writing. Of course, he was right and I think I learned something from the experience.[4]

The Coming War

Layton and the rest of the *News Chronicle* staff were delighted when Vernon Bartlett won the Bridgwater by-election in November 1938 from the Tories as an Independent, campaigning on the policies he had been expounding in the *News Chronicle* as diplomatic correspondent. From Layton's point of view, Vernon Bartlett's victory was the only goods news, apart from the birth of his first grandchild, for a long time. He was in the United States and France in early 1939 and found little but gloom about the international outlook. Then came the takeover of the whole of Czechoslovakia by Hitler in March 1939 and Mussolini's invasion of Albania in April.

Like many Liberals, Layton believed that Hitler could only be restrained if the Anglo-French guarantee of Poland was backed by Russia. In this he was strengthened by his talks with Maisky, who went on advocating such an agreement until the Ribbentrop–Molotov pact of August. However, Layton was worried because Maisky seemed determined that Britain should make all the concessions in the negotiations with the Russians.

The *News Chronicle* policy conferences – now weekly – form a good record of the period. In April they were agonizing over conscription – on the whole against – unless wealth was conscripted too. Layton wanted the formation of a national Cabinet led by Halifax, which would include Lloyd George.

In May the Labour Party Conference turned down the idea of a Popular Front, thus making constituency agreements impossible. So the *News Chronicle* policy conference decided that as many Liberal candidates as possible ought to be put up at the next election, expected to take place the following autumn, with the prospect of Chamberlain then winning a larger majority. In June there was some apprehension about the planned Ministry of Information that would be necessary in wartime being headed by Lord Perth (Layton's old boss at the League of Nations when he was Sir Eric Drummond). The Germans were reported as planning to retake the Cameroons. There was talk of Winston Churchill coming back into the Cabinet. The question was whether such an appointment would do anything to restrain Hitler. By late July, Layton was ruling that the *News Chronicle* should give as much space as possible to the new militia (the 18–20 years old age group was in the process of being called up) but without any implied glorification of war. The idea was to strengthen the idea of service. The leader on 4 August, the twenty-fifth anniversary of the Great War, was to underline the menacing nature of the situation but point out the grounds for hope since all countries were aware of the horrors of war. When the Ribbentrop–Molotov pact came on 22 August, Gerald Barry and Vernon Bartlett were in favour of Poland being advised to negotiate, but Layton and Laurence Cadbury thought that any such advice would be to undermine Polish confidence in the British guarantee.

War was now inevitable and Layton concentrated on how best the country might mobilize its resources. He had, for some time, been keeping in touch with those who were concerned with the rearmament programme, and drawing on his experience of the Ministry of Munitions in the First World War, was ready with his advice when war broke out on 3 September 1939.

CHAPTER ELEVEN

Arms and the Plan for Total War, 1940–3

The Phoney War

For Layton, as for a great many other people, life was surprisingly normal and yet rather unreal in the months following the outbreak of war on 3 September 1939. The expected air raids did not happen for nearly a year, and the sun shone on London from a peaceful blue sky nearly every day and all day during the first few weeks of the war. There never was such a beautiful September.

Like many of his friends, Layton longed for a government job which would make use of his considerable First World War experience. But except for a request for a paper on munitions from Hore Belisha, the Secretary of State for War, no summons to Whitehall came until Churchill became Prime Minister. In spite of Layton's hesitations at the time of Munich, the *News Chronicle* was judged too trenchant a critic of Chamberlain for him to be trusted with real responsibility.

So Layton continued to run the *News Chronicle*, but found some solace in the meetings of the 'Old Dogs' group, consisting of Keynes, Salter, Beveridge and Hubert Henderson, who by that time was in the Treasury. The group met weekly to discuss ideas about how the country might best prepare itself for war. It is not clear whether Keynes or Layton suggested regular meetings, but already on 7 September Layton was writing to Salter to say that Keynes, who was gradually recovering from a serious heart attack, would very much like a talk at his house in Gordon Square. In spite of still being convalescent, Keynes produced several papers in the following six weeks on price policy, on the financial principles of the blockade, on wheat as contraband, and the first sketch of his postwar credit scheme.[1]

Beveridge put in a paper on contraband and Salter proposed that a reciprocal arrangement should be negotiated with the German government, by which certain essential foodstuffs, especially wheat, should be exempted from the blockade and counter-blockade. Keynes agreed with the idea of exempting wheat from the British blockade on Germany on the curiously mercantilist ground that it would use up Germany's foreign exchange and because it would humanize the war a little and, perhaps, make bombing of civilian populations less likely. It would also have a favourable effect on opinion in neutral countries, since we could not be accused of starving innocent women and children. But more realistic than Salter, he finished his paper by saying: 'We should not get reciprocity if we ask for it, and we should lose the psychological gain that we are seeking of showing the neutrals that we behave differently from Germany.'[2]

Layton's contribution was on war aims. In particular, he outlined a proposal for a postwar settlement in Europe by which there would be two regional federations of Scandinavia and Central Europe in order to strengthen the small countries, but with a European Association to keep the peace through a mutual assistance pact and the pooling of national air forces under an international authority. It was the first sketch for a united Europe and for a Human Rights Convention on which Layton was to spend so much time and energy after the war. Keynes liked Layton's paper and went on to comment in a letter to Layton of 30 October:

> 1. The French point of view must be taken into account. A dangerous veil of separation is forming between British and French public opinion.
> 2. I have never been so much of a League of Nations man as you. But my plan for the future would include the constitution of a European league on pretty drastic lines.
> 3. What about a third federation, comprising the Baltic states, Poland, Bohemia and Slovakia?
> 4. I am sure the French would be happier if there were a fourth federation of the Rhineland (permanently dimilitarised) Germany, East Prussia and Austria.

5. The constitution of these various federations would greatly help the balance of power in my new European league.

In November, Keynes's sketch for postwar credits was published in *The Times* and Layton published his Allied War Aims in the *News Chronicle*. He had anticipated Keynes's advice by asking Paul Mantoux to keep him informed about French war aims. According to Mantoux the French were well behind the British in postwar planning. Layton himself, however, persisted by commissioning Madame Mantoux to send him cuttings from the French Press about French war aims. She could not find much material to send, and in a letter to the author, recalls ruefully how Layton was pressing her for yet more newspaper cuttings in May 1940, just when she and her husband were leaving Paris to escape the advancing German armies.

Work at the *News Chronicle* went on as normal, except that the paper shrank as newsprint became scarce. Indeed, Layton was soon appointed to the board of the Newsprint Supply Company set up at the start of the war, as the sole buyer of newsprint for all papers. Beaverbrook was the chairman and Rothermere the vice-chairman. Layton attended the Friday meetings of the board right through the war, and in 1945 he became the chairman of the Rationing Committee, because the other newspaper proprietors trusted him to be fair.

While waiting for a war job, Layton spent more time at the *News Chronicle*. His family had been evacuated to Twittens at the outbreak of war, but the railway journey from Sussex was too time-consuming. So in November he and Dorothy moved into a flat in Marsham Court, Westminster, and Brett House became a convalescent home for Czech refugees. A direct telephone line was installed between Marsham Court and the *News Chronicle* office so that Layton could always be kept in close touch.

To make more certain that his views prevailed in the leader columns, policy conferences at the *News Chronicle* were now held weekly. It was decided to oppose Lloyd George's arguments in favour of a negotiated armistice, to back Keynes's postwar credit scheme and to give space to Layton's war aims, which were also published as a pamphlet. For the rest Layton's views were understandably derived from his First World War experience. The demand for manpower from the Forces, the munitions industries and the Home Front should be properly balanced; equipment for the army should be speeded up; there should be a general plan for economic warfare, the blockade on Germany should be tightened and a clash with Russia over Finland avoided. Perhaps out of loyalty to his old chief, Lloyd George, Layton was prepared to support him in preference to Churchill as Chamberlain's successor in May 1940, always provided that Lloyd George had a strong team to support him. Layton believed that if Lloyd George took over it would have 'a terrificly heartening effect here and a correspondingly depressing effect on Germany'. Layton doubted that Churchill was up to his last war standards of efficiency. It is odd that he failed to observe that Lloyd George certainly was not.

Fortunately, Churchill got the job instead of Lloyd George, though Churchill offered him a place in his Cabinet, and Layton and the other 'Old Dogs' were all brought back into war work in the following few months. Layton recorded in his Memoirs:

> In May 1940 when Winston Churchill stepped into Neville Chamberlain's shoes, I sent him a short quotation from *The World Crisis* in which he refers to 'Sir James Stephenson, his close colleague Sir Arthur Duckham, and the young profound Professor Layton ... these three constituted for me the mainspring both of action and of review by which the central control of the immense organisation [the Ministry of Munitions] was exercised.' I added: 'The survivor of the three is still awaiting his marching orders.' Winston sent me back a message to say that Herbert Morrison would in all probability be the new Minister of Supply and he (Winston) would like me to give the new Minister the benefit of my experience. So there we were (from the Keynes group) – back again at last.

The Ministry of Supply was to prove the place where Layton could best use his talents and experience. There had been a proposal for him to go to the Air Ministry as Director of Statistics, but that would have been far too narrow a job. Churchill also offered him a peerage so he might become a junior minister, but Layton preferred to become Director-General of Programmes at the Ministry of Supply, a Civil Service job.

Layton in Whitehall and Washington

While Layton got the job he wanted, it might have been depressing to have the task of building up Britain's armaments for the second time in his life, and this time almost from scratch, as so much had been lost at Dunkirk. But Layton showed no sign of depression, partly because of the satisfaction he felt in having a real job to do at last, and partly because he found himself working with old friends. Jean Monnet had been running the London end of the organization responsible for joint Anglo-French armament orders in North America. In the first half of June, he and Arthur Salter were preoccupied in persuading Churchill and the Cabinet to adopt their proposal for an Anglo-French Union, which might prevent the French armies surrendering. But Monnet also played his part when surrender seemed imminent, in getting French orders for munitions in North America transferred to the British. At that time Monnet was living in Arthur Salter's flat in London. Salter himself was shortly to become the chairman of the new North American Supplies Committee in London. Layton was thus well placed to assess the armaments position in so far as this was possible in the confusion following Dunkirk.

He saw to it too that his small staff in the Ministry of Supply was strengthened by the recruitment of people he knew, such as Geoffrey Crowther. He was glad to find that Hugh Weeks, who had run Cadbury's statistics at Bournville, had been at work on Supply statistics since early in the war. Already on 4 June, a day or two after he had taken up his job, Layton was writing minutes to Herbert Morrison, the Minister of Supply, reporting that the BEF had been compelled to leave practically the whole of its fighting equipment, except for some rifles, in the retreat to Dunkirk. Some 880 field guns had been lost as against only about 400 still available in England. Similarly, 852 anti-tank guns had been lost while the stock in England was only 120. In effect, the artillery available in England was mostly of old First World War type, and the army's position as regards munitions was very grim. Perhaps the only consolation was that even if the army had not been driven out of France, the supplies of ammunition available would have been totally inadequate to support continuous action against the enemy.

The situation was slightly eased a few weeks later by the Americans selling Britain 600,000 First World War Springfield rifles. These were of the wrong calibre, being .300 rather than the .303 used by the British army, but at least they armed the local defence volunteers, as they were then called (later the Home Guard). Layton took great interest in this transaction, since he had been involved during the First World War in the vain attempt to get the Americans to use British rifles. Instead, they decided to make their own Springfield rifles, which could only be produced after a long delay through having to change over from British-type machinery. In the event, the American troops fighting in France in 1918 had to be issued with British rifles, but now at last the Springfields manufactured at that time were being of some use.

At times, from his minutes of this period, it looks as if Layton was fighting the First World War over again, since he often referred to production figures in 1918. In fact these figures were useful in putting the very doubtful estimates in the production forecasts up to 1941 into some sort of perspective. It was essential to get a complete view of the munitions situation as quickly as possible. Layton and his staff achieved this by the end of August, when he gave Morrison a paper for Cabinet.[3] This was the first of a long series of comprehensive papers which he produced in order to focus the strategic decisions ministers had to take. Layton must have been satisfied with this highly secret Cabinet paper, which set out the precise position of the army's equipment at the time and the supplies coming forward in the next few months, since he kept three copies together with a number of Ministry of Supply files. Indeed, it is remarkable that a conscientious and, presumably, security-minded man should have hoarded so many secret papers and taken them away with him when he left government service in June 1943, still in the middle of the war. Perhaps he wanted them for the autobiography he hoped to write some day.

This first paper was short and clear. It showed the progress in rearming the army since Dunkirk, the forces that could be deployed by Germany, and Germany's war potential in terms of steel production compared with that of the UK. It went on to set out the UK production programme of guns and tanks and ammunition, and the scale of armaments likely to be available from North America, ending with a review of the raw material and labour situation.

The next step was to give the Americans a full exposition of UK requirements needed to meet immediate shortages and to provide some insurance against damage to production that would result from the heavy bombing the Luftwaffe was expected to inflict in the coming months. It was also very probable that the Germans would attempt some invasion by land which would have to be repelled.

There had already been a number of special missions sent to Washington, where Arthur Purvis, an outstanding businessman who had run ICI's Canadian companies, was in charge of the British Purchasing Commission, but these were concerned with the details of the three services' individual needs. The time had come to give both the United States and Canadian governments a comprehensive view covering the coordinated needs of all three countries' forces.

Arthur Salter was convinced that Layton was the right man for the job. He wrote on 19 August to Herbert Morrison, who was reluctant to be without Layton's help in London, that there was not anyone else available with the right personal qualities, experience and authority: 'Taking into account the absolutely vital importance of the USA as our second arsenal, and the present critical stage here, I want to appeal to you to agree to Walter Layton going practically at once, at whatever inconvenience.' After some hesitation Morrison agreed that Layton should go just for a month with instructions from the War Cabinet that he should give the US government a general picture of the British supply of munitions and requirements, report on the manufacture of munitions in the United States and put forward proposals about how the British Purchasing Commission might best be reorganized.

Layton left London by train in the late afternoon of 6 September when the sky was darkened by great clouds of smoke from the burning London docks. At Waterloo Station the flames from the docks gleamed on the glass of the station roof. In spite of air raid warnings, Dorothy came to see him off. Next morning, while waiting for the flying boat at Poole in which he was to fly to Lisbon on his way to Washington, Layton and his three colleagues heard the church bells being rung to call out the local defence volunteers all round the coast. It seemed that invasion was imminent. He wrote to Dorothy from Lisbon two days later:

> Field and I both have a horrible feeling of running away at a critical moment. But that's a prompting of the heart rather than the head and orders are orders. Nevertheless, I shall be thinking of you day and night. I feel

singularly unable to give you any advice as to what you should do; but I imagine you will go back to Twittens and find someone who may want asylum. One thing I am certain of and that is that in any crisis your great contribution will be that you will keep your head. That is enormously important. Whatever other defects the family may have, I don't believe anyone of us would ever panic. I am sure one and all will show the poise that I should wish to show if I were with you.

Layton had to spend ten agonizing days at Lisbon waiting for the flying boat service, which was disrupted by weather, and cut off from any contact with England other than the BBC news at the height of the Battle of Britain. He wrote to Dorothy that he would have returned to London if he could, but later letters show that he had overcome any guilt feelings of leaving her just when the danger really threatened.

I suppose I ought to have a guilty feeling at leaving you all to face the music without being at your side. But to my surprise that idea does not register. You all have your parts to play and will I know play them with pride and courage. I have my marching orders and will carry them out to the very best of my ability.

Layout spent one afternoon writing out from memory a statement of his finances, so that Dorothy should know how much would be available if he were killed. He estimated his total assets before death duties at about £35,000 plus an *ex gratia* payment that could be expected from the government if he died on active service. There would also be an annuity of about £800 a year. Layton had managed his finances prudently but, although comfortably off, he was not a rich man. He sent the statement under cover of a letter saying he had heard that a bomb had missed (his secretary) Gwyneth's flat by twenty feet. 'Do tell her she can take refuge in Marsham Court if it gets bad. It is better built than her ramshackle house in Pimlico.'

Each morning Layton and the rest of his team packed their bags in the hope of being able to get away at dawn and then two hours later returned to their hotel. Eventually, however, he got a plane via the Azores and Bermuda and landed at New York. Although he was ten days late, he managed to find time to see his ten-year-old son Christopher, who had been evacuated from London early in the war. Walter reported to Dorothy:

Christopher, who had not been told I was coming, looked very well. A tinge of red round the eyes from excitement which quite went off after lunch. He took me out onto the cliff to explore the grounds and when we sat down on the warm turf he buried his face in my shoulder and held me tight for about ten minutes. Then all was well, and for the rest of the day he was his normal self. He was wearing a 'Vote For Roosevelt' button. No tears at my departure.

Throughout Layton's stay in Washington he could send messages to Dorothy through telegrams and telephone calls via Arthur Salter, so though his return was delayed week by week until Christmas, he could keep in some sort of touch with his family. He was thus in a favoured position compared to most people.

Layton got to Washington on 20 September and started work quickly with Arthur Purvis, Jean Monnet and Lord Lothian, then British Ambassador, whom he had known as Philip Kerr when they were both on Lloyd George's staff in the First World War. Lothian had also worked with Layton on the Liberal *Yellow Book* and was a keen exponent of federal union in Europe just before the war, when he wrote a book called *The Ending of Armageddon*. Although Lothian had been prominent as an appeaser of Hitler, which may have led Chamberlain to appoint him Ambassador in Washington, he had remained one of Layton's close friends.

Layton's first task was to draft, with Monnet and Purvis's advice, a general memorandum about British needs for Morgenthau, the Secretary of the Treasury, designated by President Roosevelt as the man with whom the British should deal. But before Layton got down to detailed business with Morgenthau he had half an hour's talk with President Roosevelt on 27 September. He recorded how Roosevelt asked for weekly reports about relative needs for fighters and bombers, and understandably was thinking in the short term. After all, it was not yet known whether the Germans would invade England or not. Layton, however, emphasized that the critical time would be the following spring and summer. It was essential to get as quick delivery as possible for orders already placed, but a strategic plan for beating Germany had to be worked out. 'The President interrupted with the remark "Starve them out". The Germans, he said, were not like "us"; they would hold out to a certain point and then break down completely, whereas "we" would give way only gradually. He had always urged that we should bomb the Germans everywhere, not merely at a few major points.'[4]

The full submission to Morgenthau was ready by 2 October. It was a masterly summary of the strategic position, assessing the balance of strength between Britain and Germany until the end of 1941. It set out the immediate orders to be filled to meet deficiencies and to provide insurance against bombing. But the paper also made it clear that the integration of the British programme with that of the United States was necessary to prevent duplication and to lead to the speediest growth of America's war potential. The paper was, in effect, the outcome of the piecemeal ordering of arms that had taken place since Dunkirk, all on a short-term horizon, and a debate about the longer term between Purvis, Monnet and Salter on the one hand and the Ministry of Supply and the Treasury on the other.

Purvis and Monnet wanted joint planning with the Americans which would build up US arms capacity for the long-term benefit of both the British and the Americans. In 1940 the United States arms industry was small; it was virtually three years behind Britain's. There were few armaments that could be bought off the shelf or from current production, since the United States, too, was building up its forces. Purvis saw that American rearmament was the United Kingdom's opportunity in the long run, but it had to be on a really big scale. It was wrong to order only what could be afforded at the time. The UK and US programmes must be complementary, so as to draw the United States in the direction of alliance. American capacity must be developed to the maximum regardless of the use to which the munitions might ultimately be put. As Salter wrote: 'The products will be available for our war effort, if by us – good; if by the Americans themselves – better still.'[5] This thinking was dependent on a belief that the Americans were most likely to enter the war within a year or so. Indeed, Monnet made this belief explicit on several occasions and Duncan Hall has written: 'From November 1939 to March 1941 Morgenthau and Purvis worked almost as closely together as two Ministers in the same Cabinet.'[6]

The Ministry of Supply in London was reluctant to follow this line.

It went against the grain to order beyond the army's stated requirements and without regard to the amount of dollars available. Moreover, if the Americans were encouraged to produce armaments on a rapidly increasing scale, existing British orders would suffer as scarce machine tools and raw materials were switched to US needs. Also there was bound to be uncertainty in September 1940 as to whether the United States would come into the war, or if they did, whether they would allocate the arms the British needed. In any case, the United States production targets were a matter of faith. Actual production was low.

Naturally cautious, and responsible as he was for trying to meet the army's immediate needs, Layton tried to find a way through these conflicting arguments. His advice before leaving London was that: 'To get a substantial output from the United States we must either a) adopt a common type of weapon and share in a joint programme, or b) get the goodwill of the Americans in helping forward such orders of British types as they agree should run parallel with their own orders.' In fact, Layton found when he got to Washington that the Americans were not prepared to adopt British types of weapon for their own use and were most reluctant to manufacture them except for a few weapons such as rifles, anti-tank guns and medium artillery. Their view was that to manufacture British types would hold back total production of all kinds. Layton's thinking, therefore, came more into line with that of Purvis, Salter and Monnet. In Washington that autumn, once it was clear that the Americans would not provide more British-type weapons than the small range agreed, the way out of the impasse was for American-type equipment to be ordered for an additional force of, say, ten divisions, the arms to be allotted either to American or British Commonwealth divisions as the course of the war dictated once they had become available by early 1942. Layton records in his Memoirs that this idea was put to him by an American industrialist. It was, in fact, a revival of a proposal tentatively submitted by Purvis in June,[7] but which had never been seriously considered by the British Government. However, by October it suited the Americans who, by their own orders, were creating capacity considerably greater than was needed for the scale of production they could afford with the existing funds at their disposal. If the British were prepared to take American-type armaments, the capacity could be more economically employed and they could be given the priorities they needed for deliveries.

Layton was quick to see the great advantage of this scheme, which had emerged at a meeting on 23 October. He at once went to see Stimson, the Secretary for War, who had with him General Marshall, the Chief of Staff, to find out whether the equipment for the ten divisions would be ready by the end of 1941 and whether, subsequently, priority would be given to allocating supplies to the ten divisions and maintaining them in the field. General Marshall gave assurances on both points, even though it might mean allocating nearly the whole of the new output for American weapons while American divisions at home were still equipped with old weapons. Layton then sent a telegram to Churchill asking for approval, in principle, for the scheme:

> I have pointed out that such a scheme means that the United States would in fact be equipping an expeditionary force equal in size to the British Expeditionary Force of May last but with its supply base in the United States, and that the British General Staff could only make plans on such a basis if there were the clearest undertaking (a) that the amount of armament involved would be forthcoming at the times indicated (b) that a force so equipped, wherever it might operate, must be continuously provisioned from the United States and (c) that in allocating output between the United States Army and such a force, the latter must have absolute priority to the fullest extent of its military needs. . . .
>
> The scheme has strategic attractions. Such a force might suitably be based in Canada and could be available for direct transportation to Africa or to the East. . . .
>
> You can assess for yourselves the chances whether this equipment will in fact be used by American or British Expeditionary Forces. In the latter event, the fact that orders are placed in the name of Great Britain would be important in ensuring that the War Department's suggestions should be carried into effect.
>
> In view of the almost negligible character of the financial commitment involved, the scheme seems an excellent way either of speeding up America's rearmament or of giving us a free call on America's output which might prove exceptionally valuable to ourselves.

Churchill wrote 'Yes' on Layton's telegram but sent it to General Sir John Dill (CIGS at the time), who agreed rather grudgingly: 'It is better to have American equipment than none.' Churchill was much more enthusiastic in his reply to Layton on 28 October: 'This is splendid. We should, at once, accept offer. Action accordingly.'[8] He recognized that while Britain would not have the manpower for an additional ten divisions, the plan opened the way to a much larger American army in case of need.

Layton wrote to Churchill on 12 November:

Dear Winston,

I am glad you liked the 10 Division plan. It exactly fits the present temper here, it pleases the soldiers, it is readily adapted to devices for avoiding large payments, it is elastic and it will have helped things forward if America comes into the war.

We cannot, however, assume that this last will happen in the near future. The country does not yet quite believe that this is America's war and it is a very alluring argument that if Hitler cannot cross 20 miles of Channel in Europe how can he hope to reach the USA across 2,000 miles of ocean. Hence the arguments that the country is not prepared for war and that for America to enter the war would prejudice help to Britain have become, even in the minds of our best friends, a justification for the election promises of both parties.

So for the present such devices as the 10 Division plan hold the field. If the temper of recent months persists these plans may in due course double or treble in size.

Indeed, short of sending men, the President and the country are, I think, ready to throw America's industrial resources into the balance on a very big scale indeed. But if this is to be done, we need to put before the Administration not a series of demands in terms of specific material, but a picture of what is required to win the war. For example, in order to be sure of victory in 1942 or 1943, we should need a front line strength of X-thousand planes, Y-flotillas of destroyers, so many cruisers, 50 additional Army divisions, 3,000,000 tons of new merchant ships, and so on. America loves record-breaking figures and will not be frightened by the scale of any such statement, and in due course there is much to be said for announcing some figures, both for the benefit of the American public, which would like to feel they were up against something which will really test their capacity, and for Mr Hitler's edification.

The President also needs something of the kind, both as a focus for the policy of the Administration and also in order to be able to put over the necessary interference with a peacetime production. This could, of course, most readily be done by a declaration of war, but as this is not probable in the near future the next best thing is that of a very simple and big programme which is disclosed to the public. The President has

> in fact to get the country to accept war time restrictions and a war budget without actually being at war, and this is by no means an easy task.
>
> He must, however, get to work quickly. The public are in the mood to do something for the war. For example, they will collect their aluminium pots and pans with the greatest enthusiasm. But if their activities are not quickly developed there is real danger of the agitation for feeding France, or the discussion of compromise peace terms, seizing public attention.
>
> The President's suggestion to Purvis about renting merchant ships (which I think came from London via Kennedy), is capable of many variations. For example, a Naval flotilla or the equipment for 10 or 20 divisions might be hired out at a reasonable figure, which might even in the end be a mere peppercorn rent – until such time as federation makes it common property.

Layton's letter points the way to two further developments then very much under discussion in Washington. First was the drawing up of a consolidated balance sheet showing the amount of combined UK and US production needed to win the war, and the second, how best to finance US arms supplies to Britain. As Layton suggested, it might be possible to hire them at a peppercorn rent.

These ideas took concrete shape soon through Arthur Purvis working out a balance sheet showing the armaments needed by Britain to defeat the enemy, the expected output of British production in 1941/42 and the deficiencies to be made good by the United States if the war was to be won. A little later President Roosevelt came out in favour of Lend-Lease, which solved the financial problem. Layton certainly did not claim that he played a great part in originating either of these ideas, which were of the greatest importance in the winning of the war. Indeed, Monnet wrote to Salter on 15 November very much on the lines of Layton's letter to Churchill and it was Monnet to whom, perhaps, most credit for the balance sheet idea should be given since he was thinking on these lines from the beginning of the war, though, at first, only in an Anglo-French context.

It seems that the proposals, as worked out in a form acceptable to both the British and United States governments, emerged from discussions between a group of very able men on both sides of the

Atlantic, through a ceaseless exchange of telegrams, supplemented by visits such as Layton carried out in spite of very uncertain air communications. New ideas were tested in continuous discussion. It was fortunate that Monnet came to Washington in August to join Purvis just before Layton arrived and that Salter was in charge in London. All four men tended to think on the same lines. On the American side both Morgenthau and Stimson were helpful, and both sets of negotiators were backed up by exceptionally able younger men. On the British side there was Hugh Weeks, R.W.B. Clarke, Geoffrey Crowther, Austin Robinson, Eric Roll and Harry Campion; and an outstanding economics section in the Cabinet Office under Lionel Robbins, including James Meade and Richard Stone. On the US side there were Stacy May and Robert Nathan (both expert in presenting figures), and Lincoln Gordon, who proved extremely able in the allocation of raw materials.

In Washington, Monnet played a leading part through his skill as a simplifier (some people thought he oversimplified) of seminal ideas which he then managed to inject into the White House through having the right contacts. Layton, like Monnet, was a simplifier of ideas and knew how to present them in a striking way. He also had the great advantage of being trusted in Whitehall, both by Churchill and Beaverbrook. He in his turn trusted Monnet, and in November 1940 was pressing Salter to see that Monnet was appointed vice-chairman of the British Supply Council in Washington, in spite of being a French citizen. Monnet himself recorded in his Memoirs his appreciation of the people with whom he worked in Washington: 'Their blend of ability and enthusiasm enabled them to take the measure of a situation where everyone else was baffled, to invent ingenious machinery which no one else had thought of or to act as a link between two incompatible national systems.'[9]

Although Layton got Churchill's ready agreement to the ten division plan, to run in parallel with a programme of orders for British-type weapons, and the President had virtually committed himself to these programmes in an election campaign speech on 30 October, inevitably there were second thoughts in Washington about the conditions to be attached to both programmes. As is still true today, it has always been difficult to know whether an agreement reached with a given government department in Washington will, in fact, stick. These difficulties kept Layton in Washington all through November, and he was there to help in the drafting of the Prime Minister's long letter of 7 December to the President which set out the war position as Churchill saw it and showed how the United States, though non-belligerent, could help bring victory in a common cause. The letter left the problem of how to finance the enormous amount of supplies that Britain required firmly with the President to solve.

In October Layton had visited Ottawa for talks about Canadian supplies and had delivered a speech Lothian was to have made in Boston. He had also seen his son Christopher again at school in New York, and arranged for him to go to Arthur Purvis's house in the mountains above Montreal to ski at Christmas. He had written frequently to Dorothy, telling her he expected to be back in a few days, but there were always postponements. In the end it was a question whether he could get home by Christmas. There were no places on ships or on the flying boats. The only chance was to fly in a flight of stripped-down Hudson bombers, being ferried from Gander in Newfoundland.

Layton's journey home was overshadowed by Lothian's sudden death. Lothian had returned from London to the Embassy (where Layton was still staying) in poor health. He would go to sleep at meals and leave Layton and Purvis to deal with his guests. By 8 December he had become worse and asked Layton to act as host for a dinner party for Sir Walter Citrine the following night. Next morning Lothian had partially collapsed. Layton asked whether a doctor was coming but was told that, as Lothian was a Christian Scientist, a healer was being summoned from Boston. He wondered whether he should stay but Lothian pressed him to go, taking personal messages to London. So he left by train for Montreal, which was under deep snow, and flew on to Gander in a blizzard. There he heard that Lothian had died earlier that day. Richard Casey (the Australian representative in Washington) had persuaded the healer to agree to a doctor being called, but Lothian died before he arrived.

Layton was very moved by Lothian's death and took the trouble to give a detailed account of Lothian's last few days to his relations and friends. He also reproached himself for not having insisted on a doctor being called earlier, although Lord Horder comforted him by saying that it seemed to him that Lothian could not have been saved at that late stage. The disease that killed him, uraemia, was too far advanced.

Layton had to wait five days at Gander until the seven Hudson bombers due to be ferried in one flight were ready. He spent this time drafting his report to Cabinet. The following extract gives its main thrust:

> ... neither the United States Administration nor our own Departments have fully realised the scale of assistance which has to be obtained from the United States. There has been a disposition on our side to regard America as a shop from which we can buy munitions, instead of as a country which has to be mobilized industrially in the same way that England and Germany have been mobilized. Our requirements have hitherto been stated in terms which are limited by our own financial possibilities or by our man power. In other words, except in the case of the aircraft programme, they have been supplementary to our own programmes. America's own orders, on the other hand, have been on the comparatively moderate scale required to put its defences in a reasonable condition. We have not asked the United States nor has Congress authorized the Administration to produce munitions on the scale needed to overwhelm Germany and win the war. The Prime Minister's recent letter to the President fills in the picture in many important particulars, but even that statement does not set out in terms the full contribution required from the United States in 1942.[10]

He had a cold flight to Northern Ireland in an unheated plane with one small green camp bed in an empty fuselage. The only source of heat was a tiny hole close to his head, through which warm air came from the engine. The only way he could benefit was to hold a gauntlet over the hole until it was full of hot air and then hastily plunge in his hand. The plane in which he flew landed at Aldergrove after a ten-hour flight. It took him another thirty frustrating hours to reach London, but he was in time to spend Christmas with his family.

Layton, after his three months' absence, got down to work quickly at the Ministry of Supply, where first Sir Andrew Duncan and then Beaverbrook became Minister; Macmillan was still Parliamentary Secretary. Layton, however, maintained his direct line to Churchill, sending a personal letter about Lothian's death. In the same letter he recorded his doubts about Roosevelt's stamina because of his frequent periods of inertia and enclosed a note about ways of winning the war. This note turned out to be a pretty accurate forecast of what happened in the following three years.[11] The real purpose of the letter was to emphasize the need for supplying Roosevelt, who did not read reports, with a simple statement of the arms, ships and aircraft needed up to the end of 1942 to win the war.

The pressure on Layton stayed high for the next two years, at the end of which he became quite seriously ill. During the first of these years he remained at the Ministry of Supply. Then in February 1942 he moved to the new Ministry of Production as head of the Joint War Planning Staff. Even before falling ill in January 1943 he had come to feel that he had broadly done what he could to get war production on the right lines and that he wished to resign, so as to recover his ability to speak his mind in public. His resignation took effect in June 1943.

In these two years much was achieved. In early 1941 Lend-Lease was introduced, in June Russia became an ally, and in December the United States entered the war, having been an ally in all but name during the previous eighteen months. These events gave the assurance of ultimate victory provided the Allies did not make too many mistakes. But so far as production of armaments was concerned supplies were still slender in 1941 and did not begin to be adequate until towards the end of 1942. United Kingdom and Canadian production was rising in 1941 and together was much higher than that of the United States, where production got into its stride in 1942 but did not match its potential until 1943 and 1944.

So Layton's work went on at a high pitch, directed at increasing production as much as possible within the limits of available sources of labour and raw materials. The extent to which the gap could be filled by swift mobilization of the United States economy was a constant preoccupation. That Layton, who, though determined, was no thruster, was able to have considerable influence both on home and inter-Allied policy was due quite as much to the able young men he chose to work for him as to his long-standing close links with Churchill, Beaverbrook, Monnet and Salter. Most of these young men were puzzled about what to make of Walter, who came to the Ministry of Supply with a great reputation dating back to the Ministry of Munitions in the First World War.

Geoffrey Crowther was an exception, having known Layton well from the *Economist* and *News Chronicle*. But he divided his time between the Ministry of Supply, the *Economist* and the Ministry of Information. Being an excellent expositor, he put many of Walter's ideas into order, but he was no originator. He went with Layton to the Ministry of Production and resigned about the same time as Layton. The crucial people from Layton's point of view were Hugh Weeks, who succeeded Layton as Director-General of Programmes at both the Ministry of Supply and the Ministry of Production, R.W.B. Clarke, a brilliant economist and mathematician who had been on the *Financial News* and was later to become a senior Treasury official, and Austin Robinson, an outstanding Cambridge economist who joined Layton at the Ministry of Production in 1942 from the economics section in the Cabinet Office. All three found Layton's famous silences disconcerting at first, as well as his habit of suddenly switching to a different topic. Later they discovered that, through knowing how Layton's mind worked, they could interpret these eccentricities.

Weeks thought that Layton's failure at times to get on with other people was due not so much to his silences or lack of small talk, as to his quickness of mind. He upset people, too, by exposing slipshod thinking and was sometimes in conflict with the Ministry of Supply departmental view because of his long-term synoptic approach to major problems. He depressed Weeks at first by asking for a wide range of statistics, the need for which had never occurred to him, but later put things right by complimenting Weeks on his work. He could always spot a wrong figure in a table with unerring accuracy but did not rub it in. He was highly skilled in getting facts and figures from other departments and used these to get Weeks to improve the Ministry of Supply's own statistics greatly.

Armed with accurate statistics, Layton knew that he had a good chance of standing up to other departments, and in particular to Professor Lindemann, the head of the Prime Minister's statistical section, who was, in effect, Churchill's gadfly. Harold Macmillan remembers fights with Lindemann over statistics: 'Much argument, much tribulation and sometimes recrimination followed. Walter Layton, in spite of his apparent shyness, was usually able to hold his own, though apt to be overpowered by the Prof's occasional Johnsonian tactics.'[12]

Layton recognized R.W.B. Clarke's great ability, both as a thinker and as a draftsman, and they got on well from the moment he joined the Ministry of Supply in April 1941. Clarke's main task was to discuss at length with Layton possible courses of action and then to draft the innumerable telegrams and papers on which the government machines in both London and Washington throve. Sometimes they drafted papers together. Clarke records how the first draft of the Stimson balance sheet was turned into a paper for Cabinet in August 1941:

> The operation went ahead fast. On a boiling Sunday afternoon, 10 August, I remember, Layton and I were awaiting agog at his house in Sussex for the messenger with the first provisional draft prepared by the War Department Committee, and the additional material being brought simultaneously by Stacy May. It had been arranged that the final agreed 'combined' version would be prepared in London. It is easy to recall the excitement of the occasion, to see for the first time this panorama of 'combined' war production, containing our hopes and fears for the future. As soon as it arrived, we at once sat down to work on it, and had the first conclusions ready for distribution to the War Cabinet next day.
>
> The Statement is a historic document. It was a feat of simplicity, typical of Layton's powers of presentation and exposition. The conclusions were painfully clear:
>
> (a) For Army equipment, UK and Canada were currently producing at double the rate of USA, who would not catch up until the last quarter of 1942.
>
> (b) UK and Canadian output currently exceeded USA output in two-thirds of the items: this would be reversed by the end of 1942. But UK and Canadian stocks were much the larger, so they would still lead in total quantities available by end-1942 (stocks plus production) even with no supplies from USA.
>
> (c) But UK and Canadian supplies would not be large enough to meet minimum requirements for aggressive warfare or to help others (e.g. Russia). The requisitions filed by Britain and others for Lend-Lease were already between one-third and one-half of the entire programme that had been planned in USA.
>
> (d) To perform effectively the dual task of equipping its own forces and supplying its allies' needs, USA must marshal for armament

production an amount of its production resources proportionate to that which was devoted to this purpose in Britain and Canada.[13]

Clarke considered that the main architects of the balance sheet approach to formulating policy were Monnet, Purvis and Stimson, but that the project could not have succeeded at the London end without Layton, who carried Beaverbrook with him and hence the Prime Minister.

Of Layton's departure from the Ministry of Production in 1943, Clarke wrote:

> I have never known a man with a sharper eye for the key point, a clearer and more lucid writer of reports, a wider international comprehension of war; and he was one of the few men whom Beaverbrook could not bully. Yet he was in many things indecisive; and one always sought in vain for the sharp cutting edge in his attitude to the organisations which he believed in, such as the Liberal Party and the European Movement. He was one of the most lovable of men, and I both enjoyed and learnt much from my years with him.[14]

Oliver Franks also regarded Layton at the Ministry of Supply as a superb policy planner rather than a man of action. He left the business of producing statistics to Weeks. He was no longer the solo virtuoso he had been in the Ministry of Munitions in the First World War, but he was pre-eminent in using statistics creatively and honestly. To Franks his role towards Beaverbrook was rather like that of Lindemann to Churchill. For the rest he was a lonely eminence who stood out above all his senior colleagues, to whom he did not open his heart. He would sit there, remembers Franks, almost mumbling or silent. When he spoke it was sometimes with a hint of a stammer. He gave his own views laconically, rather like Attlee, but there would be a quick flash of intelligence in his eyes. Words flowed from his pen faster than from his mouth.[15]

Beaverbrook, who became Minister of Supply in June 1941, also thought highly of Layton, having known him of old in Fleet Street. In February 1940, before either man was in government, Beaverbrook took the trouble to write to Layton about the activities of Beachcomber, who in 1937 had referred in the *Express* to the woollen statue of Sir Walter Layton in Trafalgar Square becoming unravelled: 'Beachcomber has now written another paragraph, "Sir Walter

Layton, who was so frequently knitted in the dear dead days of the Popular Front, has been unravelled and is to be knitted again for the troops". It has not yet gone into the Paper, but do you want the ragging to begin all over again? Will you tell me how you feel about it.' Apparently, Layton did not object and the paragraph duly appeared.

Layton, when he went into the Ministry of Supply, always insisted on being on the same floor as the minister in Shell-Mex House, the ministry's main offices. So when Beaverbrook was appointed, and with his great love of the sun made full use of the balcony outside his office which looked south across the Thames, Layton was nearby. This made him all the more vulnerable to the demands of Beaverbrook's working habits, which, according to Harold Macmillan entailed a daily conference at 7 pm, then dinner at the Savoy at about 9.30 pm and then more work and talk until midnight or 1 am.[16] Layton had enough moral courage to get out of some of these late nights by pleading another engagement. He still liked to have the *News Chronicle* leaders read to him on the private line from Bouverie Street to Marsham Court. But sometimes Beaverbrook swept his staff, including Layton, in a fleet of cars, down to his house, Cherkley Court, near Leatherhead, for dinner, sending them home in the small hours.

Layton's country house at Twittens, where he spent most weekends, was quite near Cherkley and in 1941 he was often summoned over for conferences on Sundays. His daughter Ruth, then aged eighteen, was living at Twittens. Having just learnt to drive, she sometimes drove him over to Cherkley and stayed to record in her diary her impressions of Beaverbrook and the way he behaved. She naturally recorded her father's own views too. According to Ruth, he pointed out forcibly to Beaverbrook how these long dinners and drives into the country wasted the time of busy men. Beaverbrook, at the time, agreed he had been thoughtless but nevertheless repeated his country dinner party the next evening. But he made Layton 'swear to tell him if he rocked the boat too violently instead of speeding it forward'. Ruth's own view was that Beaverbrook was 'a grand character but was wicked when it helps because he had too much power. . . . He ought to do as he would be done by'. No doubt her father often agreed. This must have particularly been the case on the occasion when Beaverbrook asked for weekly production figures to be delivered to him by Weeks on Sunday morning, just to be able to stir up the munition manufacturers who were falling behind. If the only man who could answer Beaverbrook's questions was on the golf course rather than in his office, a despatch rider would be sent to get him to the telephone.

Churchill had been urged on many occasions in the second half of 1941 to appoint a Minister of Production to take a grip of all war production and to lay down priorities for the use of manufacturing capacity and labour. Once the Americans were in the war in December the argument was that the British required an opposite number to Donald Nelson, who was in charge of all United States war production. Churchill wanted to make an appointment early in 1942 to help calm public opinion at a time when the war was going badly in the Middle and Far East.

Beaverbrook was, in some ways, the obvious choice but he bargained hard with Churchill about the terms on which he was prepared to take the job. The main issue was whether he would have any supervisory functions over the Ministry of Labour as well as the Supply departments. Bevin, the Minister of Labour, was totally opposed to working under Beaverbrook's guidance.

The public debate went on all through January 1942. Dorothy wanted her husband, who was very much taken up with the planning of the new ministry, to use the Press so that the right ideas could be injected into the debate. She wrote to him from Twittens: 'Don't be too modest and retiring because what you want done is vital for the future. Apparently the Prime Minister only gives jobs to those who make themselves a nuisance, and there are many of these.' Layton did not follow his wife's advice but he came to the new ministry as Beaverbrook's chief adviser and remained after Beaverbrook suddenly resigned twelve days later. Beaverbrook had already lost his claim to supervise the Ministry of Labour and was suffering at the time both from asthma and nervous exhaustion. Oliver Lyttelton, who took over from Beaverbrook, was a cheerful outgoing man and in no way an intellectual. In many ways he and Layton complemented each other well. Layton still hoped for the position of chief adviser, which Beaverbrook had intended for him, and there was some jockeying of position between himself and the Permanent Secretary, Sir Henry Self. Layton wanted his position made absolutely clear and wrote to Churchill on 15 March:

> I have talked matters over with Oliver Lyttelton. If there is to be an effective General Staff for War Production, I am ready to try my hand at organising it.
>
> But I venture to put two points to you.
>
> When I went to Supply, I lost a lot of time because there was no clear definition of my duties; nor had I any specific authority until a much later date. It is particularly necessary when fitting a new organ of Government into an existing framework that responsibility should be very definite. I therefore suggest that I should be appointed head of the War Production Staff – which would be concerned with planning both at home and overseas, but not with technical questions – and in that capacity would be Mr Lyttelton's deputy in this sphere.
>
> Secondly, if I sign on again, I cannot possibly exercise day to day direction of the *News Chronicle* and *Star*, which will continue to be in the hands of Mr Laurence Cadbury. It is true that I cannot expect ever to dissociate my name entirely from these papers either in fact or in the public mind. Nor do I wish to do so. But I hope it may be understood between us that so long as I am doing Government work I cannot accept responsibility for everything that appears in either of these papers.

Layton had already worked out the main lines on which the new Joint War Production Staff should act as a planning body relating the main strategic decisions to current war production plans. The Joint War Production Staff, which was in some ways the kernel of the new ministry, was to bring together in one committee the users and producers of war equipment in order to decide on priorities. It would control the demands of the Supply departments for weapons and raw materials from North America and elsewhere overseas. The Chiefs of Staff would be represented as well as the munition-making departments and the Ministry of Labour. Curiously, Layton does not mention in his Memoirs that he was chairman of the JWPS, perhaps because he disliked the actual job of taking the chair. Lt-General Sir Ian Jacob, the secretary of the JWPS, remembers him as being likeable and easy to get on with, but as a chairman he was long-winded and a little indecisive – probably too nice and too tired a man to make the JWPS really effective.

Austin Robinson, who joined the Ministry of Production in the spring of 1942, also found Layton a tired man, 'infinitely wise but completely incoherent', perhaps, because he had not yet got used to Layton's ways. Layton seemed to be much more interested in negotiations with the Americans than in problems at home, apart from manpower. He was skilled at finding practical solutions but was not a good administrator. He acted more as a wise man in the background.

In Jacob's view the JWPS never really got off the ground. In any case, both the Ministry of Production and the JWPS had been set up too late in the war to make really major improvements in Whitehall, since the main lines of the war production programmes had already been laid down. The role of the ministry's staff – very few in number at first – was more that of persuasion and coordination than direction. Nevertheless, there was important work for the Ministry of Production to do to help ensure that the best use was made of available resources. Layton's main contribution was in getting the JWPS to produce some first-rate surveys of the resources and manpower available to carry out the desired military strategy. In the opinion of the official war historians the survey prepared in May 1942 for Lyttelton's visit to Washington 'marked a real turning point in the official notions about the relations between strategy, war industry and manpower, for it contained the first comprehensive argument about the inevitable readjustments of combatant strength and industrial efforts'.[17]

Shortage of manpower posed serious problems, though not insuperable. The main problem was the shipping needed to carry raw materials. But the priorities had changed by September 1942, when the JWPS produced another wide-ranging survey, this time of the 1943 production programme. Before, shortage of industrial capacity had been the main problem. Now it was manpower to operate the new capacity. On current plans 2–2½ million men and women were needed for the armed services and munitions industries and nothing like that number looked like being available. This pointed to an urgent review based on the Ministry of Labour's Manpower Survey to decide how to bridge the gap. The Ministry of Labour considered the JWPS conclusions untimely and to an extent inexpert,[18] but a major review went ahead under the direction of Sir John Anderson, then Lord President. This showed that the gap to be bridged amounted to about ¾ million men.

One solution would be to cut the size of the forces to be supplied with British-made arms. But a preferable alternative (spelt out in a paper Layton sent to Stimson on 18 November while in Washington again with Lyttelton) was, after all economies had been made, to keep British forces at their planned levels and to supply them, as far as possible, from increased US production. Broadly this was the basis on which the Cabinet decided manpower allocations in December. It was very much a decision worked out in Cabinet and not one imposed by the Minister of Production, although his ministry was responsible for the allocation of manpower, within the general strategy, between the Admiralty and the ministries of Supply and Aircraft production. This allocation depended greatly on the priorities accorded to aircraft and anti-submarine vessels as against other types of munitions production. The solution was reached as a result of intensive interdepartmental work, but Layton and his staff played an important part, both then and thereafter, in ensuring that departments addressed themselves to the right questions.

How best to coordinate the British and United States programmes continued to occupy a great deal of Layton's time. He went with Lyttelton to Washington twice in 1942. On the first visit in June he stayed on in Washington after Lyttelton left to attend the first meetings of the Combined Production and Resources Board, which was intended to mastermind the integration of British and American war production programmes. This body did not come up to British expectations, partly because it was set up too late and partly because of the US War Department's conflicts with the War Production Board which was responsible for munitions. Just as the Ministry of Production turned out to be more of a coordinating body than a ministry with direct power, so the CPRB found itself tackling specific issues rather than taking strategic decisions.

Layton made use of his time in Washington to organize the return to England of his son Christopher and his daughter-in-law Dot, with her daughter Deanna, all of whom had been evacuated to the United States in 1940. All three returned with Walter to England by sea in July. The fact that he arranged their return showed his confidence in the way the war was likely to go, in spite of the middle of 1942 being marked by the fall of Tobruk, the retreat of the Eighth Army to Alamein and the German advance deep into Russia.

The November visit to Washington just after Alamein went smoothly. United States production was at last expanding fast, and broadly most of the British requirements were met. The new arrangements were set out in a letter from Roosevelt to Churchill, which was promptly circulated in Whitehall at the end of December, so that departments could take action. But as it was a personal letter there was no such corresponding circulation in Washington. Hence much embarrassment and irritating delay.

Soon after he got back to England Layton fell ill, this time more seriously than on previous occasions, and he was away from the office for about two months. Whether it was from depression brought on by his illness or because he felt that the Ministry of Production was never going to be the effective instrument he had helped plan a year earlier, Layton wrote to Lyttelton on 4 February 1943 saying that he had decided to resign, a possibility which he had already mentioned when they were in Washington together the previous November. He had three reasons for resignation. The main machinery for joint planning in the UK and the US had been set up and was functioning reasonably well; both sides were now conscious that they were parts of a greater whole. Second, Layton wanted to be able to express his political opinions publicly; he would therefore have to end his understanding with Churchill that he would not use the *News Chronicle* as a platform. Finally, his doctor wanted him to take at least a month off; his blood pressure was far too low.

Oliver Lyttelton asked him to think again and R.W.B. Clarke wrote:

> The fact is, of course, that you are the only person in the war effort who knows the programmes on both sides of the Atlantic, and can relate them to the strategy of the war. If you drop out, then we have to make do with substitutes who don't know the programmes and who don't have the imaginative facility to draw general conclusions and to propound basic policies. Perhaps at the present stage of the war this may not matter very much, the main policies having been more or less irrevocably determined, and the initiative having passed from the producers to the fighters. But I

don't think there's any point in trying to find people who can do what you can do, for they simply do not exist.

However, Layton did not change his mind. He was particularly anxious to take part in the public debate on peace aims and the reconstruction of Europe. When Lyttelton telephoned Churchill to tell him that Layton wanted to go, Churchill replied in a typically half-mocking way: 'I suppose he wants to get back to the *Daily News*', as if that paper had not disappeared thirteen years previously.[19]

While the Ministry of Production had not turned out as Layton had hoped, he recognized in his Memoirs that right up to the end of the war it had the vital task of keeping war production running efficiently at the peak levels reached by mid-1943. Characteristically on his last day in office he circulated his own detailed appreciation of the manpower and supply position. He argued that we should hold back on munition production rather than restrict the size of the forces because we could draw on the United States' vast industrial capacity: 'In 1941 deliveries from the United States of almost all war stores were more precious than rubies. In 1942 they were silver. In 1943 they are worth less than copper (now a very precious metal!), and in 1944 they will be a drug on the market.'

While Clarke and others on his staff were sorry to see Layton go, Hugh Weeks was not the only one to recognize, after the event, that the time had come for a change from Layton, the master planner, to Sir Robert Sinclair the first-rate chief executive. Lyttelton described Layton well: 'My first prop was Sir Walter Layton. He could give the best background information drawn from experience on war production in the First War. A man of saintly character and charm and high intellectual calibre, he clearly had to be supported by a team of executives.'[20]

As on several occasions in the past when he was changing his job, Layton went to see Churchill, who received him in bed. To Layton's eyes he had aged considerably and seemed unlikely to be fit enough to continue in office after the war. Churchill, having asked why Layton was leaving the Ministry of Production and what he wanted to do, said he was sceptical about planning for a postwar Britain and a postwar Europe. Great Britain would do as she had always done and face great issues as they arose. She would do this through the medium of her constitutionally elected representatives after an election. He was much afraid of diverting attention from the war effort, which still made a very great call.

Layton was not deflected by this talk from leaving government service, but he did agree when pressed by Brendan Bracken to lead a newspaper proprietors' delegation to Australia and New Zealand, which meant that he did not return to the *News Chronicle* until 1944.

CHAPTER TWELVE

The *News Chronicle*: the War Years and After

Laurence Cadbury must have been pleased that Layton became a full-time civil servant in 1940 since he and Layton changed places. Cadbury became chairman of the *News Chronicle* and felt he could now run the paper instead of being in a back seat. It was agreed between the two men that Layton would give the paper the benefit of any information he could without conflicting with his official duties. He still had a direct telephone line from his flat to Bouverie Street. He was to be consulted on important changes of policy. He would give up his salary of £7,500 a year but retain his commission on numbers of copies sold. In the event, this proved a good arrangement for Layton since, with newsprint rationing, every copy printed was sold and his commission went up from £9,000 in 1941 to over £12,500 in 1943.

Layton was in the United States from September to Christmas 1940 and again in 1942, and Cadbury himself led a mission to Russia on war supplies from June to September 1941. But Cadbury's time as chairman ended in 1944 when Layton returned from the Press Mission to Australia which he undertook after leaving the Ministry of Production. Cadbury cannot have found the experience as satisfying as he hoped since, with newsprint rationing, the paper shrank to four pages and Layton still often vetted the leading articles in spite of having become a full-time civil servant. Cadbury was also at odds with the editor, Gerald Barry, a lot of the time. He wrote to Layton on 2 January 1941 immediately after the latter had returned from an exhausting trip to Washington; 'Ever since I have been in my present position I felt that Barry has pursued a policy of heading me off effective action in editorial matters. I have been regarded as "the proprietor" whose only approach to the editorial staff should be via the editor.' Robin Cruikshank used to describe how, when Cadbury wanted to review a sensitive editorial, Barry would retire to the lavatory with the leader in question, knowing that his infuriated chairman would feel compelled to catch the 7.14 train to Birmingham. Once Cadbury had left, the editorial would be rushed to the head printer unmutilated at least for the early editions. Cadbury complained, too, that he had no influence over staff appointments, for instance that of Vicky the cartoonist in 1941, which in fact turned out to be one of the best appointments ever made to the *News Chronicle*.

Layton was too busy to do very much about these various troubles, but he did send a firmly worded note to Cadbury towards the end of 1941 against the *News Chronicle* campaigning for an early Second Front in order to take the pressure off the Russians. This was a line which Gerald Barry, who was a keen sympathizer of the Russians, wished to pursue. By February 1942 Cadbury was trying to muster up courage to sack Barry. He wrote to Layton that he hoped to get Robin Cruikshank back from the Ministry of Information, where he had been running the North American Department, in exchange for Barry, who would go to Washington. Another solution would be for Layton to come back to the *News Chronicle* for three months, in order to discipline Barry. Brendan Bracken, then Minister of Information, insisted, however, on keeping Cruikshank and suggested that Barry should be replaced by R.W.B. Clarke, who was at that time working for Layton and subsequently became a senior Treasury official. In the event, Barry stayed on, pushing the paper further to the left than Cadbury, or even Layton, wanted.

Layton resumed his chairmanship of the *News Chronicle* in 1944 apparently without considering whether the time had come to make a change. Rather he hoped to be able to buy out the Cadbury family so that he could have complete control. Laurence Cadbury refused to sell. The most he was prepared to do was to sell the *Star*, which had little attraction for Layton. So the rather uneasy partnership continued, with neither Layton nor Cadbury being ruthless or decisive enough to set the paper on a firm course.

In 1947 the Labour government made Layton a peer, much to the fury of the Liberal Party. It was said that the peerage was offered at the instigation of Herbert Morrison, who hoped that it would keep the *News Chronicle* well disposed to the government. But Layton was certainly not to be influenced in this way. He merely recorded that during the war he was sounded on accepting a peerage by all three political parties. He accepted in 1947 partly to keep up with the other Fleet Street barons but mainly because the House of Lords provided a platform for his views on matters in which he was then intensely interested – such as economic policy and the European Movement.

Although the *News Chronicle* still made profits up to 1956, circulation was on a falling trend and the stream of critical letters from the Cadbury family flowed faster as time went on. Early in 1947 Henry Cadbury complained of inadequate board control, and Layton took the criticism as a motion of no confidence in himself. In a note Layton sent to the Daily News trustees in March 1947 he agreed that he had controlled the papers' political policy 'not only in principle but in considerable detail'. He had, however, always hoped that, after reaching the age of sixty, he could free himself from office routine which started with a call from the *Star* at 9 am and ended with the delivery of the first edition of the next day's *News Chronicle* at his flat at 11 pm. It was therefore time to look for a successor to himself – though it was clear he was not suggesting that Laurence Cadbury should take over the actual running of the paper. He wanted the new man to be given a free hand by the Cadbury family.

Even though Gerald Barry left later that year, preferring to run the Festival of Britain rather than continue to edit the *News Chronicle* while subject to two masters with different political views, there was no real change in the way the paper was managed. Egbert Cadbury complained in June 1947 that although the Cadbury family had responsibility it had no effective control over the policy of the *News Chronicle*. A managing director was needed who would not only be a first-class businessman but also 'loyal to Laurence and the rest of the family'. Layton was spending too much time in the House of Lords to be able to do the job properly.

In spite of these complaints things went on very much as before, and Layton was able to ensure that the *News Chronicle* gave full coverage to the things that really mattered to him, in particular the European Movement, which Laurence Cadbury thought excessive.

Cadbury summed up his worries in a letter of 22 March 1948, in which he wrote: 'I do not think we ought to look at a concern like Bouverie Street as though it was a government department working under a single minister.' This was not at all a bad description of Layton's attitude at the time.

Although greatly restricted in size because of the shortage of newsprint, the *News Chronicle* maintained a high standard of journalism in the years immediately after the war. Robin Cruikshank came back from the Ministry of Information and became Layton's right-hand man on editorial policy until he took over from Gerald Barry as editor at the beginning of 1948. Cruikshank had little formal education but a great flair for writing. He had made his name as New York correspondent of the *News Chronicle* before returning in 1936 to edit the *Star*. He was a good Liberal and on very friendly terms with Layton. After the war the Cruikshanks shared Brett House with Layton's eldest daughter Margaret Geiringer and her family. Even though Cruikshank was close to Layton, Mary Cruikshank, his widow, remembers that he had difficulty in knowing precisely what Layton wanted. Partly because of the demands made on him by both Layton and Cadbury he worked excessively long hours, and unfortunately the illness from which he died in 1956 began to undermine his health soon after he became editor. He was never able to show his true worth.

Another future editor, Michael Curtis, joined the paper in 1947 and soon made his mark as a leader writer. Sally Chilver, later to be head of Bedford College and Lady Margaret Hall, Oxford, whom Layton had got to know in the Ministry of Production, was brought in to run the new research department. In fact, she devilled for Layton and helped him with his House of Lords speeches when he became a peer early in 1947. Sally Chilver found Layton a more masterful and energetic figure at the *News Chronicle* than he had been in the Ministry of Production, and at the same time more relaxed. Yet, to her, he was a perfectionist, meticulous about the presentation of an article. To get it right he would seem to wrench the article she had written into shape with his large bony hands. He was becoming more obsessive about small points as time went on and would go back and back over a leader, often exhausting Cruikshank as editor. But Sally Chilver remembers Layton's fondness for quoting poetry, in particular from Scott's 'Marmion'. His vitality was as great as ever.

The Budget Leak

There was a dramatic episode on 12 November 1947 when the Chancellor of the Exchequer, Hugh Dalton, was asked by the *Star* Lobby Correspondent, John Carvel, on his way into the Chamber about the supplementary Budget he was about to present. Not thinking that Carvel would use the information, or indeed realizing the speed at which the *Star* could operate, Dalton told Carvel the main items. In fact, Carvel at once telephoned the items he had heard as his forecast of the Budget without mentioning that he had the information direct from Dalton.

The telephone message was relayed at 3.17 pm and Dalton started his Budget speech at 3.32 pm, but as usual the first half of the speech was taken up with an analysis of the state of the economy. The announcements of tax changes all came after 4 pm, since, following the normal practice, tax changes were announced after the Stock Exchange had closed and were, in any event, kept to the end of the speech in order to keep up the interest of the House. Carvel's message was printed in the stop press of the *Star* by 3.39 pm, and 200 or 300 copies of the paper were on the streets by 3.50 pm and in much greater number in all central areas of London by 4.15.

The standard of Budget secrecy being much higher then than now, Dalton resigned at once when he realized what had happened, and before he knew there was to be a Select Committee of Inquiry. Any suspicion of a Budget leak for which the unscrupulous might make money was, at that time, a matter of grave concern and the Chancellor's private office took strict precautions to safeguard the Budget secrets. Indeed, even other ministers, apart from the Prime Minister, did not normally know the contents of a budget until the day before. So when the Chancellor himself blurted out tax changes to a journalist, resignation was regarded as the only honourable course. After Dalton's death, Attlee, in the course of a television interview, described him as 'A perfect ass. His trouble was he would talk. He always liked a secret to confide to somebody to please him. He did it once too often.'[1]

Layton ordered a detailed investigation of the sequence of events in the offices of the *Star* and sent a personal message to Dalton, whom he had known ever since he had attended his lectures in Cambridge. Dalton replied on 15 November tersely: 'Thank you very much for your kind personal message. As to the *Star* and other persons concerned, I think it best that I should say nothing.'

Layton's reputation in Fleet Street as a man to be trusted led him to be active in the immediate postwar years in two companies which served the Press as a whole, the Newsprint Supply Co. and Reuters. He became vice-chairman of the Newsprint Supply Company, which continued after the war as the sole buyer of newsprint, as well as taking on the difficult task of being chairman of the Newsprint Rationing Committee during a period when the severest wartime limit of four pages was continued, with only a few short-lived easements, until 1949. Even afterwards the limit on pages was kept at six until 1952 and restrictions continued until 1957.

Although the company was run by a very able general manager, George Goyder, Layton played an active part in negotiating the successive changes in the rationing scheme and in agreeing new contracts with the Canadian and Scandinavian suppliers. He visited Canada three times for this purpose. Goyder saw a lot of Layton in this period and became very fond of him. This was in spite of Layton being unwilling to delegate, so that there were often delays – infuriating for busy subordinates – while he analysed all aspects of a problem. Sometimes Layton got his way, mainly because he could tire out his opponents, but Goyder admits that he usually came to the right decision.

Sir Christopher Chancellor, the general manager of Reuters, also came to admire Layton when he became a director in 1945. He found his idealism and conscientiousness extraordinary in a Fleet Street magnate. He seemed at times more like a clergyman or a don, with little sense of humour, but nevertheless easy to get on with.

Layton was personally interested in the rebuilding of Reuters in Western Europe, both because of his work for the European Movement and because by 1948 his eldest daughter's husband, Alfred

Geiringer, as Reuters' assistant European manager, had established a strong organization in Western Germany. But Layton's main efforts went into rebuilding Reuters' links with Commonwealth countries, first with Australia (and later New Zealand) in 1946 by means of partnership agreements with the Australian Press, and in 1948 with the newly formed Press Trust of India. He was very ready to lead the Reuters team which negotiated the Indian partnership since he was convinced that it would not only preserve Reuters' position in India, but also help to keep India in the Commonwealth after independence from British rule. He also enjoyed leading the goodwill mission to India during March 1949 to cement the partnership agreement, especially as he was able to see how Indian independence was working out.

Chancellor appreciated how important India was to Layton emotionally, because of the strong impressions made on him when he was in India with the Simon Commission twenty years before and because of Dorothy's work to try to improve the lot of Indian women. After the partnership with India had broken down in 1952, because of political and financial difficulties, Layton was less active at Reuters but served as a trustee for ten years from 1953.

By and large the *News Chronicle* did well up to 1950, when Layton handed over the chairmanship to Cadbury. Its comparatively serious approach (for a popular newspaper) to political news was in tune with the mood of its readers at a time when the Attlee administration was creating the Welfare State and was implementing some of the policies originally proposed in the Liberal *Yellow Book* of 1928. So the *News Chronicle* was usually prepared to back Attlee, though being very ready to criticize his mistakes.

Layton himself was anxious that the journalists on the paper should not all come from one party. He wanted the paper to carry more serious articles but, perhaps because he was spending so much time on the European Movement, in the House of Lords and at the Council of Europe, he did not put a good many of his ideas into practice. He was, of course, hampered by the slowness with which the supplies of newsprint improved. Some of his staff thought that Layton's heart and mind were in the right place but that he was too passive. The *News Chronicle* was compared to the ruins of Athens – all columns and no roof. As a result, the sub-editors tended to dictate the presentation of news and the paper lost some of its individuality.

Most of the surviving journalists who worked on the *News Chronicle* in those years agree that Layton was a good man, fair, honest and without any hint of the grand manner. He was probably too good for Fleet Street. They also agree that he was kind and friendly, especially to the young, though rather remote. He had no small talk, and the disconcerting silences in his conversation, particularly on the telephone, became longer as the years passed. But on occasion, when warmed up, he would converse freely and was an able raconteur. He was liked and respected by most of the staff for his great knowledge and experience of public affairs.

The *News Chronicle* was a good paper to work for, particularly for those of an independent mind. By and large, journalists could write what they wanted, provided they did not run counter to Layton's favourite policies, and could count on not being sub-edited without their consent. Normally they were left to get on with the job, and morale at the *News Chronicle* was high, even though journalists were still paid less than at other papers. As against this, the leader writers sometimes felt they were submitting an essay to their tutor when bringing a leader to Layton for his approval. There was no problem over matters of high principle. Where his principles were firmly held, e.g. on democracy, internationalism or free trade, Layton would expound them with lucidity and force. But on the lesser issues which cropped up every day and where he was called upon to adjudicate on conflicting evidence he could be inarticulate and dilatory.

Some thought Layton rather like a desiccated pedantic don, a thoughtful Liberal of the old school whose influence had helped to create the earlier *News Chronicle*, but whose ideas of journalism were too refined for a popular modern paper. They suspected that, while he wanted to direct policy, often he had no policy of his own. The *News Chronicle* suffered not only because of the division between Layton and Laurence Cadbury, but also because of the division between Layton and succeeding editors from Vallance onwards.

Others thought him a tough old bird. Although he did not throw his weight about in the office, he gave the *News Chronicle* a wiry strength and held his own in Fleet Street, where he was respected by most of the newspaper proprietors, especially Beaverbrook. He had, after all, shown toughness in building up the paper's finances in the 1930s and in fighting off criticism from Liberals and others that the *News Chronicle* was becoming a socialist paper. He had also shown courage in appointing leftwing innovating editors such as Vallance and Barry, and later in standing out for commercial television when most of his friends abhorred the idea.

Perhaps a fairer view of Layton at the *News Chronicle* in the immediate post-war years was that, though meticulous and rather remote, he was certainly not desiccated. He still had plenty of energy and willingness to take on new work in Fleet Steet as vice-chairman of the Newsprint Supply Company and a director of Reuters. While his hesitations and silences could be infuriating, he was more resolute than he often seemed. He had, in fact, built up a good radical paper and he was quite clear that he wanted to keep it on the left wing of the Liberal Party. He was ready to rule on the really important issues but, for the rest, he did not seek to lay down the law, especially on matters with which he was not fully conversant. In fact, he often knew as much or more than the journalists on the paper about the topics of the day, but he was not prepared to make snap judgements trusting to hunch. He wanted the facts if he could possibly get them.

CHAPTER THIRTEEN

The Search for a United Europe

Layton managed to pack several careers into his working life of over sixty years, starting a new one roughly every decade. It is no exaggeration to call his work for the European Movement and at Strasbourg a new career, since for most men in their sixties the amount of time and effort Layton devoted would have amounted to a full-time job. He noted in his diary that from 1949 to 1957, while he was vice-president of the Council of Europe Consultative Assembly, he spent nearly a third of each year abroad attending international meetings of one kind or another. In addition, he was chairman, vice-chairman or treasurer of all the more important UK bodies of the European Movement which sprang up in such numbers from 1946 onwards.

Layton was able to take on this considerable extra burden – and there is nothing so physically tiring as attending long international meetings in overheated rooms with all the difficulty of following speeches, often in bad French or inadequate translation – because at last he had found a cause he could embrace wholeheartedly without feeling obliged to be scrupulously fair to all points of view. Looking back on the rather meagre achievements of the Council of Europe in the 1950s, the question arises whether Layton was not a little naïve for a man of so much political experience. Should he not have exhibited more of the caution for which he was criticized by the younger journalists on the *Economist* and the *News Chronicle* in the 1930s? That he did not do so was because the European Movement focused for Layton the ideas and ideals he had believed in for many years at a time when exciting opportunities for rebuilding Europe on sane lines seemed to be opening up. Admittedly the Cold War between East and West put an end to some of the ideas Layton advanced in his Sidney Ball lecture in 1944. (He then proposed a federation of all Europe except for Russia and Great Britain, which together with the United States would sponsor a loose world association in which Europe and other regional groupings, such as China, Latin America and the Muslim world, would have their say.) At the same time the Cold War gave added impetus to the need to ensure unity in Western Europe. In particular, France and Germany must be brought together and internecine wars in Western Europe be made virtually impossible. Layton had, for a long time, been convinced – mainly through his experience at the League of Nations before the war – that not much was to be expected from a world political organization such as the United Nations. The best way forward politically was through regional bodies, while world organizations were likely to be more successful if limited to specific functions, such as finance, trade and transport.

Layton was, therefore, very ready to help work out the details of the ideas Churchill propounded during his Zurich speech in September 1946. The European Movement, which soon grew up in the United Kingdom and other European countries, attracted both sides of his nature. Intellectually he had always been interested in finding ways of achieving full international economic cooperation, but the emotional pulls were even stronger. The European Movement not only harnessed his long-held idealism in international affairs, but gave him a new purpose during a period when the *News Chronicle* was getting into difficuties and Dorothy's health was poor. Perhaps almost as important, it kept him in touch with leading politicians such as Churchill, Spaak, Adenauer and Reynaud and also with old colleagues such as Monnet and Salter. On top of this the Marshall Plan discussions of the summer of 1947 pointed the way to European economic recovery being achieved within a few years.

Altogether it was a period of fresh hope, so Layton found his work rejuvenating even though physically tiring. Although he was chairman of the leading Liberal newspaper, the *News Chronicle*, and was soon to play a larger part in politics as a Liberal peer, he had no hesitation in accepting Churchill's invitation to join in the work of 'United Europe', which, though intended as an all-party group, was in fact dominated by Tories such as Duncan Sandys and Harold Macmillan with a good sprinkling of Liberals. The Labour Party was suspicious and kept aloof.

With Leo Amery, Layton visited Paris several times in 1947 to discuss with like-minded Frenchmen such as Monnet and Reynaud how best to proceed. These meetings, together with similar work going on in other countries, prepared the ground for the Hague Congress of Europe in May 1948. Layton was by that time chairman of the Committee for United Europe in Britain and played a major role in the preparations for the Congress, particularly on economic and financial matters, and on the proposals for a Convention for the protection of human rights. Churchill was president of the Congress and was accompanied by Anthony Eden and Duncan Sandys. Seven hundred delegates from sixteen countries, including Western Germany, attended. There were also observers from Eastern European countries, including some political refugees. Dorothy Layton attended in her own right as president of the Women's Liberal Federation, together with Lady Violet Bonham-Carter and Elma Dangerfield, who worked closely with Layton in the European Movement for the rest of his life.

The large British delegation was only outnumbered by the French, and it included more Tories and Liberals than Labour Party members. The Labour Party was still chary of any proposals which might interfere with the mild socialism that the Attlee government was introducing, especially as most of Europe then had Catholic parties in power which they regarded as reactionary. Moreover, the Labour government did not wish to be seen to be following Churchill's lead.

Although the Hague Congress was a meeting of private individuals and not government representatives, it was influential in persuading governments to act. There is a revealing photograph in the illustrations of the leaders of the British delegation at the congress calling at No. 10 Downing Street on their return from The Hague. Churchill is smiling to himself and Layton is looking very determined. The Congress called for political and economic union in Europe, a European Assembly and a Charter of Human Rights with a European Court to enforce it. Economic union was a long way off but the Organization for European Economic Cooperation (OEEC) made swift headway once lauched in 1948. The Council of Europe, which some hoped would become the political authority for Europe, was set up and its

Assembly held its first meeting in August 1949, while the Convention for the Protection of Human Rights was agreed by November 1950. By international standards this was swift progress.

Harold Macmillan records how he came back from The Hague, with Layton, Lady Violet Bonham-Carter and Peter Thorneycroft, in a small plane with an undercarriage which would not go down when they arrived over Croydon, so that they had to fly round for an hour to use up petrol. 'As I expected Lady Violet and Layton happily discussed the future of the Liberal Party for over an hour scarcely noticing that anything was amiss.' When they finally landed and had to jump out quickly Macmillan called out 'Women and Liberals first!'[1]

During the second half of 1948 the French government made most of the running in pressing for a Consultative Assembly as a main feature of a Council of Europe. Although Ernest Bevin, then Foreign Secretary, thought a Council of Europe might help strengthen European unity by including Germany and Italy, most of the Labour Cabinet were sceptical, and while in the end agreeing to a Consultative Assembly, were only prepared to join half-heartedly in the Council's work. Layton himself, at that time very active in the European Movement as chairman of the UK Committee, was confident that the pressure of events would lead the Labour government to realize that insistence on absolute sovereignty no longer made sense and that there would have to be some pooling of sovereignty in Europe.

The Consultative Assembly which met for the first time in August 1949 was made up of 138 representatives drawn from the national parliaments of sixteen countries. Most countries' parliaments elected their representatives directly, but the UK adopted the method of appointment by the government of the day after consultation through party whips. Layton was one of the two Liberal members all his time at Strasbourg, the other sixteen British representatives being chosen according to the number at the time of Labour and Conservative members of Parliament. Herbert Morrison, Hugh Dalton and William Whiteley, the Labour Chief Whip, led the Labour Party representatives. Churchill, Macmillan, David Eccles and Robert Boothby led the Conservatives. Layton was the Liberal spokesman.

Early on Spaak, who had just ceased being Belgian Prime Minister, became president of the Assembly.

Layton's experience of the first assembly made a great impression on him and his election as one of the seven vice-presidents set the pattern for a large part of his working life for the next eight years. His eldest daughter, Margaret, came over for a time from Frankfurt, where her husband Alfred Geiringer was working for Reuters. Walter's youngest son, Christopher, was there for a time too. Walter recorded in one of his letters how during a weekend trip into the Vosges mountains Margaret mistook the road at a hairpin bend and drove her car into the ditch. The car hit a stone wall and the front axle was broken. Walter had several large bruises but, characteristically, to reassure Dorothy he wrote that they 'did not amount to more than a momentary inconvenience'.

When it came to the election of the vice-president of the Assembly, the first of a series of clashes between Churchill and Herbert Morrison took place, much to the surprise and puzzlement of the other delegations. Morrison, who had little experience of international conferences, wanted the same procedures to be followed as ruled at the Westminster Parliament and was glad to find that Sir Gilbert Campion, a recently retired Clerk to the House of Commons, was to be present. Moreover, Morrison wanted William Whiteley to be the British vice-president. But Churchill and Macmillan held that it was wrong to appoint a minister to an office which might mean his having to argue with the Committee of Ministers, the executive of the Council of Europe. Churchill thereupon sponsored Layton for the job as being totally independent, and he is said to have declared to Layton: 'Walter, if you don't stand for vice-president I will never speak to you again.'[2]

Layton at that stage had no desire for office: as the Liberal spokesman at Strasbourg he wanted to be free to move round the committees as well as speak in the main Assembly. However, he was persuaded to stand and won the vote by a narrow margin, much to the delight of Churchill, who was one of the scrutineers. While Layton had not sought the job, Churchill had certainly made the right decision in sponsoring him. He was well suited to help build up the Council of Europe so that it might become a European political authority which, according to the oft-quoted phrase at the time, 'would have limited functions but real powers'.

The first Assembly made reasonable progress in three main directions. The Economic Committee, with Paul Reynaud in the chair and David Eccles as rapporteur, produced a long list of measures, most of which were being considered by the OEEC at the time. The Committee on General Affairs under Bidault started the study of 'Necessary changes of the political structure of Europe'. It also considered a proposal by Churchill for the admission of Germany to the Council of Europe. The Committee on Legal Questions, with Sir David Maxwell Fyfe in the chair, made most progress by producing the main outlines of a draft Convention for the Protection of Human Rights. Layton served on both the Economic and Legal committees, and became a member of the Directing Bureau as one of the vice-presidents.

Layton left Strasbourg for Bonn convinced that the Assembly had good prospects of making progress, provided its members covered a wider spectrum of views. At the first meeting there were too many representatives who were members of the European Movement, and a stronger sceptical opposition was needed to reflect the real state of opinion in most countries. However, the Assembly looked like providing a useful forum for the discussion of the central European issues of the day. The main impediment was that it was likely to be at loggerheads with the Committee of Ministers. As Paul Reynaud put it 'the Council of Europe consists of two bodies, one of them for Europe and the other against'.[3]

In Bonn, where the Allied military government was being superseded by the first postwar German government, with Adenauer as chancellor, Layton set about sounding the main political parties on the question whether Germany should join the Council of Europe, even though at that time the Allied High Commission had reserve powers over Germany's conduct of foreign affairs. Adenauer was in favour of Germany taking part in the work of the Assembly, but did not wish to be represented on the Committee of Ministers by the High Commission. The Social Democrat Party were concerned that joining the Council of Europe would antagonize the Russians further and make the reunification of Germany more difficult.

Whatever Adenauer's doubts about his ability to win a vote in the Bundestag against Social Democrat opposition, he sent Layton a telegram on 20 October 1949 asking whether an application from the German government for membership of the Council of Europe could be sure of acceptance. At that time Germany had no diplomatic representation in London, but Layton, having talked to the Foreign Office, was able to reply that the British government would support a German application for membership, but it would be prudent to consult the French. There was then a delay, as the Social Democrats wanted to link membership of the Council of Europe with a satisfactory settlement on the Saar.

They were still worried about the Saar, as well as about the possible impact of membership on the Russians, when Layton saw Schumacher, the leader of the Social Democrats, in Bonn in April 1950. Layton thought he had moved Schumacher by asking whether, if the Bundestag turned down an invitation to join the Council of Europe, Germany could hope to become reunited as a neutral state. Schumacher agreed that this alternative course was quite impracticable. Whether Layton had much influence or not, he clearly acted as a good roving ambassador for the Assembly. In the event, Adenauer got his majority in the Bundestag and a German delegation, complete with Social Democrats, turned up at Strasbourg four months later.

The Council of Europe's most striking achievement in its early days was swift agreement on the Convention for Protection of Human Rights by November 1950. Drafting had started early in 1949 in the international juridical section of the European Movement under Sir David Maxwell Fyfe and Pierre Henri Teitgen, a former French justice minister. The preparatory work done in drafting the UN Universal Declaration of Human Rights, which was never given legal effect, proved useful too. By 1949, the deteriorating atmosphere of the Cold War had increased the determination of many European ministers, who had spent most of the Second World War in resistance movements, to build defences against the resurgence of new totalitarian regimes. The draft Convention, at the time, seemed a useful defence against such developments. The European Commission on Human Rights together with the European Court were to be the keepers of the European conscience.

Layton played an important part in the 1949 discussions at the Assembly, when the Legal Committee had an all-night sitting. At that time the Labour representatives voted against the Convention, which Dalton later dismissed in his Autobiography 'as a much vaunted instrument which, in fact, led to no practical results. In countries where human rights were respected it was unnecessary; where these rights were not respected it was ineffective. But its supporters made some very emotional speeches and displayed much juridical learning.'[4]

Layton's emotions were certainly engaged but he wanted to limit the numbers of rights covered by the Draft Convention to those which were essential to preserve democracy, so enabling the Convention to be ratified quickly without losing a lot of time in legal definitions. He thought that its ratification would be a great help in building up German democracy. Once the Convention was ratified and had entered into force, he worked hard to get the British government to adopt two optional clauses by which individuals would have the right to apply to the European Court and the government would bind itself to accept the jurisdiction of the Court. This was a long process. In November 1958 Layton lobbied twenty of his fellow peers before making one of the more cogent speeches of his life. The government did not then give way, although the Lord Chancellor of the time, Lord Kilmuir had, as Sir David Maxwell Fyfe, played a major part in drafting the Convention. However, Layton lived long enough to see the Labour government adopting both optional clauses in 1965.

The Schuman Plan proposals of May 1950, for a European Coal and Steel Authority operating in a single European market, provided an early test of how far the Labour government was prepared to go towards some pooling of sovereignty. Jean Monnet had become disillusioned with the Council of Europe at an early stage and persuaded Schuman, then French Foreign Minister, to put forward his plan as a way of strengthening Europe both politically and economically. War between France and Germany would be unlikely to occur again if the two economies were bound tightly together, while setting up a single market would strengthen Western Europe's coal and steel industries.

For the new authority to be effective Monnet was convinced that it must be able to exercise supranational powers. The Labour government, while welcoming the political aims of the plan, was suspicious of the economic proposals which had only been sketched in broad outline. They feared that their policies of nationalization, socialist planning, full employment and building the Welfare State would be at the mercy of a European body unsympathetic to socialism and in which Britain would have no veto. Most Conservative politicians were prepared to use Labour's refusal to accept the principle of a supranational body (as a precondition for entering into negotiations) as a stick with which to beat the government, without committing their own party to accept the plan. But Layton and some European-minded people in both the Conservative and Labour parties, such as Harold Macmillan, Julian Amery, David Eccles, Robert Boothby and Bob Edwards, welcomed the Schuman plan wholeheartedly in a letter to *The Times* on 22 May.

Layton, speaking for the Liberal Party as a whole, pressed the case for joining in two speeches in the House of Lords on 24 May and 28 June, arguing that there were strong political and economic reasons for Britain to join. The delegation of certain limited powers to the proposed authority was no real obstacle. The government's fears were ill-founded. Until it could be seen precisely what powers were to be delegated, emotional language about sovereignty obscured the issue. It was clear that some international body with executive powers, which would be more than a forum for consultation like the OEEC, was needed to rationalize the European coal and steel industries within a single market. The main idea of pooling these industries was in no way revolutionary. Indeed, it had often been discussed in the past and the Bank of International Settlements provided a good precedent for delegating national powers within strict limits.

Already in June the government had shown that it was not prepared to accept the Schuman Plan in principle, which meant that Britain did not take part in the initial negotiations. But Layton did not give up hope. He and his son Michael helped Harold Macmillan and David Eccles work out proposals which attempted to get over the government's fears by making the authority subject to a Council of Europe ministerial committee with the right of veto.

The Macmillan–Eccles plan was rejected outright by the French and made no progress at the Council of Europe Assembly meetings in August. Layton, who had his own doubts about some aspects of this plan, tried in a speech to the Assembly on 15 August to show that in all important respects it was not very different from the Schuman Plan and that it had the great merit of enabling Britain to join. 'Because I am a Schuman fan I have supported the proposal put forward by Mr Macmillan. ... I am a Schuman fan because it is by far the most promising plan yet proposed in postwar Europe.'

The Six went on without Britain and the Schuman Plan Treaty was signed in April 1951, but Layton was still hoping that Britain would join. At the Council of Europe Assembly in May 1951 he urged British membership in a speech which Harold Macmillan recalled as 'truly magnificent. I never heard him speak so well. He spoke as one having authority.'[5] Sometimes when Layton spoke it seemed to his listeners that he was driving himself to get out every word, but on this rare occasion enthusiasm brought out real eloquence.

Although Britain only later joined the Coal and Steel Community Layton continued to be much involved in Council of Europe work. As a member of the Bureau of the Assembly, Layton had to go to four meetings a year, in different capitals, to guide the work of the Assembly's committees and secretariat in between plenary meetings. There was also plenty of lobbying to be done, both at home and abroad, and constant pressure on the *News Chronicle* staff to see that the paper reported events in Strasbourg fully and fairly. Some of the journalists who considered the Council of Europe a boring backwater resented this, but most did their best with what was rather unpromising material.

Other tasks Layton took on had rather more glamour. For instance, he acted once more as a roving ambassador for the Council of Europe when he spent the whole of June 1951 in Washington, following up the Council of Europe's invitation to Congress for a meeting to discuss problems of common interest. The job was not an easy one. Though there was much interest in the United States in the possibility of bringing about a United States of Europe, there was little understanding in Washington about the purpose and work of the Council of Europe. Moreover, Layton soon met the usual frustrations of life in Washington during the summer. He wrote:

> I now know – for a month spent on Capitol Hill has taught me – that to achieve anything in American politics you need infinite patience and unshakable obstinacy.
>
> It was, however, universally agreed that June 1951 was about the worst possible month in which to get Congress to consider an unusual, and, from the point of view of internal American politics, a remote proposition. The prolonged and continuous MacArthur hearings which broke all endurance records occupied the whole time of the Senate Committee on Foreign Relations which was unable to hold a single ordinary business meeting for nearly two months. The tropical heat and humidity were trying in the extreme and the strain reduced many Senators to physical collapse. ... Even when I could get anyone to give continuous thought to my mission I only found three or four members of Congress who had more than a vague idea about the Council of Europe.

Nevertheless, Layton persisted. He lobbied sixteen leading Congressmen and ultimately met President Truman, whose support he gained. Before he left Washington resolutions had been introduced into Congress to accept the Council of Europe's invitation. But he had to return with Spaak to build on the good will he had won and draw up an agreed agenda for the meeting which took place in November.

This meeting proved a great success, if mainly one of mutual education. It took place after the Assembly had adopted Churchill's call for a unified European army and after the setting up of the Coal and Steel Community. In 1952 the European Defence Community Treaty was signed and an ad hoc assembly was called, made up of the Coal and Steel Community Assembly and representatives from the Council of Europe Assembly, charged with the task of drafting a treaty for a European political community, intended by some to be a major step towards European federation.

Layton was one of the Council of Europe representatives at the ad hoc assembly. At that time it seemed that the Council of Europe, which had proved a disappointment to many, including Spaak (who had resigned the presidency of the Assembly in December 1951), might find a really useful role at last. Layton certainly hoped so, though he was convinced that progress could only be made by tackling specific problems such as coal and steel or defence, rather than pressing for a Federal Europe which he knew no British government would join. Layton himself was therefore pressing for a simpler arrangement by which European institutions should be coordinated through a committee of prime ministers. In particular, he wanted the OEEC to be brought under a common political authority. His close contracts with Monnet at least helped get agreement that there would be annual joint meetings of the Coal and Steel Assembly and the Council of Europe Assembly, the first taking place in June 1953.

The ad hoc assembly produced a draft treaty in March 1953 which provided in a protocol for as close links as possible between the Council of Europe and the European Community 'so that the Council of Europe may constitute the general political framework of Europe'. Layton thought this treaty the best that could be negotiated at the time. By providing for Britain and the Scandinavian countries to be closely associated with the Six, it might in time lead to their position being very little different from full membership.

The draft treaty came to nothing, largely because, with the Gaullists increasing in power, the European Defence Community was rejected in 1954 by the French National Assembly. Moreover, East-West tension had slackened following the death of Stalin and NATO seemed to offer adequate defence.

By this time Layton was speaking at Strasbourg in terms of the UK following the functionalist rather than the federalist path, because of her Commonwealth ties. This was, indeed, the orthodoxy of the time in both Conservative and Labour parties, but Layton admitted that the trouble with the functionalist approach was that it led to too many separate institutions, hence his desire for a supervising ministerial body. He also wanted international secretariats to be more independent and held that all international institutions should have a parliamentary body to subject their work to public scrutiny. He does not seem to have been depressed by a letter of November 1955 from Alexander Loveday, who had worked in the League secretariat during the inter-war years: 'The Council of Europe, which should be the leader is actually one of the weakest organisations – stuck out at the end of a limb in Strasbourg with a second rate secretariat, limited funds and limited and ill-defined functions.'

While Layton at one time hoped that Robert Marjolin, the secretary general of the OEEC, would combine that job with being secretary general at the Council of Europe so as to bring the two bodies closely together, he did not put the blame for the Council of Europe's shortcomings on its staff. Indeed, he went out of his way to try and build up the secretariat and to increase the powers of the secretary general.

Members of the secretariat at Strasbourg may have found Layton too old and too set in his opinions to provide the drive that was needed from him as one of the senior vice-presidents. Certainly, like Layton's staff on the *News Chronicle* and before that in the Ministry of Supply, they found him a quiet, self-contained man with very little small talk. He never had been a good chairman and did not become so at Strasbourg. Small meetings were much more congenial. He liked discussions with a few people over lunch, preferably in a modest restaurant. But some of his speeches at Strasbourg and in the House of Lords show by their clarity and cogency, if not in their manner of delivery, that his heart as well as his mind was fully engaged. Above all he retained his enthusiasm for a United Europe.

Some thought him a bit fuddy-duddy (after all he was seventy-three when he ceased being vice-president in 1957) because he kept losing his papers. Dunstan Curtis, the deputy secretary general, had to write any notes he sent Layton on the platform during meetings in triplicate because he was bound to lose two of them. But the British members of the secretariat were grateful for his enthusiasm. Among all the cynics he kept his faith. They thought of him as a warm, kindly man without personal ambition. He went out of his way to be hospitable during his long stays at Strasbourg, without being in any way ostentatious. The *News Chronicle* correspondents there discovered to their surprise that with their help he could become interested in good food and drink. He made real friends with Dunstan Curtis, who found him a lovable man – indeed, they remained in close touch until Layton's death. His influence at the Assembly was considerable, because he was liked and respected as a man and because he was known to be an enthusiastic European.

Layton only ceased being vice-president in 1957 because John Edwards, the Labour politician, became president, and there could only be one person of each nationality on the Bureau. While he left with few illusions about the obstacles in the way of a United Europe, he did not lose his zest for the cause and continued to work for it at home, using the House of Lords as his main platform. Indeed, in 1961 he added the presidency of the European Atlantic Group to his other commitments to the European Movement.[6]

In spite of all the setbacks and irritations inherent in working for an international organization, the experience seems to have mellowed Layton. It certainly provided a welcome contrast to the troubles of the *News Chronicle* and helped to keep him younger than his years.

CHAPTER FOURTEEN

The Search for the Field Brothers

Layton had another very different type of involvement in Europe in the 1950s, this time trying to solve the mystery of the disappearance in Eastern Europe of two brothers, Hermann and Noel Field. Hermann Field, an architect and a Quaker from New England, had worked for the Czech Refugee Fund in Poland in the summer of 1939. Being American rather than British it was easier for him to take charge of Czech Jewish and political refugees who had fled to Krakow after Hitler marched into Prague in March 1939.

Hermann Field's job in Poland was to organize the refugees into groups which left the country as and when the visas they needed to enter Britain, the United States and other countries came through. The German invasion of Poland on 1 September ended all such work and Hermann had to do what he could to save the refugees, then at Krakow, by organizing their flight from the rapidly advancing German armies. He had hoped to move the 600 refugees in his care by train, but German bombing made that impossible. The refugees therefore had to start out from Krakow on foot, with Hermann going ahead in the only available car to make arrangements for food and shelter, and, if possible, for some better transport to move them out of the way of the German army. His task was soon made more difficult when the refugees became separated into small groups as a number of German army columns cut across the roads they were trying to follow. Many were killed or wounded in the intense air raids on roads and towns and some were captured by the Germans, while others fell into the hands of the Russian armies advancing into Poland from the east. Like the other surviving refugees, Hermann and a small group of people who had been with him from the start tried to struggle through to the Polish-Romanian frontier by getting lifts. In the end he crossed the frontier with only one of the refugees, called Vilem Novy, though another ten or so joined him in Romania later.

After crossing the frontier Fields met Willie Forrest, the *News Chronicle* correspondent, who had had an equally adventurous journey from Warsaw, where he had gone to report the war. The *News Chronicle* was therefore the first London paper to carry a report of his agonizing march across Poland. Hermann also published one of the first detailed reports of German blitzkrieg methods, particularly the bombing of towns and roads in Poland. In addition, he wrote a long detailed report about the fate of the refugees to Margaret Layton, who was working at the Czech Refugee Fund offices in London. A copy of this letter went to Kate Thornycroft, who also worked at the Fund, and whose family was well known to Walter Layton. Before going to Poland, Hermann had earlier that summer proposed to Kate. This part of the story had a happy ending, as Kate and Hermann were married in June 1940 and went to New York City, where Hermann resumed his work as an architect.

Layton lost touch with the Field family until January 1950, when Kate's father, Oliver Thornycroft, asked for his help in tracing his son-in-law. Hermann Field had mysteriously disappeared while on a visit to Warsaw the previous August. He had gone to see the progress the Poles had made in rebuilding the city since a study tour of European cities he had organized for American architects in 1947, when Warsaw's achievements seemed outstanding. But on his way he had stopped at Geneva, where his brother Noel lived, being at that time a freelance journalist. Noel had left the State Department in the mid-Thirties to work for the disarmament section of the League of Nations in Geneva, and during the war, still based in Geneva, he had joined the Unitarian Service Committee, an American voluntary organization to help refugees.

At Geneva, Hermann learned from Noel's wife, Herta, that Noel had gone to Prague in May to write some articles and apparently had disappeared. Hermann and Herta went to Prague but found no trace of Noel. Then Hermann went on to Warsaw as had previously been planned, but promised to meet Herta on his return to Prague on 22 August before going to pick up Kate and their two boys in London for the flight back to the United States. He was seen off by his friends in the departure lounge at Warsaw airport but was not on the plane when it reached Prague. His name had been crossed off the passenger list. Nothing more was to be heard of him for five years.

Herta cabled the news to Kate and they exchanged several worried telegrams about what to do, but then the replies from Prague suddenly stopped. Herta had disappeared too. Kate and her father, Oliver Thornycroft, at once started enquiries through the US Embassy in London and the State Department in Washington. Both the Czechoslovak and Polish governments denied any knowledge of the three missing Fields. The Czechs were able to point out that Hermann had never turned up at Prague airport. The Poles simply denied holding him. Both the State Department and the British Foreign Office found it embarrassing to press hard when they had no evidence. Kate had started by thinking that it was best to avoid publicity, but as the weeks passed without any news she began to wonder whether it would not be better to bring public pressure to bear. Noel and Hermann's sister Elsie pointed out that an American businessman called Vogeler had only been released after his wife had protested long and hard in Washington.

The only clue that had emerged since the disappearances came in September 1949 during the trial in Budapest of Laszlo Rajk, former foreign minister of Hungary, and some other leading Communists. They were accused of giving secret information to foreign governments, and in some cases the only evidence was that the accused were friendly with Noel Field, who was alleged to have been an American spy working for the Office of Strategic Services during the war. But the Hungarians did not confront the accused with Noel Field in court, nor did they admit they held him in custody.

There was always the possibility that the Fields had been kidnapped in order to use them as evidence against those members of Communist governments who were not Stalinist enough, and were, therefore, destined to be purged at a series of show trials ordered by the Russians, for having connections with the West. But that was not at all certain in 1949. Much was written in the Press but little really known about Noel Field who, during the Alger Hiss trials of 1948 in the United States, was alleged to have been one of his associates. Kate was bound to suspect that the State Department thought that

Noel had been a Communist and that some of these suspicions would rub off on her husband Hermann. In any case, once the Fields had been interrogated and used as evidence, there was no certainty that they would be kept alive: if they were eventually to escape or be let out of prison, much of the evidence on which the trials were based could be shown to be false.

Although Kate learned later that the American Embassay in Warsaw had approached the Polish Foreign Office about Hermann fourteen times in the autumn of 1949, and in December the State Department had sent protest notes to Warsaw and Prague, at the time she was convinced that more ought to be done. She, therefore, issued a full Press statement and sent a telegram to Dean Acheson, the US Secretary of State, at the end of December. But it was doubtful whether that would bring any worthwhile result. Knowing it was no good to appeal direct to Communist governments who had publicly stated that Noel Field was an American spy, Oliver Thornycroft and his daughter Kate turned to Walter Layton for help and advice.

Layton was clearly deeply moved by this call for help. That the chapter in his Memoirs on the Field case is the most vividly written is itself some indication of his feelings. He had always been involved in the fate of Czechoslovakia since his friendship with Beněs and his lead in helping the Czech refugees before the war. During the war he had lent Brett House as a convalescent home for Czechs. He was now even more interested in events in that country, as his daughter Jean had married Paul Eisler, a Czech economist, and was living in Prague. Much of his work for maintaining peace and human rights came together with his personal life in the Field case. Layton was an old family friend of the Thornycrofts. He had taught Kate's mother, Dolly, economics at Cambridge before the First World War. He knew Kate well, since she had worked with Margaret Layton at the British Committee for Czech Refugees from the very start and by May 1940 was in charge of hostels and housing.

So Layton was from the first anxious to do all he could to help Kate and she came, as time went on, to rely more and more on his advice. He was not only in touch with those in high office in both the United States and the UK, but he was able to use the resources of the *News*

Chronicle, both in collecting information about what was going on behind the Iron Curtain and to give useful publicity to the efforts being made to find out where the Fields were being held. He started with a full report in the *News Chronicle* in February 1950, giving the known facts about Hermann and the efforts being made to find him. In March, he followed this with a report from Prague that Vilem Novy (then the editor of the Czech Communist Party's paper, *Rude Pravo*) had been expelled from the party because of his continuing to keep in touch with Hermann Field, a suspected spy. In the same issue he printed a rejoinder by Kate giving the facts about how Hermann had helped hundreds of Czechs to try and escape from Poland in September 1939, and denying that he had ever been an agent of any kind.

Layton enlisted the aid of Trygve Lie, then secretary general of the United Nations; he also encouraged Kate to continue badgering the State Department and later in March 1950, while in Washington, he followed up Kate's approaches and spoke to a number of leading Congressmen. In spite of this pressure, the State Department did not take any strong action, such as trade sanctions against either Poland or Czechoslovakia, and Kate asked Layton whether she should take up a suggestion made by Noel's sister Elsie that she should go to Washington to persuade influential Congressmen to prod the State Department. Kate did not, in fact, go to Washington, but Layton helped her with another Press statement in October and also got in touch with General William J. Donovan, who was director of the OSS in the war, in the hope that he could find out exactly how the US authorities viewed the Fields and whether they had any idea about their possible whereabouts. Donovan apparently drew a blank in Washington, but said that he had heard on reasonable authority that it would be worth talking to the UK intelligence authorities. Layton did so, but drew a blank in this quarter too.

In August 1950 the Field family had suffered a new blow. Noel and Herta Field had looked after a young German girl refugee, Erika Glaser, whom they found in a hospital in Spain when Noel was working for the League of Nations refugee section at the end of the Civil War. Erika lived with the Fields in Geneva throughout the Second World War and was treated as an adopted daughter. After the war she went back to Germany, where she married a young American officer called Wallach and settled with him and her two small children in Paris. There she received a note from an old German friend saying that if she went to Tempelhof airport in the western sector of Berlin she would be given news of her foster father, Noel Field. Her husband, after much hesitation, agreed to her going to Berlin, provided she did not go into East Berlin. But it was a trap. She could not find her friend at the airport. He was, in fact, by that time in a Communist prison, and she was persuaded to go into the Eastern sector to meet him. Immediately she crossed the frontier she was arrested and disappeared.

This was bound to be a depressing development for Kate, since it showed that the Soviet bloc countries were acting together in a most brutal manner to prevent any news about the Fields leaking out. Erika was, in fact, sentenced to death by a secret Russian military tribunal in East Berlin and then imprisoned in Moscow awaiting execution. She was only saved by the amnesty after Stalin's death in 1953, when her death sentence was reduced to forced labour in Vorkuta camp in the Soviet Arctic. From there she was allowed to send a stock printed postcard which at least showed that she was in Russia and still alive. Her husband received the postcard early in 1954, but it was not until 1955 that she got back to the West.

Layton was in Washington in June and again in September 1951 when he took the opportunity to press the Fields' case with the State Department. Kate kept in close touch with him on any public comment she made, particularly those on misleading Press articles and on the letters she herself wrote to the Press to keep the Field case before the public view. She also suggested in October 1952 that he should use his influence with his fellow Liberal, Lady Maclean, to try to dissuade her daughter-in-law, Melinda, from going to Moscow in the hope of seeing her husband Donald Maclean, who had fled there the previous year with Guy Burgess. This appeal seems to have had no effect, as Melinda went to Moscow.

Walter and Kate both continued to press the United States Embassy in London, since fresh evidence emerged that Hermann, as well as Noel, was being held to provide evidence in another show trial, this time the Slansky trial of former Czech ministers and other

Communists in Prague, who were all accused of being in touch with Western spies. In confessing their guilt in November 1952, two of the accused said that they had got to know Hermann during the flight of Czech refugees from Poland and that the Czech Trust Fund which financed Hermann's activities in Poland had been a cover agency for American and British intelligence which had recruited agents in Central and Eastern Europe for use after the war. They claimed they had renewed contact with Hermann in 1947 when he was in Prague with a party of American architects, and again in 1949. Layton himself was accused during the same trial of setting up the British Committee for Czech Refugees as a way of recruiting undercover agents for the British Secret Service. Neither Noel nor Hermann Field was produced in court during the Slansky trial in Prague, but the evidence used showed that they had been arrested and that Hermann was probably being held in Czechoslovakia.

But while Kate and Walter were glad that the Slansky trial provided another opportunity for the State Department to make representations to the Czech government, Kate could not know whether Hermann was still alive and, if he was, whether he would ever be released. So, the dogged, agonizing business of maintaining the pressure on the United States government and of keeping the case in the public eye had to continue right through 1953 and most of the following year. There was no lessening of anxiety for Kate during this time, except for the postcard from Vorkuta which showed that Erika was still alive. Layton asked the Home Office to grant Erika a visa for the UK in the summer of 1954 so as to speed up her release from Russia, but got a dusty answer.

During these long years of waiting, Kate found Walter warm, sympathetic and above all supportive. Of course she already had very real support from her parents, in whose house she lived, and also from other friends in London. But without Walter she would not have felt reassured that she was doing all she humanly could do to get Hermann released and that every step she took was the right one in the circumstances. Walter was always accessible whenever she felt the need to unburden her worries.

This long period of tension and deep anxiety was at last relieved in September 1954 as a result of a defector from the Polish secret police,

Colonel Swiatlo, admitting to the Americans, who gave him political asylum, that he had arrested Hermann in August 1949 at Warsaw airport and was responsible for his interrogation and imprisonment at Miedzeszyn just outside Warsaw. He also admitted having interrogated Noel and Herta Field in Budapest before the Rajk trials. Thereupon, the State Department sent stiff notes on 28 September to Warsaw and Budapest demanding the release of all three Fields, although at that stage there was no certainty that they were still alive. Indeed, Swiatlo had said that Noel and Herta Field had been very weak when he had last seen them in 1950.

The Poles promptly moved Hermann out of his prison into a villa, but did not admit that they had got him until 26 October, when at last he was allowed to telephone to his wife. Even then Kate and Hermann could not meet for several weeks because Hermann was in poor physical shape and, after all the kidnappings that had taken place, Kate was strongly advised not to go to Poland. Moreover, Hermann, unlike most prisoners, whose immediate objective would be to get away, insisted that the Polish authorities should release his cell-mate and that he should be put in touch with his brother Noel. He also demanded that he should be paid full compensation and that the Poles should make a declaration of his complete innocence before he left the country.

The Poles accepted all Hermann's demands, as they wished to damp down publicity about the appalling treatment to which the Fields had been subjected in order to provide bogus evidence in Eastern bloc show trials. They also tried to shift the blame from themselves by emphasizing that Swiatlo had defected to the West in December 1953 but the information he brought about the Fields was not used until nine months later. So the Americans were to blame too.

Hermann started his reorientation in a world from which he had been excluded for five years by meeting Kate in Switzerland for ten weeks' convalescence before he was ready for normal life. In those weeks Kate learnt what had happened to him. He had been arrested by Swiatlo in a small room next to the departure lounge at Warsaw airport, having gone through Customs and Immigration control. After two weeks' interrogation at the headquarters of the security police, he was driven blindfolded to a suburb of Warsaw and imprisoned in a cell in the basement of what appeared to be a converted country house. Not until his release five years later did he learn that he had been held in the Polish police interrogation centre at Miedzeszyn.

Those five years started with sixteen weeks of solitary confinement and interrogation, which became more intense and brutal towards the end. He was not told anything about his brother Noel, but he gathered that the main accusation against himself related to the work he had done in 1939 in Krakow to help Czech refugees. He was never confronted with anyone: there was no trial, there were no formal charges. Hermann was held in the basement for the whole five years, never once being allowed out of doors. He could only see a small patch of sky through an opening near the ceiling of his cell and only knew of the passing of the seasons by sounds. As the months passed he became desperate and having discovered that the Polish secret police did not want to have his death on their hands, he went on hunger strike on several occasions to try to get concessions, including communicating with his wife, and seeing the United States consul. He became extremely weak and his gaolers forcibly fed him, through which he learned that they did not want him to die in their hands. This became a useful bargaining tool. Although his main requests were refused, he was allowed pencil and paper by January 1951 and to keep him sane he was given a cell-mate.

Hermann wrote after his release: 'The hardest thing to bear was my complete isolation, my complete ignorance of what was to become of me and my complete lack of contact with the outside world. I did not see how I could ever be found, and believed I had been forgotten.'[1] Fortunately for Hermann, his cell-mate Stanislaw Mierzenski turned out to be a remarkable character of considerable ability and intelligence, qualities matched by Hermann's own. Hermann believed that Stanislaw, in effect, saved his life on several occasions. He had been in the Polish Resistance fighting the Germans during the war, but he was not a Communist. He was a highly educated man who had been a newspaper editor and after the war went into industry until his arrest in 1948.

The two prisoners were now given Polish newspapers which Stanislaw translated, but all mention of the Fields and the Slansky trials had been cut out so Hermann still had no idea what had happened. Hermann knew no Polish and Stanislaw no English, but they were able to converse in German. To pass the time they at first turned themselves into a two-man university, telling each other all they knew about history, mathematics, agriculture, science and architecture. They also told each other short stories which, in time, led to their writing together a very moving novel about a Polish Jewish girl hidden by a farmer from the Nazis in a basement of his farmhouse. Each was responsible for alternate chapters. Hermann found he was kept awake the night before his turn working out in his mind how the chapter should go. By this time they had notebooks. Having worked out each chapter together in German, Hermann wrote it down in English in a notebook which, when filled, was taken away by the guard in exchange for a new one. The novel was long and filled many notebooks, but when Hermann was at last released all of them were returned to him neatly packed in a large parcel. The novel – *Angry Harvest*[2] – was eventually published in America, England, Poland, Germany and Sweden in 1958. In 1984 it was being made into a film in Germany.

The terrible long time of waiting had ended for Kate, but she still turned to Walter for advice about the Press conference Hermann held when he came to London in February 1955. Hermann was anxious to avoid a public attack on the Poles which might harm Noel and Herta who, probably because of the accusations made against them in the United States, had chosen to remain in Hungary, and might also harm Erika who was still in Russia. Public recriminations could have led to the Poles ill-treating his cell-mate Stanislaw Mierzenski, to whom he owed a real debt and with whom he wished to work in order to produce the final version of *Angry Harvest*.

The Press conference passed off well and the whole story ended happily for Kate and Hermann, with their return to the United States in 1956 and the birth of a daughter a year later. Erika, too, eventually got out of Russia and rejoined her husband. Only Noel and Herta remained in Budapest until their deaths many years later.

For Layton there was a postscript at the time of the death in 1962 of his eldest daughter, Margaret, when he received a letter from Dr Fierlinger, who had been deputy prime minister in 1952 at the time of the Slansky trial and was now speaker of the Czech parliament, in London as leader of the Czech delegation to the inter-parliamentary union. Dr Fierlinger paid tribute to the work Margaret Layton had done for Czech refugees, and went on to express regrets for the miscarriage of justice which had occurred in 1952, when both Walter's and Margaret's names were mentioned in the Slansky trials.

Even though this letter would not have been written had not Layton's daughter, Jean Eisler, told the Czech Ambassador about Margaret's death just when Dr Fierlinger happened to be in London, it gave Layton satisfaction, especially as Fierlinger agreed that it should be published in *The Times*, together with his reply. It mattered, too, since the Eisler family were still living in Prague at the time and Jean's husband had suffered through being out of favour with the Czech government from 1951 for several years because of his Western connections. It was good to have it on public record that all charges against members of the Layton family were unjustified.

CHAPTER FIFTEEN

The *News Chronicle*: the Last Decade

When Layton stopped being chairman of the *News Chronicle* in 1950 he hoped to have more time for his many other activities, and to see more of Dorothy, who had to spend an increasing amount of time abroad because of poor health. If he had ever wanted a major public post such as chairman of a nationalized industry (as a Liberal he could not hope for a ministerial post), he must have accepted by 1950 that it would not come his way. But at least the House of Lords gave him a public platform.

Once in the House of Lords he inevitably became Liberal spokesman on economic affairs and the Council of Europe. More important, he became deputy leader of the Liberals in the Lords from 1952 till 1955, and at one time there was talk of his becoming leader. But there was objection from a number of peers who did not want to have a Press baron as leader. From the start he spoke regularly in debates affecting his main interests – economic and foreign affairs, defence, the Council of Europe, the Convention of Human Rights, the supply of newsprint and commercial television. This meant at least six major, carefully drafted speeches each year throughout the 1950s. These were speeches that read better than they sounded.

He soon mastered the procedure of the House of Lords but never acquired real eloquence. Sir Geoffrey Cox, who was the *News Chronicle* lobby correspondent at the time, considered that Layton's speeches suffered because, being so honest intellectually, he qualified every statement. But a few of his speeches were first-rate in the force of his argument, and his speech on 10 June 1947, explaining just why the Marshall Plan was of the greatest importance, showed his quick grasp of essentials. So did his speeches in May and June 1950 urging that Britain should join the Schuman Plan for coal and steel. He spoke well too at the time of Suez and when urging ratification of the Convention on Human Rights, or the abolition of the death penalty.

While Layton sometimes bored his fellow peers, since his speeches often ran to a good thirty minutes and his views were highly predictable, he was well liked. He was always punctilious in consulting his friends and possible supporters before making his speeches. When he became deputy leader of the Liberals, Beaverbrook congratulated him: 'I do not see it makes much difference. You have framed their policy for them during the past. And, of course, you will continue in the future.' Beaverbrook also sent a telegram saying he expected Layton to go on for at least another ten years, adding: 'There is nothing but misery and sorrow for those who retire.' Layton did go on for more than ten years. His last speech in the Lords was in July 1965, once more urging the abolition of the death penalty.

Whatever his hopes in 1950, Layton remained active at the *News Chronicle*, where Cadbury tried hard, when he took over the chairmanship, to improve management by bringing in Frank Waters from *The Times* as general manager. But Cadbury had difficulty in delegating and neither Cruikshank, the editor, nor Waters were allowed their heads.

Circulation continued to fall and the paper suffered a further blow in 1952 through the resignation of Vicky the cartoonist. His departure was taken as another sign that the paper was moving to the right. In point of fact it is doubtful whether Cadbury had anything to do with this incident. Vicky produced a cartoon, glancing back to 1929, of American investors jumping out of a skyscraper window, to which Robin Cruikshank took exception because he thought it was in bad taste. Vicky was used to being able to publish anything he drew, though he – being remarkably inventive – often appeared at editorial conferences at noon with several different cartoons to see which one was preferred. On this occasion, he was not prepared to accept Cruikshank's ruling and went off to the *Daily Express*. The paper also lost the services of Vernon Bartlett and Ian Mackay, a first-rate industrial correspondent, in the following years, but scored a success in recruiting James Cameron.

It was also in 1952 that Beaverbrook wrote to Layton out of the blue offering to finance his buying of the *News Chronicle* and *Star*:

> I know nothing of the facts but if you want to buy those papers I would be glad to provide money for you. The basis of the arrangement I would suggest would be as follows. The policy of the paper and also the production of the news pages would be entirely your responsibility. And I would not interfere. The business side would rest with me. You would deal with the situation openly and frankly leaving control in the keeping of yourself and your associates. We will make a community of interest between the Express and the News Chronicle which will be publicly declared ... but the community of interest would be for business management only.

Layton replied at once that there were two snags in the way of his accepting Beaverbrook's handsome offer. First of all he was sixty-eight and not fifty-eight years old. Second, the Cadburys had no wish to sell. But he promised a considered reply. Layton must have been tempted by the offer, which would have fulfilled his long-held ambition of being able to control the *News Chronicle* himself. But he realized that he could not go into partnership with Beaverbrook, whose stridently proclaimed policies included Empire free trade and opposition to the European Movement. It was a nice idea but it simply would not work. So he finally turned down Beaverbrook's offer.

Soon afterwards Layton became interested in commercial television, in which several newspapers, but not yet the *News Chronicle*, were planning to invest. He fell out with many of his Liberal friends on the question whether commercial television should be allowed. Should the BBC keep its monopoly of all broadcasting – television as well as sound – or should commercial television financed by advertisements be introduced? In a speech well above his normal standard, given in the House of Lords on 26 November 1953, Layton argued that all good Liberals should object to the BBC's monopoly, however praiseworthy the BBC programmes. 'Liberals', he said, 'dislike monopoly in all its forms but the dangers from the monopolies we dislike in the economic field are as nothing compared to the dangers from monopoly in the matters of the mind.' His speech followed that of his friend Ernest Simon, who had been chairman of the BBC and, while ready to see competition between public service bodies, was wholeheartedly opposed to a commercial service. He quoted American experience as showing that commercial television degraded the viewer. Later Simon wrote to Mary Stocks: 'Walter Layton made a speech which as a speech was well delivered but full of many wrong facts. In your words "cursed be he; he shall be known in future as 'wicked Walter'".'

In his speech Layton declared an interest in that the *News Chronicle* had applied for a licence to provide programmes earlier that year, but were waiting for the expected Television Bill before coming to any decision. When that Bill became law in July 1954, the *News Chronicle* had decided against, mainly because the Cadbury family disapproved of having anything to do with commercial television. Layton, however, became a member of the new Independent Television Authority which was set up with Sir Kenneth Clark as its chairman. He was active at the ITA in arguing the need for a news service which would be unbiased politically. At one time he thought this might best be done by a group of newspapers with different political affiliations. Certainly his ideas had much to do with the setting up of ITN.

Shortly after Layton had joined the Independent Television Authority in the autumn of 1954 he had to spend much more time at the *News Chronicle* because of the crisis which arose as a result of the grave illness of the editor, Robin Cruikshank, and the sudden death of the general manager, Frank Waters. Layton became, in effect, chairman once more, although he was not described as such. He handed over control again to Cadbury in 1956.

The crisis at the end of 1954 was symptomatic of the troubles that afflicted the *News Chronicle* throughout the 1950s. Cruikshank had been in poor health for some time before matters came to a head in September 1954 when he gave up the editorship. Since early 1954 Brian Chapman, who had been brought in from the *Express*, had been managing editor. Michael Curtis had been suggested as Cruikshank's successor, having already acted as his deputy when he was ill, but there had been a good deal of opposition to the idea because of fear that Curtis might be too young and inexperienced to command the respect of the rest of the staff. In the end, Layton's view that Curtis should become editor prevailed.

There had been much heart-searching since 1953 about the direction in which the *News Chronicle* should go. Curtis wanted the paper to become a Liberal and more spritely *Daily Telegraph*, preferably in tabloid form. His idea was to produce a quality tabloid paper, in appearance blending the best elements of the *Evening Standard* and the Paris edition of the *New York Herald Tribune*. Cadbury had wanted the paper to become more popular. Layton typically went for a compromise between Cadbury and Curtis:

> Ever since I have been concerned with the paper it has been debated whether the *Daily Express* or the *Daily Telegraph* is our best exemplar. Both have succeeded and are succeeding in finding an increasing audience for their type of paper. The short answer is that we should slavishly copy neither. We have to create a paper with a different kind of personality – one which, if we succeed, will attract to us a loyal and increasing readership. ... The case for the *News Chronicle* is that the present generation includes a growing number of people, virile, keenly interested in the dazzling march of science, with unique resources at their disposal for sport, amusement and travel, pitch-forked into the problems of 'one world', yet conscious of many social stresses and unsolved moral problems. To such their daily paper must be lively, wide awake, lightened by a sense of humour, quick to seize and portray the dramatic incident and adequate in its news coverage. But it must also appeal to the intelligence and carry the conviction of its honesty, and sincerity of purpose. The reader should feel that he has been entertained, but also that he has been well and accurately informed and given a mental stimulus. If there is no such public there is no raison d'être for the N.C. This amalgam needs the brightness – but not the shallowness and sensationalism – of the *Express* and the thorough news coverage – though not the dullness of presentation – of the *Daily Telegraph*.

Although Curtis took over as editor in October 1954, the vital decisions for a change of course were not made. Layton decided he would have to take action and on 4 December wrote to Cadbury that, in his view, much firmer guidance from the chairman and the board was needed. Cadbury, as chairman, had failed to intervene when Cruikshank fell ill. There were no regular policy discussions. Even when there was some attempt to put the paper onto a new course, as had happened at the beginning of 1954, the decisions reached were not implemented. There had to be a full-time executive head at Bouverie Street – it was not possible to run the paper by remote control. To some extent Layton was accusing Cadbury of those sins of omission of which others accused him. Perhaps just because he himself found it so difficult to take quick decisions, he was sensitive to the same failing in others.

Cadbury did not resist this onslaught and quickly agreed to hand over the chairmanship, provided it was only for one year, and he remained as vice-chairman. In the event, Layton simply joined the operating boards and Cadbury stayed on as nominal chairman until he resumed full chairmanship in April 1956. The change was announced to the world, that in view of the personnel losses the newspapers had sustained recently, Layton would resume his membership of the boards of both papers during a period of reorganization.

With Layton spending more time at the *News Chronicle* and Curtis, his own man, as editor, some expected a real improvement in the paper's fortunes. But, in fact, profits declined fast in 1955 compared with the two previous years and were replaced by a loss in 1956. Layton did not accept Curtis's proposal for a tabloid format; nor, perhaps, was it surprising that he was no more decisive at the age of seventy-one years than he had been ten years before. His son, Michael, became a director but was not given responsibility to match his energies and resigned after a few years. Layton did score a success in November 1955 by taking over the *Daily Dispatch*, with its 460,000 mainly elderly working-class readers in the Manchester area, 300,000 of which were retained until Suez, when the *Chronicle's* anti-Eden policy led to the loss of many whose politics were staunchly Tory. So the success was short-lived.

After April 1956, when Cadbury resumed full control, the financial position of the papers continued to deteriorate. Layton was at odds again with the Cadbury family at the time of Suez when he backed Curtis's fierce criticism of Eden just as he backed the *Economist*, of which he was chairman, taking the same line.

An effort was made to improve the management of the paper by the recruitment in early 1957 of John Coope, who had been deputy chairman of the *Daily Mirror*. But the general drift downwards of both the *Chronicle* and the *Star* led to Cadbury and Layton actively exploring the possibility of a merger between the *News Chronicle* and another major daily, and of an outright sale of the *Star*.

In 1957 Layton was involved with active negotiations with

Beaverbrook, Rothermere and Duncan of Odhams Press, which owned the *Daily Herald*. The most promising solution for the *News Chronicle* was a merger with the *Daily Herald*, producing a new independent paper of the moderate left, not tied to any one party. Michael Curtis set out the two choices as he saw them – either merge with the *Herald*, the editor's independence being protected by trustees, as had been done for the *Economist*, or carry on with a new-look tabloid *News Chronicle* at a cover price of 3d. (as opposed to the then 2d.), designed both to attract *Daily Herald* readers and to rival the *Daily Telegraph*'s news coverage.

Frank Cousins (who was at that time general secretary of the TGWU) put paid to a merger with the *Daily Herald* by persuading his colleagues on the TUC that they must retain political control over the *Herald* and over any successor paper in which they had a financial stake. So Curtis's proposals for revamping the *News Chronicle* came to the Daily News board early in August when he was away on holiday, and were turned down.

At the same meeting, it was decided that Layton and Cadbury should both resign from the operating boards of the *News Chronicle* and *Star* and that John Coope should, in effect, become chairman of both papers. Curtis, who did not want to work under Coope, wrote a furious letter to the Daily News board members who had turned down his proposals without his being present to defend them: 'If this is really the board's intention – knowing how strongly I feel on the subject – I must presume that they no longer have any confidence in my judgement – a sentiment which in the circumstances can only be mutual.' When Cadbury remonstrated with him, Curtis said he would resign the following month. Cadbury asked him to resign at once. On 22 August Curtis wrote a personal note to Layton saying he had refused to resign until he was certain there was no chance of the board changing its mind. He added: 'So long as Laurence remains in command I am certain the paper is doomed to die. You know that as well as I do.' Cadbury for his part appealed to Layton that Curtis should go at once.

Because of a further delay while Geoffrey Crowther was brought in as chairman of the Daily News trustees, Curtis did not finally resign until 23 September, and up to the last moment proclaimed his desire to stay on if his management and policy proposals were adopted. In particular: 'The *News Chronicle* should move gradually but consistently towards becoming a more serious newspaper and we should cease to attempt to compete directly in the same sphere as the *Daily Express*.'

Layton, partly because he saw no alternative to putting John Coope in charge, reluctantly gave up the fight to keep Curtis. Instead of urging the Daily News board to review its previous decision, he sent Cadbury a detailed financial analysis of the whole business. He also announced his intention to resign from the board and hence, in effect, to sever all connection with the business once two conditions were satisfied. The first was that a rise in the selling price to 2½d. should take place. This was to make it clear to the *News Chronicle*'s bankers that the paper's overdraft would be repaid and thus avoid any doubts they might have because of Layton's resignation. The second was that the assets of the company should not be pledged to raise funds to such an extent as to endanger the fulfilment of the moral commitment to the paper's pensioners. Layton made it clear in his letter of 23 September to Cadbury that his decision to resign had nothing to do with Curtis's departure. His reasons were:

> As you well know I have always had to step warily between my personal views as expressed inside the Liberal party organisation, in Parliament or at Strasbourg and the views expressed in the *News Chronicle*. I have for this reason always refused office in the party. Since 1950 my responsibility for *News Chronicle* policy has greatly diminished; my public activity has increased. As the gap has widened it has become increasingly evident to me that the situation could only end either by my ceasing to have any responsibility for the *News Chronicle* or by my taking over full responsibility again. While the second of these courses might have been possible when we discussed this matter two years ago, it is now too late in the day for me to be either able or willing to undertake such a task even if the Trustees wished me to do so. It has, therefore, only been a matter of timing the first alternative.

The accompanying financial review explained in detail why Layton had not supported Curtis's proposal for a 3d. paper. The trouble was that, while the *News Chronicle* and the *Star* taken together had made adequate profits in every year (except 1952) until 1956, unlike their competitors, virtually all their eggs were in one basket.

Losses could not be covered by profits from publicity activities or television.[1] The *News Chronicle* was caught in a trap, since with circulation of about 1.3 million it would be counterproductive to try to compete with papers with circulation over 2 million by putting up its cover price before they did likewise. To do so would lose too much circulation. The only way out of this trap was either by a merger, taking the *News Chronicle* into the over 2 million readers category, 'or by climbing into the "class" group by successful exploitation of a specialised readership'. Layton, presumably because he was resigning, did not say which of these courses he was advocating. However, his request to the board not to use assets to make good current losses beyond the point necessary to finance pensions clearly meant that there was a definite limit to which the Daily News Ltd could go in financing losses before it would be necessary to sell out.

The End of the *News Chronicle*

In the event Layton's resignation from the Daily News board did not take effect, since he was not satisfied that adequate provision had been made for the firm's pensioners, although a start was made in February 1958 when £300,000 was set aside for this purpose. Layton felt that by 1959 he could do nothing to save the *News Chronicle* but at least he could help the pensioners.

It was in 1958 that the detailed negotiations for a merger with the *Daily Mail* started. These were carried on by the managing director, John Coope. Layton acquiesced in these negotiations, which did not reach any conclusion until March 1959. Even then the arrangement with Associated Newspapers, which owned the *Daily Mail*, was in the form of an option whereby the Daily News Ltd could sell the *News Chronicle* and *Star* to Associated Newspapers any time up to 31 May 1959 for £1,925,000, plus ten shillings for each reader gained by the *Daily Mail* over 300,000. If this option was not exercised by the Daily News Ltd by 31 May it could be renewed repeatedly for another three months if both parties agreed to do so.

John Coope at that time had every hope that it would not be necessary to implement the plan, which came to be known as the 1925

Plan. It was renewed every three months until May 1960 when Coope wrote to Laurence Cadbury warning him that, with increasing losses, the Daily News assets would be dissipated to the damage of both the shareholders and the pensioners. This letter went to the whole board and the trustees. Circulation was declining and by June 1960 the *News Chronicle* was selling 1,160,000 copies compared with 1,500,000 in 1951 in spite of the purchase of the *Daily Despatch* in 1955. The *Star* was down to 735,000 copies compared to the 1,230,000 in 1951. Losses of both papers had increased from £237,000 in 1959 to £300,000 in the first nine months of 1960.

Negotiations with other possible purchasers had gone on since the spring of 1960, but those with the Australian Sir Frank Packer came to nothing by July, as did the last-minute negotiations with Roy Thompson in September and October. The Daily News board was therefore confronted in July 1960 with three options: 1) to continue to produce the *News Chronicle* and the *Star*; 2) to put the company into liquidation; 3) to implement the 1925 Plan. It was clearly impossible to go on as before because of mounting losses. Voluntary liquidation might well raise less than the 1925 Plan and there could be no guarantee that there would be adequate compensation for the staff. So the Daily News board decided to enter into talks with Associated Newspapers to implement the 1925 Plan. The agreed date, because of time needed to get out of an obligation to print the *News of the World* northern editions on the *News Chronicle* Manchester presses, was Monday, 17 October 1960.

While some of Layton's friends, especially members of the Liberal Party, found it difficult to believe that he had agreed to sell the *News Chronicle* to the *Daily Mail*, he clearly shared the views of the rest of the Daily News board that there was no real alternative. He explained his reasons publicly in a letter he and Geoffrey Crowther wrote to *The Times* on 20 October, three days after the *News Chronicle* had stopped publication:

> As the only members of the Daily News Trust who are not connected with the Cadbury family, we would like to place on record the fact that we entirely concurred in the decision to sell the *News Chronicle* and the *Star* to Associated Newspapers Ltd. To our infinite regret we could see no preferable alternative.

Public comment seems to be overlooking three vital points. First, the decision to sell the papers now was made in the interests of the staff. No doubt they could have struggled on for a long time yet. But that would have been justified only if there were a real hope of getting back fairly quickly to a profitable basis. We lost this hope some time ago.

The economics of the newspaper industry are very cruel to a popular paper with a relatively small circulation. It can sell less advertising space than its rivals, and therefore can give its readers less editorial matter to read. Inevitably it appears to offer less for the money. So its circulation ebbs away, and advertisements are still harder to get. Whether it would have been possible earlier on to break out of this vicious circle is a matter of opinion, and it is easy to be wise three years later. But once the spiral is revolving we think the public does not realize how much effort – and in particular how much money – is needed to escape from it.

Would the critics really have preferred that the *News Chronicle* and the *Star* should have been carried on until the last gasp, until all the assets had gone, until they no longer had a saleable value, and until there was no hope of compensation for the displaced staff or of security for the pensioners?

The second point follows from the first. Why did we not accept any of the offers that were made to buy the papers and continue them? If the interests of the staff were to be protected, any prospective purchaser would have to establish that he had enough money not only to provide working capital and to meet the trading deficits but also, if and when he eventually failed, to provide the very large sum for the staff that is now available. No offer backed by any such sums of money was ever made.

Thirdly, why all the secrecy and the suddenness? Why was there no prior consultation with the unions, other newspapers, the Liberal Party, and everybody else who is now claiming that he might have been able to think of something that might have helped? The reason for this is obvious. Associated Newspapers Ltd (who have acted with great patience and understanding), were willing to pay a very substantial sum of money for the two papers – but only on the reasonable condition that they should have the maximum possible start over their competitors in the effort to hold the circulation of the *News Chronicle* and the *Star*. This would not have been possible if all Fleet Street had known what was in the wind. To keep the negotiations completely private was an essential condition of such an operation.

It is understandable that, at the moment, people should be indignant. With full knowledge of the facts, we can give an assurance that, once the inevitability of closure was accepted, the governing consideration – indeed, virtually the *only* consideration – in all the actions that have been taken has been to provide the fullest possible protection for the staff of the two papers.

Most of the blame for the collapse of the *News Chronicle* undoubtedly fell on Laurence Cadbury, who had continued as chairman of the Daily News board. The junior staff, at least, had thought that the *News Chronicle* was safe to the last bar of Cadbury chocolate and there was much resentment. Of the many obituaries of the *News Chronicle* which appeared in the Press at the time, probably the most trenchant in its criticism was that written by James Cameron in the *West London Press* on 21 October:

> The death of the *News Chronicle* is the biggest journalistic tragedy for many years – I think it is the most meaningful collapse the newspaper business has seen this generation. For the vestiges of independence in Fleet Street the writing on the wall is up to 72-point. If the *News Chronicle* could not survive, with its extraordinary advantages of tradition, and loyalty, and talent, who can outside the great chain-stores of the trade? ...
>
> Here is the most insoluble problem of what we rather fulsomely call the 'Free Press': how is it possible to equate the commercial success that is indispensable to a liberated paper with the business interests that will always encroach upon that liberation?
>
> Well, as far as the *News Chronicle* is concerned, it couldn't be done. It should have been done, and there are many who will say that with a little guts and intelligence at the top it might well have been done.
>
> The newspaper with the most admirable free-thinking radical traditions withered on the bough precisely at the moment when the nation was ripe to appreciate these liberal qualities.
>
> Its greatest opportunities opened out before it, and it surrendered, because there was nothing at the top but timidity, conventionality and emptiness. In its closing days, the *News Chronicle* was a potential warhorse ridden by grocers. And thus it died, and great numbers of the most gifted, loyal, frustrated, trained, perceptive and heartbroken men and women are now without a job, while the grocers survive.

Layton himself received a very bitter letter from Lady Violet Bonham-Carter:

> I found it impossible to exchange casual trivia with you at Lady Samuel's birthday party – for reasons which you can well imagine – and it would have been impossible on such an occasion to do anything else.
>
> You must (of course) realise the pain and the utter bewilderment which the tragedy of the *News Chronicle* has brought to those who have given it their unswerving love and loyalty for countless years. Not only the fact of its death – but the manner of it – has shocked thousands who did not share its ideology and looked to it for light and leading and the expression of their faith.
>
> But for those who, like myself, who love *you* and trusted you and would

have laid down 'my sleeping life within your hands' in absolute confidence, the pain and the bewilderment have been doubled.

You were a Director, and your assent was necessary to all that has happened – the agreed 'marriage' with the *Daily Mail* (why not the *Express* or the *Mirror* if ideology and tradition went for nothing?), the treatment of the staff (according to their own accounts in print) and the refusal to enlist or even to allow an attempt at rescue from the paper's devoted Liberal friends – who would have done anything that lay within their power to save it. I heard from many journalist friends and others that the paper was in trouble about four months before the end (possibly a little longer). I knew also that the staff were throroughly unhappy under Cursley (which did not in the least surprise me) and the business-manager (whose name I forget) and had made their disquiet known in signed memorial. Jo [Grimond] and other Liberals had heard much the same from other sources. My first impulse was to communicate with you direct – then I thought Mark [Bonham-Carter] might be better at discussing the business angle with you. He saw you twice and elicited nothing from you. Byers saw Cadbury who simply said to him 'No comment' (as to an importunate reporter). Mark asked Geoffrey Crowther to see him about the *News Chronicle*. Geoffrey Crowther said he would be delighted to do so, but was very busy for the next two days. When Mark rang up again after these two days Crowther had left for America. (The same thing you will remember he did with you when you telephoned to him about the *Economist*'s attack on Liberals – and he was in his bath). Jo also made an abortive attempt to see one of you – (I think it was Cadbury but cannot be sure). All the *News Chronicle*'s best friends and would-be helpers were deliberately fobbed off and brushed off by its trustees – until it was too late and the deed was done. As you know the staff was not informed until the day before the paper died.

What could one feel? What could I say to the hundreds who have questioned me about it? and who all stressed 'But you knew Walter Layton well. He is one of your oldest and closest friends. How could he consent to such a procedure? What has he said to you about it'? I could only reply 'Nothing' which is the fact. Can you be surprised at my bewilderment – and that of thousands? The disinherited readers, the staff scattered and dealt out like a pack of cards among other newspapers with wholly alien creeds.

If Laurence Cadbury did not feel willing to continue to lose £100,000 a year at the paper no-one could force him to (though his TV station, acquired by right of having a paper, must have helped to cushion the loss). But surely you could, or should, have given its friends a chance of saving it – body and soul? Which they might well have done. The compensation money of £1½ million would not have been necessary had it (the paper) continued in being. And it could have been made a better paper. Cursley was a hopeless Editor (not the least interested in politics). Michael Curtis was the last good one (his proposals were as you know turned down by the board). What – I wonder – old dear Robin Cruikshank would have felt today? It could not have happened had he lived. I did not dream that it could have happened with *you* there.

I am surprised to have had no word from you about it – knowing as you surely did how much it would mean to me and all I care for and believe in. You cannot be surprised at my bewilderment and inability to understand what has happened, and your part in it. You have always been my dear close friend. Apart from my own feelings I mind being quite unable either to explain or defend you (people say to me, 'This was a great Liberal newspaper. Liberals talk about relations between employers and employees – joint consultation, etc. Look at the way they treated the staff of the *News Chronicle*.) What am I to say? or to think? or to write? (My postbag is still heavy with letters from heart-broken Liberals throughout the country who have read the *News Chronicle* since birth and ask me for an explanation). To them it seems the betrayal of a trust and of a great tradition. With Liberal fortunes on the turn throughout the country they are offered the *Daily Mail* for daily bread – (with the name of the *News Chronicle* as bait – a bait which savours to them (and me) as blasphemy). I had hoped for some word from you – but since it has not come I must break the silence between us.

Walter Layton fell ill soon afterwards and Violet Bonham-Carter relented and sent him a letter of sympathy. He was again her 'Dearest Walter'.

There were also recriminations from some members of the *News Chronicle* staff. One wrote commenting on the letter to *The Times* which Layton and Crowther had published on 20 October:

I remain completely mystified as to how two supposedly alert businessmen (or economists) could have let a concern with which they were connected – and from which they were and perhaps still are, drawing fees, collapse so miserably. . . . You knew that the managing director and the chairman were not up to the job – the former had been sacked by the *Mirror* for heaven's sake! You knew you had to get a good editor if you wanted the paper to survive – or even have a chance to. You weren't unaware of any of the facts: or if you were then you are as guilty as the grocer himself.

Indeed, so far as I can make out, both you and Sir Geoffrey sinned greatly because you could have brought matters to a head – and in time – by resigning or threatening to resign from the board or the Trust years ago. As the outside experts you had power over the Cadbury family that no single faction within it could have had.

Whether, if Layton had applied himself wholeheartedly and perhaps whole-time to trying to restore the *News Chronicle*'s fortunes, it would have been possible to save the paper must be very doubtful. In fact, Layton had largely withdrawn from management of the *News Chronicle* by the end of 1957, even though – against his original intentions – he remained a director.

In the first half of 1958 he spent an appreciable amount of time in building up the Tyne Tees Television Company in which the Daily News Ltd had taken a stake and this was to be a considerable call on his time for the next few years. Moreover, Dorothy's health had been poor and after what she and Walter called the best holiday in their life in Sicily in 1958, they decided to sell Twittens and the flat in Marsham Court and to move into Exeter Court, a block of flats overlooking Putney Heath, where they would be near several of their children and grandchildren.

In June 1958 Dorothy fell ill again and by October it was clear that she had cancer. From then until Dorothy's death in the following March, Walter spent more and more time at her bedside. He was to write a most remarkable account of her last illness in *Dorothy*, a much franker account of a death from cancer than was usual at the time, though others have followed Walter's example in recent years.

At first Walter carried on attending essential meetings, but from the end of January 1959, seeing Dorothy's distress at his late return home due to fog, he stayed with her until the end. Their daughter Jean had come back from Prague to nurse her mother. The last three months of Dorothy's life, though deeply distressing for her family and friends, were amazingly serene and, in a strange way, happy. Walter refers in his book to her 'Indian Summer of happiness' right up to the time when she knew she was going to die soon.

After her death, Walter found some comfort in writing *Dorothy*, which took much of his time up to the summer of 1960. When it was published in January 1961 Lady Violet Bonham-Carter summed up the book perfectly:

> This book has been truly described by its author as 'a great love-story'. It is flawlessly told. Though art plays no conscious part in its telling it is a work of art – born of an impulse as irresistible as the spring from which a river flows. Reading it one feels that the writer had no choice whether it should

> be written or to whom, or how. This was a story that he *had* to tell, and to tell exactly as it happened. Hence its deeply moving quality of authenticity and truth. Again – though we are allowed to share the intimacies of 'a love that after 50 years is as vivid as at the beginning ...' we have no sense of eavesdropping or intrusion.[2]

This was a remarkable achievement for a man of seventy-six who normally concealed his feelings and was famous for his silences. The book shows that Walter was a far warmer and a much more feeling and emotional character than many who had met him at work had ever realized.

While he was going through these traumatic experiences it was not surprising that the decline of the *News Chronicle* took second place in his attentions.

CHAPTER SIXTEEN

Keeping Going, 1960–6

After Dorothy's death and the collapse of the *News Chronicle* Walter showed considerable courage in facing an old age which could easily have been lonely and sad. By 1960 he was seventy-six years old, and the slight tremble in his hand had become much more marked. He grew a beard when he was ill at the end of that year, and to avoid the risk of cutting himself, stopped shaving. So, with white hair and with white beard he looked his age, though he was still slim and his eyesight and hearing were good.

He stayed on at the Exeter Court flat in Putney so as to be near his children and grandchildren. Here he had a housekeeper to look after him and cook him good meals. It was a time when he turned more to his family and found he could talk more freely to them and to his friends, especially when he had time to warm to some favourite topic. He much enjoyed the company of his grandchildren, with some of whom he formed close relationships. But he missed Dorothy greatly. He told Olive when she met him at the airport after some trip abroad how much he hated returning to an empty flat. And to Jean, who was staying with him when letters praising Dorothy came pouring in after he had published his book about her, he said 'All true, and I never told her.' He suffered another blow when his daughter Margaret died in 1962 and at that time relied very much on his children and his son-in-law, Alfred Geiringer, for consolation.

He certainly felt lonely for some years after Dorothy died, and found comfort in the company of those of his women friends with whom he could talk easily. Among these he numbered Alice Bellamy ('Old Nanny', who first came to the family in 1915), a lively-minded person who was quite able to beat him at Scrabble, which they usually played when she came to stay. Dolly Thornycroft found him relaxed, tranquil, and very ready to talk openly about the past, when she spent an evening at his flat. Elma Dangerfield sometimes persuaded him to come out for a quiet dinner at her house. Gwyneth McCleary, of whom he was particularly fond, even got him in 1965 to hear Joan Sutherland sing at the Handel Opera Society. He had, thanks to Gwyneth, become a founder member of the society but had hardly ever attended a performance.

As the years went by and he settled down to writing his Memoirs, Walter seemed to the friends who visited him to have come to terms with living on his own and to have won his way through to a degree of serenity. Willie Forrest and many other people with whom he had worked came to discuss draft chapters. If they came in the daytime they usually found him working at his desk – and as mentally alert as ever. He remained deeply interested in current events and even when he had company in the evening insisted on listening to the nine o'clock news. On television one of his favourite programmes was the series of Perry Mason courtroom dramas.

So he succeeded in keeping loneliness and depression at bay by continuing to lead a very active life for a man of his age. He felt he had at least three major tasks to complete: the *News Chronicle* staff must be won the maximum compensation possible; the *Economist*, of which he was still chairman, should continue to expand on sound lines; and he should follow *Dorothy* with a second volume which would be his autobiography.

He had always been determined that, if the worst happened and the *News Chronicle* collapsed, the staff should get adequate compensation. So he now went to great efforts to help work out the best possible compensation scheme. But in February 1961, Mr Hall Parke, the son of Ernest Parke, a former editor of the *Star*, issued a writ against the Daily News Ltd arguing that the proposed payments were illegal since the money to be used belonged to the shareholders. Hall Parke got an interim injunction, with the result that the money could not be paid out as expected by the staff. The main case was not heard until May 1962. Hall Parke's counsel then argued that his client had never received a dividend from his shares and that the entirely laudable scheme to pay compensation to the staff should be carried out with Cadbury money and not that of Hall Parke or other shareholders. The defence maintained that the payment of compensation was the essential key to the '1925 Plan' and that the payments, in effect, formed part of the contract of sale.

The verdict given on 7 June 1962 was in favour of Hall Parke. The judge laid down that: 'The defendants were prompted by motives which, however laudable and however enlightened from the point of view of industrial relations, were such as the law does not recognize as sufficient justification.' A way round this judgement was found by inviting the shareholders to hand over voluntarily the money they received for their shares, to the trustees of the Daily News Compensation Scheme. About 86 per cent did so, so that more than £900,000 became available. Layton saw to it that his family shares were given in this way and where, in the case of his daughter Margaret, who had just died, the shares were in the hands of trustees, and therefore could not be touched, he made up the difference from his own pocket. The staff finally got their money in the summer of 1963, but concern about the outcome of the Hall Parke case helped increase public pressure for the governmental redundancy scheme, covering all employees, which came into effect in December 1965.

About the time of the collapse of the *News Chronicle* and the *Star* two Sunday papers, the *Empire News* and the *Sunday Graphic*, also ceased publication. Early in 1961 Mr Roy Thomson and the Daily Mirror Group were competing for Odhams Press, including the *Daily Herald*. The resulting concern that even more national newspapers might disappear led to the government giving way to pressure for a Royal Commission under Lord Shawcross to inquire into the economic and financial state of the Press generally.

The evidence submitted by the *Daily News* about the reasons for the decline and fall of the *News Chronicle* and the *Star* attracted considerable attention. Laurence Cadbury gave the main evidence, which showed how the *News Chronicle*, because of its low prewar profits, suffered more than most of its competitors from the wartime excess profits tax. A higher proportion of the profits that were easily made in wartime, thanks to newsprint rationing and a thirst for news, were taxed away than for other papers. So reserves could not be built up.

Even more important, the relaxation of newsprint rationing after 1952, and its abolition in 1957, meant that the *News Chronicle* no longer got the advertising revenue which had been diverted to it when other papers had little space, just at a time when commercial television was taking away more and more advertising business from all newspapers.

Layton gave evidence in his capacity as chairman of the *Economist* but also touched on the *News Chronicle*, though he avoided some questions because the Hall Parke case was then in progress. He did, however, say that he had discussed possible long-term plans for the *News Chronicle* in 1957 with a number of other newspaper proprietors: 'Not one of them was ready to tackle the problem of the *News Chronicle*. All thought they could not keep it alive as a separate newspaper.'

Beaverbrook in his evidence was quite clear why the *News Chronicle* failed:

> It had no management. It passed from one weak management to another – weak management with divided counsel. It had no will to survive. If they had placed it in the hands of any good young man he would have been able to build it up. It wanted leadership and they had no leadership.

In their report the Royal Commission inevitably touched on the reason for the *News Chronicle*'s fall:

> We are bound to say that the majority of witnesses who expressed their opinions on the matter blame the management of the newspaper for the result. It is no part of our function to apportion responsibility in this matter, but we cannot escape the conclusion that the failure of the *News Chronicle* was not entirely the result of the inevitable law of newspaper economics; different and more consistent managerial and editorial policy might have saved this newspaper.

Cadbury protested that the operative word in this sentence was 'might', and deplored the fact that most newspapers in reviewing the Commission's finding put the blame on the management of the *News Chronicle*. Cadbury thought far more notice should have been taken of another sentence in the Commission's report which read: 'The problem is not so much why the *News Chronicle* could not survive with a circulation of 1¼ million, but how it could get anywhere near to surviving in competition against newspapers with a circulation of over 4 million.'

Whether, in fact, Layton could have done more to keep the *News Chronicle* going must be very doubtful. The story might conceivably have been different if he had been twenty years younger and had been able to buy out the Cadbury family interest. But his abilities did not lie in management and he was certainly not the type of ruthless newspaper magnate who would have been needed to save the paper.

Layton finally resigned from the Daily News board in June 1963, nearly six years after he announced his decision to resign once the position of the staff was safeguarded. Now that compensation had been paid out and the pension fund had been financed, he felt free to resign so as to have more time to write his Memoirs. Characteristically he wanted to continue as a member of the Daily News Trust, so the link with Bouverie Street starting in 1927 continued until his death thirty-nine years later.

It was also in 1963 that Layton handed over the chairmanship of the *Economist*, which he had held since 1944, to Geoffrey Crowther while remaining on the board as vice-chairman. Since the end of the war the *Economist*, with Crowther as editor, had developed into a vigorously written weekly with a circulation on both sides of the Atlantic, climbing in the 1950s towards 60,000. The *Economist* had by then moved its offices to Ryder Street, just off St James's. Although there was plenty of room Layton did not have a separate office there as chairman. But he took his duties seriously and was, indeed, a good chairman though sometimes indecisive. To the young members of the staff he was old-fashioned, but in no way an old stick. Most liked and admired him.

Donald Tyerman became editor in 1956 but Crowther stayed on as managing director, hoping in vain to succeed Layton quickly as chairman. There was criticism from time to time of the new editor, but Layton had no doubt about backing him on the strong anti-Eden line he took at the time of the Suez crisis. In 1960 a plan for the *Economist* to buy Penguin Books was well advanced when Allen Lane, the founder of Penguin, suddenly withdrew. Whether it would have been wise for the *Economist* to diversify its activities in this direction must be doubtful. Another more successful example of Crowther's business enterprise, in which Layton took a great interest, was the scheme launched in 1961 to build, on the site of the existing offices, a small skyscraper, much of which would be let, as well as two other buildings for letting, grouped around a raised piazza. The result was highly successful architecturally and financially. Although entirely modern in design the *Economist* buildings fit in well with the Georgian clubs in St James's and are in marked contrast to a peculiar tubular edifice recently erected at the corner of St James's Place.

Layton had some grave doubts about the proposal in 1964 that the basement should be used as a staff canteen for lunch and as a public restaurant at night. He sent a note round to the board: 'It is essential that we should avoid giving the slightest impression that the *Economist* has gone into the nightclub business in any form. Ever since I first joined the *Economist* in 1908 I have regarded the authoritative character of its articles – political, economic and commercial – as a major factor, perhaps the major factor, in building and maintaining its high prestige. It may easily damage it.' He abstained from voting and the proposal went through. In the event the restaurant was never a real success and was closed down.

During the last five years of his life Walter spent much of his time in writing his Memoirs, which he hoped to have published by Collins as a sequel to *Dorothy*. He consulted many of those who had worked with him from the First World War onwards and went to great efforts to check his facts. By 1964 he had completed the first draft, extending to 180,000 words, covering most of the main events in his life up to the 1950s, only to have it virtually rejected by Collins on the grounds that it was concerned much more with the history of the first half of the twentieth century than with the history of himself. His own role, feelings and reactions should have provided the connecting thread, but they had been so played down as to make the book seem a series of unconnected episodes. The book, therefore, would have to be reconstructed before it could be published.

Collins were right, in that most of the Memoirs make dull reading. Only when Layton was prepared to reveal something of himself, as in the chapters about his childhood and Cambridge, or his descriptions of the Milner Mission or the search for the missing Field brothers, did his writing come alive. This was not just because he had written his Memoirs in old age. It was typical of the man that he found the events much more important and interesting than the part he played himself. He had never pushed himself forward in his various jobs and he was not going to blow his own trumpet now. So it is quite possible that, even if he had written his Memoirs ten years earlier, he would not have injected into his writing the feeling and sympathy that light up his book on Dorothy.

Writing his Memoirs gave Walter ample opportunity to reflect on the course his life had taken ever since he was a choirboy at St George's, Windsor. He told his daughter Olive that he had had a marvellous life and that if he had another chance he would like to lead the same life all over again. He had gained much from his nonconformist musical parents and from his ten years at pre-1914 Cambridge with all its intellectual excitement. He had had a happy marriage and children and grandchildren of whom he was proud. He had lived a full life always doing work he found interesting and worthwhile. He liked being stretched and he had been stretched to the utmost, both by his regular jobs and by the many additional demands on him to help find practical solutions to a wide range of political, economic and financial problems at home and abroad.

He was lucky in being able to pursue his interests right up to the time of his death. He continued attending House of Lords debates and board meetings of the *Economist* up to the very last. Indeed, it was after a board meeting in January 1966, at which he had had to take the chair, that he denied himself the luxury, to him, of using an office car to travel straight home to Putney. Instead he went by tube and, unfortunately, went round the inner circle the wrong way. When he finally got to Putney Bridge Station he had a long time to wait for a bus and caught cold, which very soon turned to pneumonia and resulted in his death shortly thereafter.

It would be wrong to try and sum up such an exceptional man as Walter Layton in a neat final paragraph. One can agree with much of the *Economist* obituary. He was certainly a quiet and self-contained man. 'He was determined rather than decisive, punctilious rather than downright, honestly square to all the arguments rather than dynamic.' One can agree too that he was a good man who did his duty and indeed more than his duty in giving freely of his time whenever he felt he could help. But it is more difficult to agree with the *Economist*'s conclusion that he was 'all the time, behind a sensitive and sometimes austere reserve, a simple and delightful person'. That side of his character was certainly apparent at times, but at others a more complex side emerged. He was too highly strung a man, driving himself very hard most of his life and paying the price for doing so, to be as straightforward as that. In summing himself up one feels that he would have qualified whatever he wrote with the words he used so often in *Economist* leading articles – 'Time alone will show.'

A hundred years have now passed since his birth. Perhaps more time is needed to put his life in proper perspective, but it is already clear that Walter Layton was one of a comparatively small group of men and women who did much to ensure that, for most people, Britain became a better country to live in during the first two thirds of this century.

Notes

Chapter One

1 From Walter Layton's unpublished Memoirs, on a draft of which he was working at the time of his death.

2 Leonard Woolf, *Sowing* (Hogarth, 1960), p. 20.

3 In 1982 there were three times as many undergraduates – 9,600, of whom 3,300 were women – and in addition there were 2,500 postgraduate students, of whom there were very few in Layton's time. So the whole student body in 1982 was about 12,100 – 930 of them from overseas, and over 30 per cent of them women. In Layton's time there were just a few overseas students, mostly from India, and women made up only 10 per cent of the whole student body, a percentage which was maintained until the great changes of the early 1970s when women were admitted to men's colleges.

4 Now about 50 per cent come from independent schools which include many old grammar schools as well as public schools.

5 Woolf, op. cit., p. 157.

6 A.I. Tillyard, *History of University Reform* (Cambridge, 1913).

7 It was not only the rich and sporting undergraduates, spending much of their time at the Newmarket races, who read for pass degrees. Many intelligent but not academically minded people profited from taking pass degrees which covered a number of subjects at a level of abstraction they could understand rather than being subjected to lectures intended for those taking the Tripos, which would have gone over their heads. Indeed, some senior dons with long memories at Cambridge now regret the demise of pass degrees.

8 Woolf, op. cit., p. 160.
9 Ibid., p. 147.
10 Keynes himself in 1935 wrote the best account of the Apostles' discussions in his essay 'My Early Beliefs', printed in *Two Memoirs*, (Rupert Hart Davies, 1949). These discussions were based on the view that 'Nothing mattered except states of mind, one's own and other people's of course, but chiefly one's own.' When Layton came to review (in the *Economist* in 1949) 'My Early Beliefs', in which Keynes set out his mature reflections on the fashionable philosophy of his undergraduate days, he was worried that Keynes's scintillating style would hide 'the deep fund of human sympathy and understanding that underlay the caustic wit and devastating epigram'. So he came to the rather curious conclusion that he would have preferred this gem of Keynes's writing not to have been published until after Sir Roy Harrod's biography of Keynes, then being written, had appeared.
11 Ben Keeling, *Letters and Recollections*, ed. E.T. (George Allen & Unwin, 1918), p. 9.
12 R. Skidelsky, *John Maynard Keynes*, vol. I, *Hope Betrayed* (Macmillan, 1983), p. 267.
13 G.M. Trevelyan wrote in his Autobiography (Cambridge, 1949, p. 22): 'When his heavy bearded figure moved majestically across the Great Court under the shadow of his huge Archdeacon's hat, he seemed to have walked into our world out of Trollope's Barchester. He could have met Archdeacon Grantly on equal terms. But he conceived and carried out a new idea of the place Economic History should occupy in academic studies.' Cunningham's book *The Growth of English Industry and Commerce* (Cambridge, 1882), was a classic, and is still read today.
14 Later it was common for professional economists to read some other subject for the first part of the Tripos. Gerald Shove read classics before going on to economics, as did Dennis Robertson, who won the Craven Scholarship for classics and the Chancellor's Medal for English Verse. Hubert Henderson read law. The same was true of Oxford economists such as Roy Harrod, who read Greats, and James Meade, who read Honour Mods (classics) before going on to Modern Greats. The view that it was right to

stretch the mind on some other subjects before going on to economics persisted in Cambridge, and particularly at King's, until well after the Second World War. In 1934 Maynard Keynes told the present author, when he announced his intention of reading economics, that the first part of the Tripos was mainly descriptive and that to train his mind he must read moral sciences. Gerald Shove, in 1946, asked the Tutor at King's to dissuade freshmen from taking Part I Economics for the same reason. Layton himself, of course, had taken a degree in history at University College before taking up economics full-time at Cambridge.

15 Numbers built up from a total of 20 in 1907 when Layton graduated, and varied between 40 and 60 in the years 1910–14. This compares with about 450 today.

16 This, at any rate, was the view of Mary Paley (Alfred Marshall's wife), who went to Newnham in 1872 and became one of the first women economists. She wrote in her book *What I Remember* (Cambridge, 1947, p. 14): 'In 1870 the Moral Science Tripos, which had been leading a rather feeble existence for twenty years, was the only one in which economics found a place and as it required neither mathematics nor classics, it seemed suited for girls who had done little of either.' Mary Paley persisted, and although not allowed to attend men's lectures, achieved results, thanks to the teaching of Henry Sidgwick and her future husband, about which her examiners were equally divided whether she was in the first or second class. She went on to teach economics and to help Marshall with his books, only to be rewarded by Marshall vigorously opposing the granting of degrees to women on the grounds that they could not play a full part at a residential university like Cambridge because women would be preoccupied with their primary duty of looking after their aged parents!

17 Charles Llewellyn Davies at the Treasury, 1889–1924.

18 Francis Williams, *Magnificent Journey* (Odhams Press, 1954), p. 251.

19 But he was elected a Fellow at Caius in 1909.

Chapter Two

1 Lord Layton, *Dorothy* (Collins, 1961).

Chapter Three

1 Layton's experience at this time led him in 1939 to ring up Austin Robinson, who was a Cabinet Office economist at the beginning of the Second World War, emphasizing the need for a manpower budget.
2 Lloyd George, Speech in the House of Commons, June 1915.
3 J.M. Keynes, *Collected Writings*, vol. XVI (Macmillan, 1971), p. 110–15. For an excellent discussion of Keynes's point of view see R. Skidelsky, *John Maynard Keynes: Hopes Betrayed* (Macmillan, 1983), chapter 13.
4 Lloyd George, *War Memoirs*, vol. III (Ivor Nicholson & Watson, 1934), p. 1587.
5 But there was some continuity. The Order of St Stanislaw, 1st Class, which the Tsar would have conferred on Layton, was confirmed by the Kerensky government. The insignia, however, were not given him until February 1918, by which time Kerensky was in exile, having been ousted by the Soviets.
6 Martin Gilbert, *Winston S. Churchill*, vol. IV, Companion Vol., *Part 1* (Heinemann, 1982), p. 123.
7 Martin Gilbert, op. cit., Companion Vol., *Part 2*, p. 130.

Chapter Four

1 Other honours came his way. The French made him an Officer of the Legion of Honour and the Italians, not to be outdone, made him a Knight Commander of the Crown of Italy as well as an Officer of the Order of St Maurice and St Lazarus.
2 He worked as much as he could out of doors, using the revolving summer house built for Professor Marshall, which Mary Marshall gave him in 1926 after the Professor's death. In the Ark, as Marshall had called it, he could always be in the sunshine, or

at least out of the wind, by cranking the enormous cog wheel on which the summer house turned.

3 Thomas Jones, *Diary with Letters* (Oxford, 1954), p. 267.

4 It was probably because of Layton's directorship of the National Mutual Assurance Company, of which Keynes was chairman and O.T. Falk a director, as well as his becoming editor of the *Economist*, that led to his being invited to join the Tuesday Club in 1922.

The Tuesday Club had been started in 1917 by O.T. Falk, who was then working under Keynes in the Treasury, when he invited nine people to dinner at the Café Royal to discuss a paper on inflation by Professor Foxwell. Apart from Foxwell the other guests included Keynes, Sir Charles Addis (a banker), A.W. Kiddy (a city editor) and Hartley Withers, then editor of the *Economist*. Although the subjects discussed were serious, usually connected with monetary policy, the talk was good and often light-hearted. Falk recorded later: 'Our talk tended to be aphoristic and of playful paradox . . . we were mercifully free from the intellectual dishonesty of the economist–politicians with an axe to grind'.

In any case the Club went on meeting monthly and continues thus today. At first the numbers of members and guests were limited so that the discussion should be informal and confidential. There were not at first to be more than thirteen members, though the limit rose to sixteen in 1920. So it was an honour for Layton to be invited to become a member in 1922, having first gone as a guest the previous year to open a discussion on the subject of 'Foreign competition in the Iron and Steel Industry with special reference to reparations and the territorial changes of the Treaty of Versailles'. The other new members that year were Sir Josiah Stamp, Sir Henry Strakosch and Dennis Robertson, the economist. Hubert Henderson was elected two years later. Thus Layton was very much in his element among friends and colleagues.

Chapter Five

1 John Campbell, *Lloyd George: The Goat in the Wilderness* (Jonathan Cape, 1977), p. 189.

2 Keynes, *Collected Writings*, vol. IX, *Essays in Persuasion* (Macmillan, 1972), p. 297.
3 This emergency number was printed on a small machine in the advertising department. For some reason there were not enough letter 'e's available in the available type, so just before the press deadline Layton had to rewrite his hard-hitting article using words with hardly any 'e's in them. The full edition was duly printed after the strike was over.
4 Asa Briggs, *A Study of the Work of Seebohm Rowntree* (Longmans, 1961), p. 261.
5 Ibid., p. 199.
6 Tom Jones, *Whitehall Diary*, Vol. II (Oxford, 1969), p. 130.

Chapter Six

1 Tom Jones, *Diary with Letters* (Oxford, 1954), p. 276.
2 From a taped interview with Ruth Edwards of the *Economist*, in 1982.
3 *The Brown Book of Hitler Terror and Burning of the Reichstag*. Prepared by an International Committee, with Albert Einstein in the chair (Gollancz, 1933).
4 The whole correspondence was published in the *Economist* of 23 September 1933.

Chapter Seven

1 Katherine Mayo, *Mother India* (Jonathan Cape, 1927).
2 *The History of the Times 1912–48*, Vol. IV, Part II (London, 1952), p. 869.
3 Those wanting complete self-government for India.
4 *Dorothy*, p. 104.

Chapter Eight

1 Dr Schacht, *The First Seventy Six Years* (Allen Wingate, 1955).

2 Andrew Boyle, *Montagu Norman* (Cassell, 1967), p. 247.
3 Keynes, *Collected Writings*, vol. X, *Essays in Biography* (Macmillan, 1972), p. 389.
4 *The Inter-War Years* (a selection of Henderson's papers) (Oxford, 1955), p. 71.
5 Keynes was at this time giving the Prime Minister very different unofficial advice which he was not prepared to have circulated to the Economic Advisory Council. He was convinced that Britain was virtually certain to have to go off gold shortly. As the game was up it was foolish to try and put off the evil day, either by borrowing abroad or by cutting the pay of the unemployed at home, a course which seemed to him 'a most gross perversion of human justice'. See David Marquand's *Life of Ramsay MacDonald* (Jonathan Cape, 1977), p. 610.
6 It is possible that agreement would have been reached earlier if Dr Brüning had been at Lausanne. The previous March he had invited Layton to join him at Badenweiler, where he was going for a short rest over Easter. Brüning wanted Layton to spend a few days with him so that they might have some quiet talks. In the event Layton could not go to Badenweiler and in June 1932, by the time of the Lausanne Conference, Brüning was no longer Chancellor.
7 It is worth recording that, on the outward voyage, there was on board the *Berengaria* a certain Canon Monroe, suffering from acute depression following the death of his wife. He was accompanied by his 24-year-old daughter. One night the Canon disappeared and it was clear he was lost overboard. Walter did not know the daughter at all, but had met her sister through her work at Chatham House. When told by the Captain what had happened, Walter and Dorothy took charge of the distraught young woman as if they had been old friends, and did so with great tact and thoughtfulness which she still remembers vividly after 50 years. They brought her to sit with them at the Captain's table and saw to it she was not too much alone. Walter dealt with the cables that had to be sent and protected her from the journalists on board. When the ship

arrived at New York, the Laytons kept her in their cabin so that she could avoid the many more journalists who came on board eager for details of the Canon's death.

Chapter Nine

1 Hubert Powell, unpublished draft history of the *News Chronicle*, 1961.
2 Frances Stephenson, *Lloyd George – A Diary* (Hutchinson, 1971), p. 260.
3 In A.J.P. Taylor, *English History 1914–1945* (Oxford, 1965), p. 368.

Chapter Ten

1 Iain Hamilton, *Koestler, A Biography* (Secker & Warburg, 1982), p. 41.
2 Letter to the author from Vernon Bartlett, April 1982.
3 Letter to the author, May 1983.
4 Letter to the author, May 1983.

Chapter Eleven

1 Keynes, *Collected Writings*, vol. XXII (Macmillan, 1978), p. 22.
2 Ibid.
3 W.P. (40) 339.
4 See Martin Gilbert, *Their Finest Hour* (Heinemann, 1983), p. 799.
5 In writing these paragraphs I am indebted to Duncan Hall's book on North American Supply in the official *History of the War* (HMSO, 1955).
6 Duncan Hall, op. cit., p. 73.
7 Ibid., p. 187.
8 Gilbert, *Their Finest Hour*, p. 873.
9 Jean Monnet, *Memoirs* (Collins, 1978), p. 172.
10 NAS (41), 3, 1 Jan. 1941.

11 Layton's main theme was that the air and naval power could not win the war on their own. The first task was to push the Axis powers back in the Middle East and the Mediterranean, and then to move into Southern Europe and Norway, leading to an ultimate attack on the Channel coast.
12 Harold Macmillan, *Blast of War* (Macmillan, 1966), p. 91.
13 Sir Richard Clarke (edited by Sir Alec Caincross) *Anglo-American Economic Collaboration in Peace and War 1942–1949* (Oxford, 1982), pp. 6, 8.
14 Ibid., p. 18.
15 Private conversation with Lord Franks, who was Director of Labour at the Ministry of Supply in Layton's time.
16 Macmillan, op. cit., p. 119.
17 Scott and Hughes, *The Administration of War Production* (HMSO, 1955), p. 455.
18 H.M.D. Parker, *Manpower in the Second World War* (HMSO, 1956), p. 172.
19 Private conversation with Sir Dennis Rickett, Oliver Lyttelton's private secretary at the time.
20 *Memoirs of Lord Chandos* (Bodley Head, 1962), p. 285.

Chapter Twelve

1 Granada TV interview, 1967.

Chapter Thirteen

1 Harold Macmillan, *Tides of Fortune* (Macmillan, 1969), p. 162.
2 Ibid., p. 170.
3 Richard Mayne, *The Community of Europe* (Gollancz, 1962), p. 81.
4 Hugh Dalton, *High Tide and After* (Frederick Muller, 1962), p. 330.
5 Harold Macmillan, op. cit., p. 210.
6 Layton had founded the European Atlantic Group, with Elma Dangerfield as secretary, in 1954, as a forum for discussion of

international problems by leading members of the main Anglo-European and Anglo-American and Canadian societies in London. The group is still active today with Michael, the present Lord Layton, as its chairman.

Chapter Fourteen

1 Draft of a press statement by Hermann Field, February, 1955.
2 Hermann Field and Stanislaw Mierzenski, *Angry Harvest* (New York, Thomas Y. Crowell, 1958; London, Victor Gollancz, 1958).

Chapter Fifteen

1 The Daily News board did decide a few weeks later to invest in a new company, Tyne Tees Television, of which Layton became a director. This investment turned out to be very profitable, but not in time to save the *News Chronicle*.
2 In a review of *Dorothy*, written for *Time and Tide*, February, 1961.

Index

Addis, Sir Charles, 113, 258n
Addison, Dr Christopher, 36, 39
Adenauer, Dr Konrad, 206, 210–11
Amery, Julian, 213
Amery, Leo, 207
Anderson, Sir Alan, 87
Angry Harvest (novel by Hermann Field), 228
Apostles, the, 8
Appeasement of Hitler and Mussolini, 147
Asquith, H.H., 29, 69
Atholl, Duchess of, 156
Attlee, Clement, 105, 147
Austria, Layton's mission to (1925), 100–1
Austro–German Customs Union, 100, 115

Bagehot, Walter, 32, 84
Baldwin, Stanley, 74, 141, 140
Balfour, A.J., 8, 14, 56
Balogh, Thomas, 89
Bank of International Settlements (BIS), 113–15, 213
Barry, Gerald, 96, 148, 154, 157, 158, 162, 163–4, 166, 196–7, 198
Bartlett, Vernon, 148, 162–3, 165, 166, 231
'Beachcomber', 90, 187–8
Beaverbrook, Lord, 169; Minister of Supply (1941), 183, 187–9; Minister of Production (1942), 189; respects W.T.L., 204, 231; offers to finance purchase of *News Chronicle* by W.T.L., 232, 236, 249
Bedales School, 12, 14
Bell, Richard, 21
Beneš, President, 70, 156, 222
Bensusan-Butt, David, 89, 90
Beveridge, Sir William, 35, 64, 68, 87, 167–8
Bird, Roland, 89, 90
Blackett, Sir Basil, 99, 105
Bonham-Carter, Lady Violet, 207, 208, 241–3, 244
Boothby, Robert, 208, 213
Bracken, Brendan, 87, 88, 195, 197
Brand, R.H., 54, 55
Brooke, Rupert, 12–14, 21
Brussels Financial Conference (1920), 54–6
Brett House (Layton family home), 149, 169, 199
Briand, Aristide, proposals for European Customs Union, 104, 115
Brüning, Dr, 116, 143, 260
Budget leak (1947), 200–201
Bulmer-Thomas, Ivor, 162, 164
Bunbury, Sir Henry, 162

Cadbury, Edward, 127
Cadbury, Egbert, 128, 198
Cadbury, Dame Elizabeth, 127
Cadbury, George, 127, 128–9, 138
Cadbury, Henry, 127, 128, 129, 131, 198
Cadbury, Laurence, 22–3, 127, 128, 131; his character, 134–5; unwilling for W.T.L. to acquire more *Daily News* shares, 140; *N.C.* policy conferences, 162, 160; runs the *N.C.* (1940–44), 190, 196; becomes *N.C.* Chairman (1950), 230; and Michael Curtis, 236; blamed for collapse of *N.C.*, 240–1; gives evidence to Royal Commission on the Press, 249

Caius College, Cambridge, 21, 33
Cambridge University in 1904, 10–12; 254n; women at Cambridge, 11, 254n; Triposes, 11
Cameron, James, 231, 241
Campion, Sir Harry, 181
Carter, Alice ('Old Nanny'), 38, 246
Casey, Richard (later Lord Casey), 182
Catto, Sir Thomas, 129, 130
Chamberlain, Neville, 117, 157, 158
Chancellor, Sir Christopher, 201, 202
Chapman, Brian, 233
Chapman, Sir Sydney, 99
Chilver, Sally, 199–200
Churchill, Winston S.: First World War – Minister of Munitions, 46–8; settles Cumberland miners' strike, 47–8; Second World War – offers W.T.L. a job, 170; enthusiastic about 10 Division Plan, 178; comments on W.T.L.'s resignation and post-war planning, 194; and 'United Europe', 206; Hague Congress of Europe (1948), 207; Council of Europe Assembly, 208–9
Clarke, R.W.B., 181, 185, 186–7, 193, 197
Combined Production and Resources Board, 45, 192
Cook, A.J., 73–4
Coope, J., 235–7
Council of Europe, 207
Council of Europe Consultative Assembly, 205, 208
Couzens, Frank, 236
Cowdray, Lord, 131
Cox, Sir Geoffrey, 230
Cox, Katherine, 14, 26
Cripps, Stafford, 155
Crowther, Geoffrey, 82, 89, 90, 93, 96, 171, 181, 185, 236, 239, 242, 243, 250
Cruickshank, Mary, 199
Cruickshank, Robin, 162, 197, 199, 231, 233
Cummings, A.J., 84, 135, 162
Cunningham, Archdeacon, 17, 20, 255
Cursley, Norman, 242
Curtis, Dunstan, 217
Curtis, Michael, 199, 233–6
Czechoslovakia, 156, 159–60; Czech refugees, 160–1; Czech Refugee Fund, 159, 160, 219; British Committee for Czech Refugees, 160–2

Daily Chronicle, merged with *Daily News* (1930), 128–30
Daily Despatch, take over of (1955), 235
Daily Mail, 145, 238–9
Daily News Ltd., holding company for *News Chronicle* and *Star*, 139, 238–9, 241, 244, 250
Daily News, 22, 65, 82, 128; merger with *Westminster Gazette*, 130
Daily Worker, 155
Dalton, Hugh, 13, 22, 200–1, 208, 212
Dangerfield, Mrs Elma, 207, 247, 262
Davenport, Nicholas, 89
Dawnay, Major-General Guy, 88
Donovan, General William, J., 223
Doumergue, M. (Prime Minister of France), 40, 42
Drummond, Sir Eric (later Lord Perth), 44, 53, 56, 166
Duncan, Sir Andrew (Minister of Supply), 183
Duncan, A.C. (of Odham's Press), 236

Eccles, David, 208, 210, 213
Economic Advisory Council, 99, 119
Economists in the Civil Service, 99
Economic General Staff, 99
Economics Tripos at Cambridge, 9, 11, 16–17, 19, 255n, 256n
Economist, the, 21–2, 30, 31, 65; and Miners' Strike (1926), 72, 259n, 79; W.T.L. at the *Economist*, 82–97; 92, 250–1
Eden, Anthony, 207
Edwards, Bob, 213
Edwards, John, 217
Eisler, Paul, 222, 229
European Atlantic Group, 218, 262
European Customs Union, 104, 115–17
European Movement, 198, 205–6, 208
Evening Standard, 137

Fabian Society, 12, 14, 27
Field, Hermann, 219–29 *passim*

Field, Herta, 220–1, 228
Field, Kate (née Thornycroft), 220–9 *passim*
Field, Noel, 219–21, 228
Fierlinger, Dr (Czech politician), 228–9
Financial crises of 1931, 117–19
Forrest, Willie, 154, 158, 220, 247
Franks, Oliver (later Lord Franks), 187

Garnett, David, 28
Geiringer, Alfred, 202, 209, 246
Glaser, Erika, 223–5, 228
Goebbels, Dr, 143
Gollancz, Victor, 155
Gordon, Lincoln, 181
Goyder, George, 201

Hague Congress of Europe (1948), 207
Hahn, Kurt, 144
Halsey, Sir Lionel, 87
Hammerstein, General von, 144
Hawtrey, Sir Ralph, 99
Henderson, Arthur, 115–6
Henderson, Hubert, 22, 35, 64, 65, 76, 78, 80, 98, 99, 119, 167, 258n
Henlein (Sudeten German leader), 156, 157–8
Herbert, Mervyn, 164
Herkomer, Hubert (artist), 1
Herriot, M. (French Prime Minister), 69, 121–2
Hindenburg, President, 144
Hirst, F.W. (editor of the *Economist*), 21, 35, 84
Hitler, Adolf, 118, 122, 142–3, 145, 157
Hoare, Sir Samuel, 146, 156–7, 158
Hobson, Oscar, 84, 148
Hodgson, Stuart (editor of *Daily News*), 128
Hodson, Donald, 164–5
Hodson, H.V., 88, 90
Horder, Lord, 183
Hore, Belisha, 167
Horrabin, J. (cartoonist), 148
Hubback, Eva (née Spielmann), 26, 76, 78
Hubback, F.W., 13, 32
Human Rights, Convention for the Protection of, 208, 210, 211, 212
Hutton, Graham, 85, 89, 90, 91, 92
Huxley, Julia, 26

Independent Television Authority, 233
India: the Simon Commission, 105–8; the Simon Report, 111
Introduction to the Study of Prices by W.T.L., 33
International Monetary System, 102
Iron and Steel Federation, 50–3
Irwin, Lord (Viceroy of India) 107

Jacob, Lt-General Sir Ian, 190, 191
Jacobssen, Per, 55, 100
Jay, Douglas, 89, 90, 92–3
Joint War Production Staff, 190–1; and manpower planning, 191–2
Jones, Tom (Deputy Secretary to the Cabinet), 80

Kaldor, Nicholas, 89
Keeling, Ben, 13, 15
Kerr, Philip (later Lord Lothian), 52, 64, 136, 147, 175, 182–3
Keynes, Maynard: at Cambridge, 12, 14, 17, 22, 31, 51, 255n; in Treasury in First World War, 35, 39–40; post-war liberal policy, 54, 57, 64, 65, 66, 69, 71, 76–7, 79–80, 98; and financial crisis of 1931, 119, 260n; 'Old Dogs' Group, 167–9
Koestler, Arthur, 154

Laval, M. (Prime Minister of France), 120, 146
Layton, Alfred (W.T.L.'s father), 1
Layton, Christopher (W.T.L.'s youngest son), 60, 149, 150, 174–5, 182, 209
Layton, David (W.T.L.'s second son), 33, 52, 150
Layton, Deanna (W.T.L.'s eldest grand-daughter), 151, 165
Layton, Dorothy (née Osmaston; W.T.L.'s wife), 14, 22; childhood, undergraduate at Cambridge, engagement and marriage, 24–33 *passim*; in First World War, 38–9; becomes ill, 52; family life, 60–2,

Layton, Dorothy (*contd.*)
149–51; concern for Indian women, 106, 109; her view of Walter's work, 149; work for Basque children, 153; last illness and death, 244
Layton, Dot (née Cross; W.T.L.'s daughter-in-law), 150, 151
Layton, Gilbert (W.T.L.'s younger brother), 2, 5, 83
Layton, Jean (W.T.L.'s second daughter: married Paul Eisler), 38, 62, 150, 151, 222, 244, 246
Layton, Margaret (W.T.L.'s sister), 2, 4, 6, 14–16, 28, 39, 62
Layton, Margaret (W.T.L.'s eldest daughter; married Alfred Geiringer), 32, 33, 38, 40, 150, 160, 199, 209, 220, 229, 262
Layton, Michael (W.T.L.'s eldest son; second Lord Layton), 33, 52, 150, 213, 235, 263
Layton, Olive (W.T.L.'s third daughter), 50, 60, 61, 150, 246, 252
Layton, Ruth (W.T.L.'s youngest daughter; married Robert Pegna), 60, 150, 188
Layton, Thomas (W.T.L.'s grandfather), 2
Layton, Walter Thomas, First Lord Layton: choir boy at St George's Chapel, Windsor, thereafter at the Temple at King's College School, Strand, 2–5; and Westminster City School, 5–6; at University College, London, 6–8; at Trinity College, Cambridge, 9–21; his philosophy, 14–15; wins Gresham studentship at Caius College, 21; starts working at the *Economist*, 21–2; becomes assistant lecturer in economics, 22; engagement to Dorothy Osmaston, 27–9; marriage, 32; publishes *Introduction to Study of Prices* (1912), 39
First World War – at Board of Trade, 35; at Ministry of Munitions, 35–8; becomes indispensable to Lloyd George, 37; takes different view from Keynes on war strategy, 39–40; on Milner mission to Russia (1917), 40–4; Balfour mission to USA (1917), 44–6; offers resignation to Churchill, 46; becomes member of Munitions Council and Chairman of 'Clamping Committee', 49; Made Companion of Honour (1919), 50
W.T.L. in the 1920s – Director of Iron and Steel Federation (1919), 50; attitude to party politics, 51; as a father, 52–3, 60–2, 150–1; becomes editor of the *Economist*, 57; character and attitude to work, 58
Liberal Party and the *Economist* – W.T.L. and Keynes compared, 60; as leading member of group of liberal radicals, 64–6; runs Liberal Summer Schools, 67–72; organizes Liberal *Yellow Book*, 75–81; editor of the *Economist*, 82–97; doubts about Keynes' new theories, 93; defends the *Economist* against complaints of being party-political, 94–5
W.T.L. as Economic Advisor – mission to Austria (1925), 100–1; Financial Assessor to Simon Commission, 104–11; Reparations and Bank of International Settlements, 112–15; negotiations for a European Customs Union, 115–17; financial crises of 1931, 117–19; most of W.T.L.'s main economic policy objectives not achieved until after Second World War, 124–6
News Chronicle and *Star* – statement of *N.C.*'s policy, 132; relations with Laurence Cadbury, 135; rebuts charges *N.C.* was pro-Labour, 139–41; seeks higher salary and to reinforce his position as *N.C.* chairman, 135–9; visits Hitler in Berlin (1933), 142–4; W.T.L. and *N.C.* play leading part in League of Nations Union Peace Ballot, 145–6; not an appeaser, 147–8; attitude to Communists, 154; The Henlein pamphlet (1938), 157–8; work for Czech refugees, 159–62; returns to *N.C.* after war service (1944), 197; gives up chairmanship of *N.C.* (1950),

Layton, Walter Thomas (*contd.*)
230; returns to *N.C.* (1955–6), 235; desire to resign from *Daily News* Board, 237; writes letter to *Times* justifying sale of *N.C.* and *Star* to Associated Newspapers, 239
Second World War – the 'Old Dogs' Group, 167–9; W.T.L.'s 'Allied War Aims', 169; joins Ministry of Supply, 171–2; mission to Washington (1940), 173–83; The 10 Division Plan and President Roosevelt, 177–80; relations with Beaverbrook, 187–9; Head of Joint War Production Staff at Ministry of Production, 190–1; visits Washington with Oliver Lyttelton, 192–3; resigns from Ministry of Production, 193
European Movement: W.T.L.'s Sidney Ball lecture (1944), 205–6; goes to Hague Congress of Europe (1948), 207; as Vice-President of Council of Europe Assembly, 209–17; supports the Schuman Plan, 213–14; the search for the Field brothers, 219–29; becomes Deputy Leader of the Liberals in the House of Lords – his speeches, 230–1
Layton, Wilfred (W.T.L.'s elder brother), 2, 3, 6
League of Nations, 53; First Assembly (1920), 56; search for collective security in the 1930s, 147
Leith Ross, Sir Frederick, 55
Liberal Summer Schools, 58, 67–70
Liberal *Yellow Book*, 58, 75–81
Lie, Trygve, 223
Lindemann, Professor (later Lord Cherwell), 185–6
Lloyd George , David, 21, 35; becomes Minister of Munitions, 36; writes to Dorothy Layton, 37; in conflict with Reginald McKenna on munitions policy, 37; criticizes Lord Milner's failure to foresee Russian revolution which W.T.L. forecast, 43; advises W.T.L. to join League of Nations secretariat, 54; at Liberal Summer School, 69; his Liberal *Yellow Book* weekends, 75–9; Council of Action (1935), 94; concern about *N.C.*, 136, 141, 165, 169, 170
Lothian, Lord, *see* Philip Kerr
Loveday, Alexander, 55, 216
Lowes Dickinson, 13, 19, 20
Lyttelton, Oliver (Minister of Production), 189, 190, 192–4

Maclean, Melinda, 224
McCleary, Gwyneth, 152, 174, 247
Macdonald, Ramsay, 99, 100, 121–2, 123, 141
Mackay, Ian, 231
Macmillan, Harold: *Reconstruction* and *The Middle Way*, 80, 94; at the Ministry of Supply, 183, 186; European Movement, 206, 208; Schuman Plan, 213–4
M'Taggart, John, 8, 17
Maisky, Ivan (Russian Ambassador), 70, 86, 156, 165
Manchester Guardian, 103
Mantoux, Professor Paul, 49, 54, 169
Mantoux, Mme, 169
Marshall, Professor Alfred, 15, 16, 17–18, 20, 24, 31, 32, 51
Marshall, Mrs Mary (née Paley), 24, 256, 257
Marshall, General, 178; Marshall Plan, 125, 206, 230
Masefield, John, 70
Masterman, Charles, 64, 75, 76
Maxwell Fyfe, Sir David (later Lord Kilmuir), 210, 211, 212
May, Stacy, 181, 186
Meade, Professor James, 181
Melchior, Dr Carl, 118
Meredith, Hugh, 8, 20, 22
Mierzenski, Stanislaw, 227–8
Milner mission (1917), 40–4
Miner's Strike (1926), 72–5
Monnet, Jean, 49, 54, 56; munitions in Second World War, 171, 175, 176, 180–1; Europe, 206, 207; Schuman Plan, 212
Monroe, Canon, 260n
Montagu, Edwin, 39

Morgenthau, Henry (Secretary of US Treasury), 175, 176, 181
Morrison, Herbert, 171, 208, 209
Mosley, Sir Oswald, 141, 145
Mother India by Katherine Mayo, 106
Munition programmes, co-ordination by the Allies in First World War, 44
Murray, Professor Gilbert, 64, 68, 69
Mussolini, 141

Nation, the, 65, 79, 85
News Chronicle, 22, 82; formed from merger of *Daily News* and *Daily Chronicle* (1930), 131; circulation, 132-3; accused of being pro-Labour Party, 135–9; a good paper to work for, 148; and profitable, 152; help for Basque children, 153; during the phoney war, 169–70; Laurence Cadbury becomes chairman (1940), 196; W.T.L. takes over again (1944), 197; post-war circulation falling, 198; *N.C.* staff's view of W.T.L., 202–4; Michael Curtis' proposed reforms, 234; merger negotiations, 236: with Odhams (*Daily Herald*), 236; with Associated Newspapers (*Daily Mail*), 238; with Sir Frank Packer and Roy Thompson, 239; sale to Associated Newspapers (1960), 239; compensation for staff, 238; the Hall Parke case, 247–8; Royal Commission on the Press, reasons for *N.C.* collapse, 248–9
New Statesman, 65
Newmarch Lectures, 8
Newsprint Supply Co., 169, 201
Niemeyer, Sir Otto, 99
Nitti, Signor Francesco, 69
Noel Baker, Philip, 22, 64, 65, 116, 220, 223
Norman, Montagu (Governor of the Bank of England), 55, 99, 113–4
Novy, Vilem, 220, 223

Observer, 79
'Old Dogs' Group, 167
Organisation for European Economic Co-operation, 207, 213, 216, 217
Osmaston, Francis (Dorothy Layton's father), 25, 29

Parkinson, Hargreaves, 84, 89, 90, 95
Parratt, Sir William, 3
Peace Ballot, 145
Pearson, Clive (of the Cowdray family), 136, 137
Philips, Hubert, 76
Pigou, Professor A.C., 7, 17, 19, 22, 31, 98
Production, Ministry of, 189
Purvis, Arthur (head of British Purchasing Mission, Washington 1940–1), 173, 175, 176, 180, 181, 182

Rajk, Laszlo, 221
Rama Rau, Sir Benegal, 107, 110, 111
Rathbone, Eleanor, 68, 106, 111
Reeves, Amber, 14, 27
Reid, Leonard, 84
Reuters, 201–2
Reynaud, Paul (French statesman), 206, 207, 210
Reparations, 68, 102, 112–3; Wiggin-Layton Committee, 118; BIS Reparations Committee, 120; Lausanne Conference (1932), 121–2
Rist, Professor Charles, 100, 101, 120, 121
Robbins, Lionel (later Lord Robbins), 88, 181
Robertson, Sir Dennis, 22, 64, 69, 98, 258n
Robinson, Professor Sir Austin, 93, 181, 185, 190–1, 257n
Roll, Eric (later Lord Roll), 181
Roosevelt, President, 175
Rothermere, Viscount, 169, 236
Rowntree, Seebohm, 35, 64; Miners' Strike (1926), 73–5; Liberal *Yellow Book*, 77–8
Royal College of Music, 1, 2
Royal College of Organists, 1, 2
Royal Commissions: on the Coal Industry (1925), 72; on the Supply of Food and Raw Materials in Time of War (1905), 9; on the Press (1962), 248–50

INDEX

Runciman, Sir Walter, 87, 88

Saint George's Chapel Choir School, 2, 3
Salter, Sir Arthur, 35, 49, 54, 64, 113, 167–8, 171, 173, 176, 206
Samuel, Sir Herbert, 69; Miners' Strike (1926), 72–3; Liberal *Yellow Book*, 75, 138
Sanger, C.P., 7–9
Schacht, Dr Hjalmar (President of the Reichsbank), 113–14, 142, 143
von Schleicher, General 144
Schumacher, Dr (leader of German Social Democrats 1949), 211
Schuman Plan, 212–14
Schuster, Sir George, 107, 110, 111
Scott, C.P. (editor of the *Manchester Guardian*), 67, 155
Shove, Gerald (economist), 22, 256n
Simon, Sir John, 69, 75, 76, 87; Indian Statutory Commission, 105, 106–8, 111
Simon, Ernest (later Lord Simon of Wythenshawe), 24, 64, 65; Liberal Summer Schools, 67, 71–2: Liberal *Yellow Book*, 75–8, 87; views on commercial television, 233
Slansky trial (1952), 224–5, 227–8, 229
Snowden, Philip (Labour Chancellor of the Exchequer), 114, 116, 119
South Kensington School of Art, 1
Spaak, Paul-Henri (Chairman of Council of Europe Assembly), 206, 209, 215
Spanish Civil War, 153
Stamp, Sir Josiah, 35, 64, 76, 87, 258n
Star evening newspaper, 128, 129, 130, 138, 139; loses libel case to Mosley, 145
Steed, Dr Wickham, 156
Stimson, H.L. (US Secretary for War 1940), 178, 181, 187
Stone, Sir Richard (economist), 181
Strakosch, Sir Henry, 87, 88; accuses the *Economist* of becoming party-political, 94, 95, 258n
Swiatlo, Colonel, 226

Tarriff barriers, 100–1, 102, 103–4
Teitgen, Pierre Henri (French Minister of Justice), 211
Thorneycroft, Peter (later Lord Thoneycroft), 208
Thornycroft, Oliver, 220–2
Thornycroft, Dolly, 222, 247
Times, 80
Toynbee, Professor Arnold, 84, 89
Trinity College, Cambridge, 9–11, 22
Truman, President, 215
Tuesday Club, 258n
Twittens (Layton family home in Sussex), 151, 244
Tyne and Tees Television Company, 244, 263n

United Newspapers, 130, 139
University College, London, 6–8

Vallance, Aylmer, 82, 84; at the *Economist*, 88; editor of the *News Chronicle* (1933), 135, 137; sacked, 138, 148, 153
Versailles Peace Treaties, 49
Vicky (cartoonist), 148, 197, 231

Ward, Dudley, 29, 55
Waters, Frank, 231, 233
Weeks, Sir Hugh, 171, 181, 185, 187, 194
Westminster Gazette, 128, 129; merger with *Daily News*, 130
Wiggin-Layton Committee on German debts, 118
Wilson, General Sir Henry, 40, 43, 49
Wilson, Sir Horace, 73
Wilson, James (founder of the *Economist*), 84, 86
Withers, Hartley (editor of the *Economist*), 57, 258
World Economic Conference (1927), 103–4
Workers Educational Association classes, 21, 30

Young, Geoffrey Winthrop, 144
Young, Hilton, 84